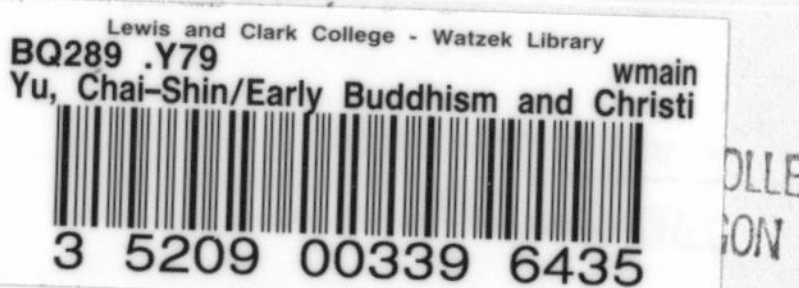

OLLEGE LIBRARY
GON 97219

EARLY BUDDHISM AND CHRISTIANITY

Early Buddhism and Christianity

A Comparative Study of the Founders' Authority, the Community, and the Discipline

CHAI-SHIN YU

MOTILAL BANARSIDASS
Delhi :: Varanasi :: Patna

©MOTILAL BANARSIDASS
Indological Publishers & Booksellers
Head Office : 41-U.A., Bungalow Road, Delhi-110 007
Branches : 1. Chowk, Varanasi-1 (U.P.)
2. Ashok Rajpath, Patna-4 (BIHAR)

First Edition : Delhi, 1981
Price : Rs. 60

Printed in India
By Shantilal Jain, at Shri Jainendra Press,
A-45, Phase I, Industrial Area, Naraina, New Delhi-110 028
Published by Narendra Prakash Jain, for Motilal Banarsidass,
Bungalow Road, Jawahar Nagar, Delhi-110 007.

ACKNOWLEDGEMENTS

I would like to express my gratitude to Professor J. G. Arapura for his advice and valuable suggestions throughout this study, and to Dr. Y. H. Jan, Dr. B. Meyer, Dr. E. Sanders, Dr. W. Whillier and Dr. J. Pringle for their many valuable criticisms, corrections and suggestions.

Finally, my thanks go to my wife for the tedious task of typing and tireless support and encouragement.

— CHAI-SHIN YU

CONTENTS

INTRODUCTION

The purpose of this study is to examine the similarities and dissimilarities between early Buddhism and early Christianity in regard to the authority of the founders, the nature of the communities, and the conception of discipline in the respective communities.

Buddhism is discussed in Part I, Christianity in Part II. A thorough examination of the topics listed above is undertaken within each group because, as observed by Max Müller, "Before we compare, we must thoroughly know what we compare."[1] In Part III, the early Buddhist and Christian communities are compared.

Each of the first two parts is divided into three chapters, dealing respectively with the founder's authority, the community, response to the founder and to his teachings, and the nature of discipline in the community. Emphasis in both parts is on the "authority" of the founder in respect of the views held by the early Buddhist and Christian disciples, and on how this authority and the founder's teachings were commemorated and followed by the members of the community in relation to the goal of unity among the followers. To the discussion of Buddhism is added a consideration of whether the early community constituted a church or an esoteric community.[2] This topic is included only in the discussion of Buddhism, because the early Buddhist community, unlike that of the early Christians, consisted of both a monastic community and a laity, and these must

1. Cited in, J. Wach, *The Comparative Study of Religions*, New York, Columbia University Press, 1958, p. xi.

2. S. Dutt, *Early Buddhist Monachism*, Bombay, India, 1960, p. 48, "Kern observes that Buddhism is properly a monastic institution, and the laity is but accessory (*Ibid.*, p. 72). Dr. Archibald Scott finds the broadest distinction between the Christian Church and the Buddhist Church in the fact that the work of the former lay outside the limits of the church. Of Buddhism, he says, "Its lay associates, however numerous, were but the fringes of religious communities. When, therefore, deterioration in the order sets in, reformation of it by the people was hopeless" (*Buddhism and Christianity*, p. 272).

be compared. In addition, the subject of the essence of the discipline which developed in response to the founder's teaching is discussed with regard to both the Buddhist and Christian communities.

This comparative study appears significant for several reasons. The two religions being considered here are both great world religions, which Matzutani called "the two most sublime religions mankind has ever had."[1] A comparative study of these religions may permit the followers of each faith to learn from the other. This may lead to a better general understanding of the religions of other peoples, and help to avoid strife among them. As Parrinder wrote, "The construction of a world-wide harmony is too great a task to be undertaken except with religious faith."[2]

But in studies of this kind attention has to be paid to something not sufficiently paid heed to so far. According to Richard Gard :

> Most of the attempts to compare or contrast Buddhism and Christianity are unsatisfactory because they tend to deal with doctrinal contexts, without sufficient reference to their historical and institutional contexts, and they usually do not employ an established comparative method of analysis or common terminology.[3]

As Gard's comments indicate, most comparative studies to date have been inadequate in their treatment of the historical and institutional aspects. To fill this void has been one of the main objectives of the present study. As Matzutani has noted:

> Usually, when two religions are compared, the analysis is biased in favor of the writer's own religion. He starts with preconceived conclusions and his aim really is to defend and uphold

1. F. Matzutani, *A Comparative Study of Buddhism and Christianity*, Tokyo. The Young East Association, 1957, p. 1.
2. G. Parrinder, *Comparative Religion*, London, George Allen & Unwin Ltd., 1962, p. 118.
3. R.A. Gard, "Buddhism", *A Reader's Guide to the Great Religions*, ed., Charles Adams, New York, The Free Press, 1965, p. 90.

his own religion and thus disparage the other. Such a comparison, however minutely it may be treated, can never be called a scholarly work.[1]

One of the purposes of the present study, therefore, has been to bring a more objective approach to bear on the comparison of Buddhism and Christianity.

Parts I and II contribute some new information and interpretations concerned with topics which themselves have been the subjects of considerable debate, e.g., the problems of Buddha's authority, the unity of *samgha*, the unity of the Church, and the nature of discipline in each community. In Buddhism, it is generally believed that *dharma*, not Buddha, was the basis of authority (see Part I, Chapter I). In Christianity the authority of Christ has generally been accepted, but the present study seeks to introduce some new points into the discussion. Many scholars have denied the existence of unity in the early Buddhist community and have, instead, emphasized individuality, but the unity of *samgha* has received equal emphasis in this study (see Part I, Chapter II). There is no dearth of books about these issues in Christianity, and theories regarding Christ as the source of both disunity and unity have been much debated among scholars. In these studies the nature and role of discipline do not appear to have been adequately discussed in relation either to Buddhism or to Christianity. Hence my emphasis on them in this dissertation.

Finally, a study of the similarities and differences of these two great religions in matters pertaining to authority, community and discipline may not only contribute to an understanding of these topics themselves, but may also help to explain the vitality and strength of these religions and partially account for their success as world religions.

The three topics discussed in this dissertation—authority, community, and discipline—are all essential aspects of each religion and are inseparably related to one another. In both, community and discipline appear to be grounded in the authority of the founders. Discipline, for example, must of necessity rest upon

---

1. Matzutani, *op. cit.* p. i.

authority. Therefore, the authority of the founder must be considered. Because discipline is practised by the community, the nature of the community must also be investigated. Discipline without the community and its founder would be meaningless. Without the founder, neither the community nor its discipline would have come into being. Early Buddhism, therefore, had the three jewels—Buddha, *dharma* (*vinaya*) and *samgha*—which were understood both in a particular and in an interrelated unitary sense. In early Christianity, too, one finds an inseparable unity between Christ, the Church and the understanding of the teaching and discipline. Further, Christ and the Church are regarded as one, the latter being the body of Christ.

The reason why the Buddhist discipline rather than *dharma in toto* has been discussed in this study is that doctrinal aspects have already been extensively discussed by other authors.[1] The primary purpose of the present author is to consider the more practical aspects. This is in keeping with an observation made by E.O. James: "...the main interest and purpose of the discipline have been the maintenance of society, the well being of mankind and the continuance of the natural order as they exist here and now."[2] Discipline was central to the whole Buddhist understanding—an understanding which was focused on the objective of the attainment of wisdom through moral discipline. In Christianity, Matthew's Gospel and Paul's letters indicate that moral teachings as discipline in Christ were a very important part of the Christian communal life. In Christianity as well as Buddhism both discipline and doctrine had soteriological significance related to the authority of the founder and to the maintenance of unity among his followers. In the present study, however, doctrinal matters have been given only secondary consideration.

In order to describe and discuss the comparable patterns in each of the early communities, the author considers the self-understanding of the disciples, instead of relying on a historical-institutional approach. This consideration of the self-understand-

1. Cf. Dutt, *Early Buddhist Monachism*, Bombay, 1960. pp. 6-9.
2. E.O. James, *Comparative Religion*, New York, Barnes & Noble 1938 (reprinted 1961), p. 305.

ing of the members of each community provides an objective basis for the discussion of these communities which could not be obtained by considering them strictly from a modern viewpoint. Original texts have therefore been used as the primary sources of information, while more recent works serve only a supplementary function.

Such topics as the influence of either of these two religions upon the other, or syncretism as the basis of both religions, or the superiority of one over the other are not within the scope of the present study.

Important sources of information on early Buddhism which have been used in this study are:

The Tripiṭakas in translation: *Vinaya Piṭaka* (*Books of Discipline*); *Sutta Piṭaka*: *Dīgha-Nikāya* (*Dialogues of the Buddha*); *Majjhima Nikāya* (*Further Dialogues of the Buddha*); *Samyutta-Nikāya* (*Book of the Kindred Sayings*); *Aṅguttara-Nikāya* (*Book of the Gradual Sayings*); *Dhammapada* (*A Collection of Verses*); *Sutta-Nipāta* (*A Collection of Discourses*); *Theragāthā* (*Psalms of the Early Buddhists*), and also Chinese translation of the original texts, namely: *Ssu Fen Lu*; *Shih Sung Lu*; *Mo Keh Sung Chih Lu* (*Mahāsāṅghika-Vinaya*); *Ta Chih Tu Lun*; *Chung A Han Ching*; *Tza A Han Ching*; *Tseng-yi A Han Ching*; *Shan-Chien-Pi-P'o-Sha* (A Chinese Version by Saṅghabhadra of *Samantapāsādikā*).

Secondary selective sources include S. Dutt, *Early Buddhist Monachism*; E. J. Thomas, *Buddha*, *The History of Buddhist Thought*; H. Oldenberg, *Buddha*: H. Kern, *Manual of Indian Buddhism*. The following Japanese works have been drawn upon: H. Ui, *Indo Tetsugaku Kenkyu* (*A Study in Indian philosophy*), Vol. 4; Watsuji, *Genshi Bukkyo no Jissen Tetsugaku* (*Practical Philosophies in Primitive Buddhism*): M. Sato, *Genshi Bukkyo Kyodan no Kenkyu* (*A Study of the Early Buddhist Order in the Vinaya Piṭaka*); A. Hirakawa, *Ritsu no Kenkyu* (*A Study of the Vinaya Piṭaka*); K. Tsukamoto *Shoki Bukkyo Kyodanshi no Kenkyu* (*A History of the Early Buddhist Order*); K. Hayajima *Shoki Bukkyo to Shakai Seikatsu* (*Early Buddhism and Social Life*); H. Nakamura *Genshi Bukkyo no Seiritsu* (*The Formation of Early Buddhism*).

The study of Christianity has been based primarily upon the New Testament, especially on Paul's letters, the Synoptic Gospels, the *Acts* — all important original sources. Later works consulted include: R. Williams, *Authority in the Apostolic Age*; J. McKenzie, *Authority in the Church*; P. Benit, *The Passion and Resurrection of Jesus Christ*; A. Schlatter, *The Church in the New Testament Period*; G. Bornkamm, *Jesus of Nazareth*; J. Weiss, *Earliest Christianity*; R. P. Martin, *Carmen Christi*; J. Jeremias, *New Testament Theology* Part I; D. L. Dungan, *The Saying of Jesus in the Churches of Paul*; J. G. Davies, *The Early Christian Church*.

Comparative studies of religions which have been consulted during the preparation of this study include: J. Wach, *The Comparative Study of Religions*; Edmunds and Anesaki, *Buddhist and Christian Gospels*; T. Sterling Berry, *Christianity and Buddhism*; Winston L. King, *Buddhism and Christianity*; Nakamura, *Hikaku Shisho Ron* (*A Study of Comparative Thought*) B. D. Kretser, *Man in Buddhism and Christianity*; R. Garbe, *India and Christianity*; Archibald Scott, *Buddhism and Christianity*; etc.

Most studies of early Buddhism have relied almost exclusively on Pāli texts. The use of Chinese translations of texts not available in Pāli, and the use of important Japanese studies of early Buddhism not available in English provide a balanced perspective on the aspects of Buddhism which are the concern of this thesis. Many previous studies have lacked such a balance.

In conclusion I would like to explain the form used in citing non-English references, the in-text use of non-English terms, and, finally, my understanding of the scope and significance of some difficult English terms which are central to this thesis.

The translation of Chinese and Japanese source materials are, without exception, my own and I must assume full responsibility for them. For the convenience of the readers I have transliterated the Chinese and Japanese characters into Roman script throughout the footnotes. Following the transliteration I have included my translation of it enclosed in square brackets. The full form, with the Chihese or Japanese characters, is given in the bibliography.

I have used translated versions of the Sanskrit and Pali texts. In the citations as well as in the bibliography the citations follow the form used by the translator; in all cases the Sanskrit and Pāli texts are given in Roman script followed by the translation of the title enclosed in round brackets.

In the Sanskrit and Pāli translations themselves two form problems occur: (1) Following the text and the translator, some key terms which are not translated into English have been used variously in their Sanskrit or Pāli form, or in both forms, i.e., Sanskrit *dharma* and Pāli *dhamma.* In my citation of the material I have not altered the translator's form. In the text of the thesis I have followed the Sanskrit forms, and where I thought it might help the reader understand the text, I have included the Pāli form in round brackets. (2) It is becoming increasingly common in "popularized" works on Indian Religion to capitalize certain key Sanskrit or Pāli terms (i.e., Dharma, Dhamma) and to overlook the academic rule that non-English terms be italicized or underlined. The general rule which is used as a guideline to capitalization in the English language — that the particular use of a term is capitalized, while its general use is not — does not apply to Sanskrit for two reasons: (1) the devanāgarī script does not have capitalized forms, so, to include them in the Romanized form of the script is artificial, and (ii) those terms which one finds capitalized most often are the very terms which have such a fullness of meaning that it is often superficial to attempt to designate between the "particular" and the "general." Because of this I have used Sanskrit in lower case and italicised all Sanskrit and Pāli terms; proper names are the only exception to this rule.

Two terms which occur throughout the thesis require brief consideration: (i) the term "early" in studies such as this often embroils one in textual-historical questions. It was not possible within the scope of this study to consider such involved questions. My intent is to put forward an interpretation of a set to religious phenomena and while attempting to facilitate this task, I have used the term "early" in a broad but not careless manner to refer to the period covered by three generations after the deaths of Buddha and Christ which, even more generally, would be about a hundred years.

PART I

EARLY BUDDHISM

CHAPTER I

THE AUTHORITY OF BUDDHA : AN EXAMINATION OF THE VIEWS OF THE EARLY DISCIPLES

In this chapter the authority of the founder according to the views of the early Buddhist disciples is discussed.

In order to discuss religious discipline in Buddhism, one should first ask: To what extent and in what way is understanding of authority related to Buddha? Another question is: What is the central authority of all of the Buddhist schools which have very different ideas, although all of them claim to be Buddhist?[1] This discussion will, however, be limited to the first three generations after the founder.[2]

1. Buddhism contained so many different schools that it is difficult to find elements common to them all. For example, while Hīnayāna is more individualistic, Mahāyāna is more universal. Tantric Buddhism (left wing) emphasized the sexual idea, which seems to be a rejection of the early disciplinary prohibition of sex for monks. Zen Buddhism in general denied the succession of the traditional scriptures and traditions and had a very practical emphasis. The Nichiren sect in Japan emphasized militancy; killing the enemies of Buddha was seen as proper action, and was praised, contrary to the original prohibition of killing. Although all these claim to be Buddhism, Tantric Buddhism appears to have been influenced by Hinduism, Zen by Taoism and Confucianism, and Nichiren by Shinto and Confucianism, although all have some common Buddhist elements.

2. From Buddha's death to the Second Council. Cf., R. A. Gard "Buddhism" C. J. Adams *op. cit.* : "The dates of the Buddha are still problematical : the Theravādins in Burma, Ceylon, and India give 624-544 B.C.; and those in Cambodia, Laos and Thailand one year later, 623-543. B.C.; whereas the Mahāyānists, especially in Japan, and most Western scholars have various opinions, such as 566-486 B.C. (the preferable date), 563-483 B.C. or 558-478 B.C.; in any case, all agree that the Buddha had a life-span of 80 years." p. 109. Cf., E. J. Thomas *The History of Buddhist Thought*, "The Cullavagga (Ch. 12) also gives an account of the Second Council. We are told that a hundred years after the death of the lord, (Buddha)." pp. 29-30.

Views vary as to whether or not Buddha was accepted as an authority. Some scholars, including Ui, Watanabe, S. Dutt, Humphreys *et al.*, answer this question in the negative;[1] others, including Keith, Matzumoto, Jayatilleke, Kitagawa, *et al.*, answer in the affirmative.[2]

An important text in Buddhism states that Buddha repudiated his own leadership and suggested truth (*dharma*) as an authority. He said:

> 'Now the Tathāgata, Ānanda, thinks not that it is he who should lead the brotherhood, or that the order is dependent upon him.' And he went on to say: 'therefore O Ānanda, be ye lamps unto yourselves. Be ye a refuge to yourselves.

1. Negative views : H. Ui says, "Buddha had no special controlling power; Buddha was one of the members of *saṅgha*." *Indo Tetsugaku Kenkyu*, vol. 4. (*A Study in Indian Philosophy*), p. 414; S. Watanabe states that the discipline of Buddhism did not have any authority but autonomy as pure independent morality; therefore, no other authority than oneself. *Bukkyo* (Buddhism), p. 91; According to S. Dutt, "In Buddhism there existed no central authority or central control... *Buddhist Monks and Monasteries of India*; C. Humphreys states "There is no 'authority' in Buddhism." p. 28. *A Popular Dictionary of Buddhism*, pp. 38-39.

2. *Positive views* : A. B. Keith states, "Thus happily enough, is a bridge built between the final authority of Buddha and the demand of the individual for respect to his intellectual independence." *Buddhist Philosophy in India and Ceylon*, p. 35; B. Matzumoto says that during Buddha's life time and also for a hundred years after Buddha's death, it was not believed that anyone existed who could be the vicar of Buddha. Their respect for Buddha could not be transferred to any other person : So says *Bukkyoshi no kenkyu* (*A Study of Buddhist History*), p. 18; K. N. Jayatilleke states "The Arahat...had to accept on faith and therefore almost the whole theory of Buddhism had to be accepted on the authority of Buddha alone." *Early Buddhist Theory of Knowledge*, p. 400; J. M. Kitagawa says, "During his lifetime, Buddha was the final authority in the life of the Community, deciding all matters of doctrine and practice even though he may not have meant his decisions to be binding in the years to come. It is said that Buddha on his death-bed urged his followers to depend solely on the Dharma as the guiding principle of their path. But the Dharma was not self-evident : it was the Dharma taught and interpreted by Buddha that his followers accepted." *Religions of the East*, p. 171.

Betake yourselves to no external refuge. Hold fast as a refuge to the Truth.'[1]

S. Dutt suggests that it is not unreasonable to accept this statement from the early Buddhist texts. Whether or not these are the actual words of Buddha, they provide a record of the belief held by the first Buddhist disciples that such was, in effect, Buddha's last pronouncement.[2]

If one accepts this statement, it can be interpreted to mean that Buddha denied his own authority during his lifetime and developed *dharma-vinaya* as the authority for the Buddhist community. The question might still be asked whether the early Buddhist disciples neglected the question of the Buddha's authority.

If Buddha's disciples neglected this question, why should Ānanda have asked Buddha himself about leadership or authority and about his successor, instead of asking other *arahats ?* The very fact that he put this question indicates that Buddha's opinion on the matter was essential, that is, Ānanda regarded Buddha's opinion as the most authoritative one. If they accepted *dharma-vinaya* as an authority, is it not still the case that it was Buddha's teachings which were the basis of what was considered authoritative, however impersonal those teachings may have been in the *vinaya* form? This would seem to indicate that the question of authority should not be too closely tied to the purely historical question of Buddha's personality as a leader.

The author's argument in this section, therefore, is that Buddha's authority was affirmative in the historical sense in that the early Buddhists accepted their founder's teachings as authoritative, although, ultimately, these teachings were to be transcended.

Let us first examine the relationship between Buddha and *dharma.* In his lifetime Buddha denied any claims to authority

1. *Dīgha-Nikāya* (*Dialogues of the Buddha*), Part II, Vol. III, by T. W. Rhys Davids, Pali Texts Society tr., Mahā Parinibbāna-Suttanta II, 100, pp. 107-108. The term "*dharma*" is discussed at length in p. 6 fn. 1 below.
2. S. Dutt, *The Buddha and Five After-Centuries*, p. 96.

as master of the Order, and also declined to nominate a successor. On the contrary, he suggested *dharma* as the principal authority for his disciples. After his death, therefore, they recognized the *dharma* as the guide of the community and thus solved the problem of authority in obedience to Buddha's own mind. It seems natural that after Buddha's death his disciples should interpret authority in accordance with the founder's teaching. This appears to have been a primary characteristic of early Buddhism. *Dharma* is the universal law,[1] which was discovered by Buddha through his enlightenment. It was, let it be

1. Cf. S. C. Banerjee, *Dharma Sutras, A Study in Their Origin and Development*, p. 1. But, "*dharma*" is one of those Sanskrit words which defy an exact rendering into English. While "religion' is rather a loose English equivalent of "*dharma*", "duty" fails to convey all the senses in which the word has been used in ancient Indian literature. The best definition of "*dharma*" appears to have been given by Jaimini in the words "*codanālakṣaṇo 'rtho dharmaḥ*" that is to say "*dharma*" consists in beneficial directions. These directions, however, are manifold : they direct us in our lives as individuals and also as members of society. They teach us how to conduct ourselves in matters both religious and secular. Cf. Th. Stcherbatsky, *The Central Conception of Buddhism*, Susil Gupta, pp. 62-63. Stcherbatsky notes : "The conception of a *dharma* is the central point of the Buddhist doctrine. In the light of this conception, Buddhism discloses itself as a metaphysical theory developed out of one fundamental principle *viz.*, the idea that existence is an interplay of a plurality of subtle, ultimate, not further analysable elements of Matter, Mind and Forces. These elements are technically called '*dharmas*', a meaning which this word has in this system alone. Buddhism, accordingly, can be characterized as a system of Radical Pluralism (*saṅghātavāda*) : the elements alone are realities, every combination of them is a mere name covering a plurality of separate elements. The moral teaching of a path towards Final Deliverance is not something additional or extraneous to this ontological doctrine, it is most intimately connected with it and, in fact, identical with it.

The Connotation of the term "*dharma*" implies that—

1. Every element is a separate (*pṛthak*) entity or force.

2. There is no inherence of one element into another, hence no substance apart from its qualities, no matter beyond the separate sense-data, and no soul beyond the separate mental data (*dharma*=*anātman*=*nirjīva*).

3. Elements have no duration; every moment represents a separate element; thought is evanescent; there are no moving bodies, but consecutive appearances, flashings, of new elements in new places (*kṣaṇikatva*).

[Contd.

repeated, *discovered* by Buddha and not created by him. As his title itself indicates, he became a knowledge-conqueror ever since he attained enlightenment, or, more strictly speaking, he won it by a struggle.[1] As it is stated in a *sūtra*: "The world's Honored One, Buddha, in the world of all the *devas*, demons, Brahman,

4. The elements co-operate with one another (*saṃskṛta*).

5. This co-operating activity is controlled by the laws of causation (*pratītya-samutpāda*).

6. The world-process is thus a process of co-operation between seventy-two kinds of subtle, evanescent elements, and such is the nature of *dharmas* that they proceed from causes (*hetu-prabhava*) and steer towards extinction (*nirodha*).

7. Influenced (*sāsrava*) by the element "*avidyā*", the process is in full swing. Influenced by the element '*prajñā*', it has a tendency towards appeasement and final extinction. In the first case streams (*santāna*) of combining elements are produced which correspond to ordinary men (*pṛthag-jana*); in the second the stream represents a saint (*ārya*). The complete stoppage of the process of phenomenal life corresponds to a Buddha.

8. Hence the elements are broadly divided into unrest (*duḥkha*), cause of unrest (*duḥkha-samudāya*=*avidyā*), extinction (*nirodha*), and cause of extinction (*mārga*=*prajñā*).

9. The final result of the world-process is its suppression. Absolute Calm : all co-operation is extinct and replaced by immutability (*asaṃskṛta*=*nirvāṇa*)." Cf. Conze, *Buddhist Thought in India*, pp. 92-94. Also, "In an ontological sense *dharma* is (1a), a transcendental reality which is real in absolute truth and in the ultimate sense... (1b) *dharma* is 'the order of law of the universe, immanent, eternal, uncreated.'... As reflected in the conduct of life, *dharma* means the moral law, righteousness, virtue, right behaviour, duty and religious practice... The dharmic facts of 1 and 2 as interpreted in the Buddha's teaching. The word then means 'doctrine', 'scripture', 'the truth' (cognitive, and not ontological as at 1a), 'sacred text' or a 'doctrinal text' (often as distinct from *vinaya*)." Daito-Shuppansha in the *Japanese-English Buddhist Dictionary* p. 107. says of the term: *dharma* / *dhamma* : "Etymologically, it means something that always maintains a certain character and becomes a standard of things. I. Laws, truth, righteousness. II. The universal norms or laws which govern human existence. III. The Buddha's teachings; the Buddhist canon. IV. Good deeds that have no defilements... VI. The whole universe as the object of thought."

1. H. Oldenberg, *Buddha*: *His Life*, *His Doctrine*, *His Order*, tr. William Hoey in English, p. 84.

monks, Brahmin, only Buddha was able to attain and realize the Great Wisdom (*mahāmati*) or omniscience by himself."[1]

Dharma or the doctrine was taught by Buddha. He gave it utterance. Without *dharma,* there was no Buddha, but whether there was a Buddha or not, *dharma* would always exist. Being the '*eternal dharma*', it was inherent in the true nature of things, and Buddha rediscovered what had presumably been discovered before but had in course of time been lost.[2] Therefore, whoever could find *dharma* and thereby attain kinship with Buddha's enlightenment, would be attuned to the reality which Buddha proclaimed. Buddha said that through respect and whole-hearted study of this *dharma,* one would attain enlightenment.[3] Thus Buddha's injunction to his disciples to go directly to *dharma* was perfectly consistent with his understanding of himself and his relationship to it. Buddha was an independent man who accepted no authority other than his experience which showed to him a truth. This truth was subsequently expressed by him in the positive form of *dharma.* If *dharma* was the Universal Law, whoever attained Buddha's enlightenment, would be akin to him in his relationship to *dharma.*

This is all theoretically true, but the principal question for us is, "How did his disciples react to him and to his authority?" Did they take his injunction literally and actually act according to it, or did they take the injunction and the man

1. *Tsa A Han Ching*, Vol. 3, *P'o-l'uo-men Ching*, 7, 82 (53) :

"世尊於諸世間諸天魔梵沙門婆羅門中，大智能自證知"

Cf., *Saṁyutta-Nikāya* (*Kindred Sayings*), Part 1, by Mrs. R. Davids, Pali Text Society tr. The *Brahmin Suttas* 7, 1 : 'O *brahmin,* I know of no one throughout the world of gods, Maras or Brahmas, recluses or *brahmins,* no one human or divine, who could so admonish that Exalted One, Arahat, Buddha Supreme. Nevertheless, go thou, *Brahmin,* and then thou wilt know.' p. 200.

2. Cf., E. J. Thomas, *op. cit.*, p. 175.

3. Cf., *Saṁyutta-Nikāya* (*Kindred Sayings*), Part 1, "This Norm (*dharma*) then, wherein I (Buddha) am supremely enlightened—what if I were to live under it, paying it honour and respect !" p. 175. Cf., H. Matzutani *Toyo Shiso no Keisei* (*Formation of Eastern Thought*), p. 269. Cf., *Hsiang ying pu ching Tien Majjhima-Nikāya*, 6, 2, "Kung ching" (Nan Chuan pp. 238-240) Tza a han ching, 44, 11 (*Taisho* 2, 32, 1-2.)

as the author of the injunction in some inseparable unity which became integral to their understanding of the *dharma*? The latter seems to be the case. The disciples, moreover, depended on Buddha's authority during his life-time itself and especially afterwards. If they were not dependent on his authority, why then did Ānanda ask Buddha, not others (*arahats*), about his successor and the leadership and instruction of the community?

In *Majjhima-Nikāya*, there is a report that Vassakara and Gopaka-Moggallana asked Ānanda about their master's successor after his death, a report that runs as follows:

> As to this, the brahman Gopaka-Moggallana said to me: Is there even one Monk, Ānanda, who is possessed in every way and in every part of all those things of which the good Gautama, perfected one, fully Self-Awakened One, was possessed? When this had been said, I brahmom, spoke thus to the brahman Gopaka-Moggallana: 'There is not even one monk... But the disciples are no way following after him." "Is there, good Ānanda, even one monk who was designated by the good Gotama saying; 'After my passing this one will be your support, and to whom you might have recourse now?' " There is not even one monk, brahman, who was designated by the Lord who knew and saw, perfected one fully Self-Awakened One, saying: 'After my passing this one will be your support, and to whom we might have recourse now.' But is there even one monk, Ānanda, who is agreed upon by the order and designated by a number of monks who are elders, saying: 'After the Lord's passing this one will be our support, and to whom you have recourse now?' "There is not even one monk, brahman, who is agreed upon by the order... and to whom we might have recourse now."
>
> "But as you are thus without a support good Ānanda, what is the cause of your unity?"
>
> We, brahman, are not without support; we have a support, brahman. Dharma is the support."[1]

1. *Majjhima-Nikāya* (*The Middle Length Sayings*) Vol. III, by I. B. Horner, 108, *Gopakamoggallanasutta* III, 8-10, pp. 58-60.

However, Ānanda said that no monk appointed by Buddha's successor or by Buddha himself was to take his place. Then both of them asked, 'If this was so, without having a leader (one to guide them), how could the community have unity?' If the community did not have a head, who would control the monks, so that there would be harmony and peace in the community? At that time, religious communities in India were generally led, controlled and regulated by their leaders. It was accordingly assumed that Buddha controlled his community. But was there a leader after his death? Ānanda's answer was that there was no one like Buddha who possessed *dasa pāsādaniyā dharma*. The meaning of this statement is that if there was anyone equal to Buddha, he could succeed him, but, clearly, in Ānanda's mind there was nobody equal to him. Therefore, there was no question of succession. Buddha's authority as the head of the community was not transferable. He was the head by virtue of having discovered the *dharma* and known it as no other man had. So Ānanda said that we must depend on *dharma*.[1]

Buddha, however, taught that the individual monk should find his own *dharma*. The disciples, moreover, generally accepted Buddha's *dharma* as authoritative, apparently depending on the impersonal authority of the master, as contained in his collective teachings. Also they did not appoint a leader either because they were obeying Buddha's word or because they could find no person who was fit to take his place. The question of the unity of the community also seems to have been in the minds of the disciples. They did not want to jeopardize it. Therefore, they accepted the impersonal authority of Buddha for the sake of the unity of the community.

Professor Nakamura develops an argument contrary to the position I have taken from the fact that there was no distinction between the first five monks and Buddha. If Śākya was superhuman, he suggests, then his disciples could not attain a status equal to that of Buddha. His superhuman status, he thinks, is a later concept developed by theologians and

1. M. Sato "Genshi Bukkyo no Kyodan Rinen" (The Community Idea in Early Buddhism), Ed. S. Yoshimura, *Bukkyo Kyodan no Kenkyu* (*A Study of Buddhist Community*), p. 85.

constitutes a distortion of the historical truth.[1] Nakamura's statement suggests the equality of the monks and Buddha inasmuch as the *arahats* did attain a status equal to that of their spiritual master. This appears to be historically true. Accordingly, one could assume that Ānanda asked Buddha to name his successor after his death in that Ānanda was not one of the *arahats*, and therefore did not possess any knowledge of the equality between Buddha and the *arahats*.

The above opinion runs counter to certain facts: if the *arahats* and the elders enjoyed equality with Buddha, why should the monks in the First Council ask Ānanda to propound Buddha's teachings on *dharma*? Furthermore, when they compiled the *dharma-vinaya* they looked for its foundation in Buddha's own words. One disciple's report is as follows:

> 'Thus have I heard from Buddha, in the first place, brethren.' From the mouth of the Exalted One himself have I heard, from his own mouth have I received it. This is the truth, this the Law, this the teaching of the Master, 'Verily, this is the word of the Exalted One, and has been well grasped by that brother.' This, brethren, you should receive as the first Great Authority.[2]

The Buddhist scriptural reports mention the place, the time, the people who were there, and the situation resulting in the preaching of the *dharma*. They state that *dharma-vinaya* was not based on the monks' own knowledge, but on what Buddha had taught. Although all of the *dharma* which they recorded could not actually have been Buddha's own words,[3] they put many of those words in Buddha's mouth in order that they might be endowed with the weight of authority.

1. H. Nakamura, *Gotama Buddha* (*Life of the Buddha*), p. 238.
2. *Mahā-parinibbāna-suttanta* (*The Book of the Great Decease*), pp. 125-126.
3. Cf. S. Dutt, *Early Buddhist Monachism*, p. 7.

This indicates that if the early Buddhist community wanted to establish or even change *dharma-vinaya*, it realized that Buddha alone had the authority to do so. Thus, although in theory no one could alter the *dharma-vinaya* after Buddha's death, some modification was effected and stamped with legitimacy by invoking Buddha's name.[1]

In the light of the above discussion, it appears that Ānanda asked Buddha to name his successor not because he was not an *arahat*, but because he represented the Buddhist monks who had adopted the same attitude as he. In the First Council, when the first lines of Buddha's words were presented by Ānanda, every elder and monk wept and "laid down his head under the master's words."[2]

Matzumoto states that during Buddha's life-time and for a hundred years after his death, his disciples were unable to find anyone who could replace him. Their respect for the master could be transferred to no other person.[3] Nakamura himself qualifies his view regarding the equality of Buddha and the monks with the suggestion that it was not true historically but only theoretically.

It is essential now to try to see what Buddha thought of this question. He evidently did believe in equality in the ideal sense but in practice he allowed distinctions which many scholars[4] have overlooked probably because they were much too concerned with the question of equality. There is no doubt that Buddha himself believed in complete democracy concerning the possibility of attaining the realization of the *dharma*. The *saṁgha* was a democratic community which basically had no caste discrimination; all members practising *dharma-vinaya* were equal and all aimed at the same goal, i.e., *nirvāṇa*. Oldenberg states:

1. Y. Takahashi. "Kai To Sono Kiban" (Discipline and Its Foundation : Problems in Discipline), Ed. Nihon Bukkyo Gakukai, *Bukkyo Ni Okeru Kai no Mondai* (*Problems in Buddhist Discipline*), p. 2.

2. Matzutani, *op. cit.*, p. 318.

3. Matzumoto, *op. cit.*, p. 18

4. Cf. Ui, *op. cit.*, p. 414; H. Nakamura, *Genshi Bukkyo* (*Primitive Buddhism*), p. 146.

No caste in this band (of Buddha) : Whoever will be Buddha's disciple renounces his caste. In one of the speeches which the sacred writings put in Buddha's mouth, it is said on this subject : "As the great streams, O disciples, however many they be, the Gaṅgā, Yamunā, Aciravatī, Sarabhū, Mahī, when they reach the great ocean, lose their old name and their old descent, and bear only one name, these four castes, Nobles, Brahmans, Vaiśya and Śūdra, when they, in accordance with the law and doctrine which the perfect one has preached, forsake their home and so into home-lessness, lose their old name and old paternity, and bear only the one designation: 'Ascetics, who follow the son of the Śākya house'."[1]

If Buddha's disciples saw the difference between the Buddha and the *arahats*, what were the main reasons for this distinction ? "Buddha" means "enlightened one." During Buddha's life-time, the name "Buddha" was applied only to the Buddha himself in the community; his disciples, enlightened through his teachings, were called "*arahats*" (holy ones, respected ones) but not "Buddhas."[2]

According to the *Majjhima-Nikāya*, Ānanda declared :

There is no monk entirely and completely endowed with those qualities with which the Lord, the Arahat, the all-enlightened, was endowed. For the Lord was the producer of the unproduced path, the preacher of the path. But now the disciples are followers of the path, being endowed with it afterwards.[3]

The *arahats* and the Buddha differed in that the latter was the originator of the Path, the discoverer and knower of the Unknown and the preacher of the Unpreached.[4]

1. Oldenberg, *op. cit.*, p. 152.
2. Cf. T. W. Rhys Davids, *Early Buddhism*, "There are distinct traces in our earliest documents of a development of thought in the views of his followers regarding the personality of their master, in their Buddhology." p. 48.
3. Thomas, *op. cit.*, p. 212, *Majjhima-Nikāya* (*Middle Length Sayings*), III, 8.
4. A. Shastri, *An Outline of Early Buddhism*, pp. 25-26.

He was also omniscient (*sarvavid*) in a sense in which the *arahats* were not.[1] When Buddha was claimed to have been omniscient and the concept of 'emancipation by intellectual knowledge alone' (*paññāvimutta*) had developed, there would have been a wide and unbridgeable gulf betwen the Buddha and the *arahats*. The *arahats*, not having developed the *jñānas*, could not and did not verify the fact of rebirth through *karma*. It was a truth which they accepted on faith.[2] Also, while Buddha had ten powers (*daśa-bala-mahā-balasā*), only three types of knowledge were shared by the *arahats*.[3] Although the *arahats* were also enlightened, they could not reach the true perfection which Buddha had, for he claimed the power of remembering his previous existences in which he had cultivated his virtue to an extraordinary degree. The *arahats*, not having this power, could not reach the perfect life style of Buddha, and therefore sometimes made mistakes in this life.

Furthermore, *dharma-vinaya* was equated with Buddha himself and not with the *arahats*, because the monks believed that only the Buddha's wisdom and virtue constituted the perfect nature : what he said and what he did were synonymous. One of his great disciples states : "The world's most venerable Buddha is this eye, this wisdom, this righteousness, this Law. Buddha is Dharma-lord, and Dharma-general. His speech explains righteously the categories of reality; all righteousness is explained according to him."[4]

Conze observes :

If the doctrine of the Buddha had been just a saying of some person or individual, it would lack in making authority. As a matter of fact, it emerged from the spiritual principle, from the Buddha nature, which lay hidden in that individual

1. E. Conze, *Buddhist Thought in India*, p. 169.
2. Jayatilleke, *op. cit.*, p. 400.
3. Shastri, *op. cit.*, pp. 26-27.
4. Chung A Han Ching, Vol. 128 :

迦旃延嘗 '世尊. 是眼. 是智. 是義; 是法. 法王' 法將. 說眞諦. 諦義, 現一功義

Śākyamuni, and which as we might say 'inspirited' him to understand and to teach the truth. His disiciples considered the Buddha the Tathāgata, or speak of his dharma-body.[1]

Even though Buddha was a historical person and the son of a man, the nature attributed to his character differed from that attributed to others. Through his longer cultivation of virtues, he must have attained an ideal character. Thus, as seen by his disciples, he had an ideal supernatural character which they could not reach.

His chief disciple, Sāriputta, praised him thus :

> All monks observed that Buddha had no defects in body, speech or mind (or will) ... in three realms (*trailokya*), he is the only honoured One. There is nobody able to equal him. Because he is Supreme, and most honoured one ... Buddha had committed no sins in his relationships with the people ... [2]

This represents Buddha's character as being superior to that of an ordinary human being.

In the disciples' views, *dharma* is impersonal, yet in Buddha it harmonized with his personality and thus appealed personally to his people ; his thirty-two marks, for example, expressed his omniscience.[3] Thus Buddha was not only different from and

1. Conze, *op. cit.*, pp. 35-36.
2. *Tseng-yi A Han Ching*, Vol. 24, (Shan Chu P'in Vol. 32) :

"觀察如來 無身口意過 … 三界独尊 無能及者，最尊最上 如來無咎於"

Cf., *Suttanipāta*, (*A Collection of Discourses*) *op. cit.* : "Adoration be to thee, O Noble man, adoration be to thee O thou best of men; in the world of men and gods there is no man equal to thee." p. 94. Cf., B.C. Law, "Early Buddhist Brothers and Sisters", p. 39, "The early Buddhist brothers and sisters belonged to a distinct religious Order and school of thought in respect of which the position of the Buddha was that of Saṁgha (founder of an Order), Gaṇi (leader of a following), and Gaṇa (a band of followers), the epithets usually applied to the contemporary founders of different Orders and leaders of different schools of thought." *Digha*, 1. p. 48; *Suttanipāta*, (*A Collection of Discourses*) *op. cit.* p. 39.

3. A. Hirakawa, *Ritsuzo no Kenkyu* (*A Study of the Vinaya-Piṭaka*), p. 516.

superior to men, including the *arahats*, but also his teaching represented an unparalleled authority for his disciples. Thus it was that his personality blended with his teaching.[1]

Professor Warder states that, "The doctrine, not the teacher (Buddha), was the center of interest throughout."[2] This author agrees in general that the doctrine was the center of interest but would add that the doctrine was manifest in the teacher. At least, the historical truth seems to be that Buddha's doctrine, as interpreted by his disciples' understanding, is grounded in his authority as the great teacher.

Let me now illustrate Buddha's personal authority as the great teacher more fully. If the Buddha had no spiritual authority of character as a great teacher, how could his doctrine be trusted and accepted by his disciples ?

Buddha proclaimed himself as the Enlightened One and said :

Victorious over all, omniscient am I
Among all things undefiled,
Leaving all, through death of craving freed,
By knowing for myself, whom should I point to ?

For me there is no teacher,
One like me does not exist,
In the world with its devas
No one equals me.

For I am perfected in the world,
A teacher supreme am I,

1. Cf. I. B. Horner, "Buddhism : The Theravāda", ed. by R. C. Zaehner, *The Concise Encyclopedia of Living Faiths* : "The Dharma I have taught and the Vinaya I have laid down—that after my passing is to be your teacher", (*Dīgha-Nikāya*, III, 84), the body of *dharma*, applicable only to the Buddha and not even to *arahats*, points in this same direction, so the *Milindapañha*, a later and post-canonical work, could say : "The Lord can be designated by means of the *dharma*-body" (*Milindapañha* 75), even though he himself has entered on *parinirvāṇa*... Thus while the unending *dharma* exists the Lord exists and cannot be called extinct. p. 282.

2. A. K. Warder, *Indian Buddhism*, p. 43.

I alone am all-awakened,
Because cool am I, nibbāna-attained.

To turn the dharma-wheel
I go to Kāsi's city,
Beating the drum of deathlessness
In a world that's blind become?[1]

In the same context he said, "I am the knower of everything and winner of everything", therefore "come to me." Herein he claimed and proclaimed that a pure moral character and a perfect wisdom were united in him.

The story of the founding of the Buddhist community illustrates this understanding :

> Then I, monks, walking on tour, in due course arrived at Benares, Isipatana, the deer-park and the group of five monks. Monks, the group of five monks saw me coming in the distance, and seeing me they agreed among themselves, saying, 'Your reverences, this recluse Gautama is coming, he lives in abundance, he is wavering in his striving, he has reverted to a life of abundance. He should be neither greeted, nor stood up for, nor should his bowl and robe be received : all the same a seat may be put out, he can sit down if he wants to. But as I, monks were not able to adhere to their own agreement: having approached me, some received my bowl and robe, some made a seat ready, some brought water for washing the feet, and they addressed me by name and with the epithet 'your reverence.' When this had been said, I, monks, spoke thus to the group of five monks : 'Do not, monks, address a Tathāgata by his name or by the epithet 'your reverence'.' Monks, the Tathāgata is one perfected, (172) a fully self awakened One. Give ear, monks, the deathless is found, I instruct, I teach *dharma*.[2]

1. *Majjhima-Nikāya*, (*Middle Length Sayings*) Vol. I by I. B. Horner, 26. *Ariyapariyesanāsutta* I, 171, pp. 214-215.
2. *Ibid*., p. 215.

This episode tells us that though Buddha's former companions had resolved to treat him without respect, they changed their minds and respected him because his attitude and figure were somehow different from theirs: they advanced to meet him and then washed his feet. They respected him and were attracted to the authority of his personality. They paid him homage without having heard his teaching. It was later that his teaching impressed them.

An episode of the *Mahāvagga* in the *Vinaya Texts*, further supports this fact because, before becoming a Buddhist, Sāriputta met Assaji and asked,

> 'Your countenance, friend, is serene; your complexion is pure and bright. In whose name, friends, have you retired from the world ? Who is your teacher ? Whose doctrine do you profess?'
>
> Assaji replied, 'There is, friends, the great Samana Sakyaputta an ascetic of the Śākya tribe; in His, the Blessed One's name have I retired from the world; He, the Blessed One, is my teacher; and His, the Blessed One's doctrine do I profess,'[1]

However, *vinaya* always presented similar patterns of those who led a homeless life. Most of these monks searched for the teacher and, having found him, became his disciples. It is clear that they embraced the teacher first and then explored his teaching.

Buddha's disciples, brimming over with respect for his personality, formed the small community of both monks and lay

1. *Vinaya Texts*, Part I, *Mahāvagga*, *op. cit.*, 23, 3-4, p. 145; cf., S. Dutt, *Buddha and Five After-Centuries* : "The questions which the wanderers used to ask on meeting one another for mutual recognition and acquaintanca. (see supra pp. 34-35) imply that, in the formation of a sect in the wanderers' community, there were three constitutive principles, viz. (1) Headship or the existence of a recognized Teacher (*Sattha*), (I1) A distinct system of Faith (*Dharma*), and (III) Discipleship (*Uddesa*). The Buddhist sect must have originally had this common organization." cf., M. Sato, "Genshi Bukkyo no Kyodan Rinen" (Ideal of Early Buddhist Community) *Bukkyo Kyodan no Kenkyu*, *op. cit.*, Says, "In *Suttanipāta* and *Āgama*, Buddha is called as the person who possessed *saṁgha* (*saṁghin*) and the person who has gaṇa." p. 84.

people.[1] They forsook their wives, children and relatives, and abandoned their household belongings and valuables to enter the *saṁgha*. Because Buddha exhibited genuine worth, they respected him and responded to him. To them, he was more important than life and property, more important than anything else in their lives.[2] To them the historical Buddha was the person who grasped *dharma*, but he was also the living embodiment of truth, the teacher of men and of gods. Thus the people recognized his absolute authority and followed his leadership. They believed in him as the immovable truth. The Path (*dharma*) which he treaded was the way to enlightenment, which they were constrained to follow.[3]

Among them there were two differing attitudes. One group sought to imitate Gautama Buddha's life, to adopt his life style, and to become like him. Others sought to be enlightened as he was, but failed to adopt his life style.[4]

When they became his disciples, they confessed :

> 'I take my refuge with Buddha; I take my refuge in the Doctrine : I take my refuge in the Order.' At the fortnightly confession, the liturgy of which is among the oldest of all the monuments of Buddhist Church life, the monk, who leads in the confession, charges the brethren who are present, not to conceal by silence any sins which they have committed, for silence is lying, 'And intentional lying, O brethren, brings destruction; thus hath the Exalted One said.' And the same liturgy of confession describes monks, who embrace heresies, by putting in their mouths these words : 'Thus I understand the doctrine which the Exalted One hath preached etc.' Throughout, it is not an impersonal revelation, nor is it the individual's own thought, but it is the person, the word of the Master, the Exalted One, the Buddha, which is regarded as the source of the truth and holy life.[5]

1. Nakamura, *Genshi Bukkyo*, *op. cit.*, p. 144.
2. Matzutani, *op. cit.*, p. 14.
3. Watsuji, *Genshi Bukkyo no Jissen Tetsugaku* (*Practical philosophies in primitive Buddhism*), p. 170.
4. Yoshimura, *op. cit.*, p. 3.
5. Oldenberg, *op. cit.*, p. 75.

The Three Jewels (*triratna*) were central to the Buddhist community as the guiding principles for Buddha's disciples who lived in obedience to this authority. Buddha was accorded the first place among the Three Jewels of the Buddhists. His disciples were influenced by his great personality, while people took refuge in him spiritually;[1] they trusted in him and in his exposition of the *dharma*.[2] Not only the lay people but the *arahats* also had to accept him on faith; in fact, almost the entire theory of Buddhism had to be accepted on the authority of the Enlightened One alone.[3] B.M. Barua has written on the nature of this faith :

> The Abhidharma definition of faith assumes a popular character when it is restated in terms of Buddhaghosa's commentary, 'Faith is a trusting and taking refuge in the Buddha and other Jewels—the Doctrine and the Order. It is an act of believing in the sense of plunging, breaking, entering into qualities of the Buddha and the rest, and rejoicing over them.'[4]

The disciples started with a faith which was grounded in knowledge. One could not think of the doctrines of the master by the independent light of reason; they had to be taught and explained. According to Keith,[5] faith was the means by which one might cross the depth of the river of existence to the safety of *nirvāṇa*. He also observes on the nature of faith :

> The teaching of (the) Buddha saves him who has faith, but destroys the faithless. Ratnakūṭa tells us 'Here the Tathāgata

1. Mizuno, *op. cit*., p. 27.
2. Mrs. Rhys Davids, *A Buddhist Manual of Psychological Ethics*, p. 14.
3. Jayatilleke, *op. cit*., pp. 400-401.
4. B. M. Barua, "Faith in Buddhism," B. C. Law Ed. *Buddhistic Studies*, pp. 332-333; cf. *Atthasalini*, p. 145.
5. Keith, *op. cit*., pp. 34-35.; cf., *Dīgha-Nikāya* II, *op. cit*., 88-89, XVI, *Mahāparinibbāna Suttanta*, 34 : The Exalted One beheld the people who wished to cross to the opposite bank looking some of them for boats and some of them for rafts of wood, and some of them for rafts of basketwork; and as he beheld them he break forth at that time into this song.

[Contd.

alone is my witness, the Tathāgata knows, I do not know but I shall try to discover or verify this myself;[1] boundless is the enlightenment of the Buddhas.' Those who have mere faith and mere affection for the Buddha are destined to heaven. However, faith means confidence, trust, and belief in the instruction of the teacher Buddha.[2]

Buddha emphasized that his disciples should not accept his teachings out of mere respect. He enjoined that they should test his personality and his teachings for themselves in order to find out whether they were true or false, and through their own reason and experience to fully realize the truth. In addition to faith, then, reason was an important aspect of Buddhism. This point is made by Jayatilleke when he says,

> This attitude is well expressed in a late verse, which appears in the *Tattvasaṁgraha* (3588) and the Tibetan version of the *Jñānasamuccayasāra* (cf. V. Bhattacharya, *The Basic Conception of Buddhism*, Calcutta, 1934, p. 11, fn. 9). It reads as follows : 'Just as wise men (test a claim to be gold) by burning, cutting and rubbing (on a touch stone), my statements, O monks, should be accepted after examination and not out of respect for me.' This verse is not found in the Nikāyas but it reflects the attitude of the Buddha as often represented in the Nikāyas. The Buddha is anxious to see that his statements are not accepted out of respect for his authority as the teacher—the very thing that he condemns in the *Kālāma Sutta*. On one occasion he asks, 'would you, O monks, knowing and seeing thus say, "our teacher is respected, we say out of respect for our teacher" (*M*. I. 264).' The monks submit that it is not so.[3]

Indeed, Buddha suggested to his disciples that they should understand his truth, all truth, with the help of analytical

'They who have crossed the ocean drear
Making a solid path across the pools
Whilst the vain world ties its basket rafts—
These are the wise, these are the saved indeed.

1. *Ibid.*, pp. 35-36.
2. Jayatilleke, *op. cit.*, pp. 34-38.
3. *Ibid.*, pp. 390-391.

reasoning. One can thus assert that the Buddhist faith is reason-oriented. Moreover, Buddha's teachings (on suffering, on 'five *skandhas*', and on 'twelve links') were analytical and capable of being understood through reason. Nevertheless, Buddhist *dharma* could not be grasped by logic alone (*D.N.* I p. 187). Buddha is said to have left unexplained (*avyakta*) the ten questions regarding the eternity or non-eternity of the soul (*jīva*) with the body (*śarīra*), the difference between them, and the nature of the Tathāgata after death.[1] Reason was chained to practical experience. The disciples had to trust the Exalted One and his teachings and to verify them through practice and experience. Early Buddhism emphasized the enlightenment experience.[2] This stemmed from an initial trust in Buddha's personality and teachings which were accepted as authoritative without entirely sacrificing the rational aspect of freedom. Thus a bridge was built between the authority of the master and the demands of the disciples for their intellectual independence.[3]

It was not possible to acquire *dharma* without acceptance of this authority. Evidently it was believed to be impossible to acquire *dharma* without accepting the authority of Buddha as an omniscient teacher and following the example set by him. Buddha's disciples regarded their master as being superior to Brāhmaṇas, other men and even gods, because his teaching was great and because his personality and moral virtue outdid those of the others.

If we compare and analyze the story of "the conversion of Sāriputta and Moggallana" and the story of "Devadatta", they would give some indication of Buddha's authority; the general authority of a teacher in Buddha's time appears evident in the first episode. When Sārripputta and Moggallana wanted to move from the community led by Sañjaya to the Buddhist community,

1. Shastri, *op. cit.*, pp. 157; 423. See also, N. Dutt, *op. cit.*, pp. 44-49.

2. Cf., Keith, *op. cit.*, stresses Buddha's superhuman knowledge and argues against thinking that his name was founded on "dialectic accompanied by reasoning or experience, made of individual intuition" p. 35; cf., *M.N.* i, 71; cf., *S.N.* iii, 103.

3. *Ibid.*, p. 35.

Sañjaya attempted to stop them. He promised them that he would divide his community leadership into three parts and that he would give each of them one part of the leadership, retaining the third part for himself. The three of them would lead the community. Sāriputta and Moggallana rejected this offer and moved to the Buddhist community. If we interpret Sañjaya's words correctly, a teacher had absolute authority of leadership; if he chose to hand over the leadership to someone else he could do so. While, in practice, this differed from the situation in the Buddhist community, the people of that time generally viewed the question of leadership in Buddhist community in this light.[1]

Next, let us examine the story of Devadatta. Toward the end of Buddha's life, Devadatta, his cousin and one of his disciples, wanted to assume the role of the leading authority in the Buddhist community and asked Buddha about it. Kern provides an account of Devadatta's position : "Sometime afterwards, the story goes, when the Lord, sojourning in the Bambu grove, was preaching the Law, Devadatta rose from his seat, and reverentially made the proposal that the Lord, on account of his age, should leave the leadership of the congregation of monks to him, Devadatta."[2] This request was made three times but was refused by Buddha. "Buddha told him that he was not going to name any successor of his, not even his best disciples like Sāriputta and Moggallana, not to speak of an evil-minded person like him."[3] Upon his refusal, Devadatta conspired with King Ajātaśatru to kill him. He first hired sixteen men to murder him, but these men became his followers instead. He next attempted to kill him by hurling on him a large rock, but succeeded only in injuring his foot. Devadatta then sent the wild elephant, Natagṛha, to kill Buddha, but was unsuccessful again.

1. M. Sato, *Bukkyo Kyodan no Seiritsu to Tenkai* (*Formation and Development of Buddhist Community*), p. 25.

2. H. Kern, *Manual of Indian Buddhism*. He also says, "Already long before the epoch enmity had sprung up in the breast of Devadatta against the Lord, whose growing fame and influence filled him with jealousy." p. 38.

3. N. Dutt, *op. cit.*, p. 107.

If Buddha did not have the authority to bestow the right of leadership, why then did Devadatta propose that he should transfer it ? Why did the Buddha refuse ? When Buddha refused to give Devadatta the leadership, why did Devadatta attempt to kill him, three times, and finally start another community ? There are two reasons why Buddha did not transfer his authority to Devadatta. First, Buddha's authority was based on his own personal attainment, and hence not as such transferable. Secondly, he obviously did not think that Devadatta was the fittest person to wear the mantle of chief disciple. On the other hand, when Sāriputta and Moggallana followed him, he said : "This pair of disciples will be my chief, my eminent pair !"[1] It was on the basis of this that the early Buddhist communities generally recognized these two as the chief disciples.

In the *Sutta-nipāta* we read the following :

Sela :
Wholly awake thou dost profess to be,
Rajah of Dharma and without a peer;
Thou say'st; By Dharma do I roll the wheel ?
But who's thy marshal, Gotama, thy squire,
The Master's man ? who keeps a roll for thee
This wheel of Dharma thou hast set aroll.
The master (Buddha) :
The wheel by me set rolling, said the Lord
The wheel of Dharma, Sela, without peer,
'Tis Sāriputta who keeps, that aroll
He is the heir born to the Man-thus-come.[2]

When some mendicants wished to move to a western province to live, they came to Buddha to seek permission. He asked them, "Have you got leave, brethren, from the venerable Sāriputta ?" "No master...", they replied. "Then get leave from...Sāriputta. He is the patron of those who live the righteous life along with him."[3]

1. Horner, "Buddhism : The Theravāda", *op. cit.*, p. 281.
2. *Sutta-nipāta,* (*A Collection of Discourses*) tr., E. M. Hare, Vol. III and IV, 555-557, p. 88.
3. *Saṁyutta-Nikāya* (*Kindred Sayings*) Vol. III, *op. cit.*, p. 6.

Furthermore, in the early sources of the Jain scriptures, Sāriputta appears as the leader of the Buddhist community and Buddha himself is ignored. It is important from a historical point of view that an outside source mentions Sāriputta's position as the leader of the Buddhist community.[1] However, it is important to note that Sāriputta was the leader of the community precisely because Buddha appointed him his chief disciple and representative in the community.[2] Sāriputta's general career was highlighted by his role as an interpreter of Buddha's doctrine and as a catechizer.[3] (He would appear to be the Buddhist counter-part of Simon Peter, but we shall later see how similar and dissimilar the two are.)

Sāriputta praised Buddha as follows :

> Buddha had no defects in body, speech, or mind... In three realms, he is the only honoured one (Buddha). There is nobody able to equal him, because he is supreme and most honoured one. Buddha had committed no sins in his relationships with the people.[4]

Unless Buddha believed in the right to give authority to another and unless his disciples accepted the leadership role vested on Sāriputta; how could Sāriputta possibly have been appointed his chief disciple ? We shall notice later how this is

1. Cf., Nakamura, *Genshi Bukkyo no Seiritsu*, *op. cit.*, p. 390. Cf., *Isibhasiyam*. "Ein Jaina-Text der Frühzeit." Von Walter Schubring. *Nachrichten von der Akademie der Wissenschaften in Göttingen*. Philologisch-Historische Klasse. Jahrgang 1942, Nr. 6; 1952, Nr. 2. Vandenhoeck und Ruprecht in Göttingen. ch. 38 (Pali : *Sāriputta Buddha*=Sanskrit : *Sāriputra Buddha*.)

2. Cf., *Majjhima-Nikāya*, (*Middle Length Sayings*), Vol. III, 29, p. 81, "Monks, if anyone speaking rightly could say of a man : "He is the Lord's own son, born of his mouth, born of dhamma, formed by dhamma, an heir to dhamma, not an heir to material things'—speaking rightly he could say of Sāriputta : 'He is the Lord's own son, born of his mouth, born of dhamma, formed by dhamma, an heir to dhamma, not an heir to material things."

3. Law, "Early Buddhist Brothers and Sisters", *Journal of the Asiatic Society of Bengal*, Vol. XI, 1945, p. 48.

4. See p. 15, fn. 2.

still different from the power by which authority was transmitted by Christ to Peter and the other disciples.

The *Mahā-parinibbāna Suttanta* relates an episode which is of interest :

> Now at that time the venerable Mahā-Kassapa was journeying alone the high road from Pava to Kusinara with a great company of the brethren, with about five hundred of the brethren... Now the venerable Mahā-Kassapa saw the naked ascetic coming in the distance; and when he had seen him he said to that naked ascetic; 'O friend ! surely thou knowest our Master ?' 'Yes friend ! I know him. This day the Samana Gotama has been dead a week ! ...' On that of those of the brethren who were not yet free from the passions, some stretched out their arms and wept, and some fell headlong on the ground, and some reeled to and fro in anguish at the thought.... Now at that time a brother named Subhadda, who had been received into the order in his old age was seated in that company ! And Subhadda the recruit in his old age said to those brethren : — 'Enough, sirs ! Weep not, neither lament ! We are well rid of the great Samana. We used to be annoyed by being told : — 'This beseems you, this beseems you not ! But now we shall be able to do whatever we like; and what we do not like, that we shall not have to do !'[1]

The episode indicates that one of his former disciples maintained that the strict rules given by Buddha were mandatory for his disciples during his life-time, but upon his death, they ceased to be binding. Accordingly, the disciples called the First Council and compiled the *dharma-vinaya.* This confirms my point that the Buddha was authorized by the disciples to control the community.

During the life-time of the founder, the Buddhist order or *saṁgha* was unified under the leadership of the Buddha. One *sūtra* illustrates this point clearly :

1. *Mahā-parinibbāna Suttanta* (*The Book of the Great Decease*), *op. cit.*, *D.* ii, 162, (19-20), pp. 183-184.

Buddha asked a monk 'How old are you monk ?' He said 'I am one year old. At that time there were many Buddhist monasteries in the districts, but if he belongs there he was as if he were one year old without Buddha's acceptance : So that Buddha was always the center.[1]

Many local *saṁghas* were democratically organized, but where-ever Buddha was present the place became the center of the general Buddhist community.[2] Buddha laid down laws for the disciples; he alone was the law-giver. Each rule which purported to be a statement of right was stipulated in a serious deliberation by Buddha after a particular situation had actually arisen; therefore he was also the judge.[3] Early Buddhists claimed that the scriptures were given by Buddha, and not formulated by them. In fact, the scriptures could be given by Buddha in part only; later additions were numerous.[4] The disciples generally claimed that they formulated no *dharma*, but that they accepted Buddha's *dharma* as authoritative.

Buddha had authority as the leader who was both law-giver and judge of his disciples. He craved for a democratic way of life for his community, and he chose not to exercise strong authority over the teachers of other religious communities of his time.

We come now to consider Buddha as the "King of Dharma" (Pāli : *cakkavatti* = Sanskrit: *cakravartin*). What manner of king was he ? He was not a king in the secular sense—that was obvious. But, then, was he the son of a king ? Oldenberg answers this question thus :

A widespread tradition represents Buddha as having been a King's son. At the head of this aristrocratic community

1. M. Sato, "Genshi Bukkyo no Kyodanrenen" ("The Community Idea of Primitive Buddhism"); S. Yoshimura, Ed. *Bukkyo Kyodan no Kenkyu*, *op. cit.*, p. 90.
2. *Ibid.*
3. S Dutt, *Early Buddhist Monachism*, *op. cit.*, p. 23.
4. Cf., S. Dutt, "Vinaya Piṭakam", *Journal of the Department of Letters*, Vol. X, Calcutta, India, 1923 : "Rules which are inconsistent with each other and which clearly belong to different stages in the evolution of Buddhist monachism are thus placed on the same chronological level by putting them into the mouth of Buddha." p. 26.

there must certainly have been someone leading man, appointed, we know not by what rules, with the title of King, which can scarcely in this case have indicated more than the position of *primus inter pares*. But the idea that Buddha's father Śuddhodana enjoyed this royal dignity is quite foreign to the oldest forms in which the tradition regarding the family are presented to us: rather, we have nothing more or less to contemplate in Śuddhodana than one of the great and wealthy landowners of the Śākya race, whom later legends first transformed into the "great King Śuddhodana."[1]

The above statement appears to have been accepted by some scholars.[2] But, even though he was not a king's son, if the early Buddhist disciples took him for the "Son of King", or for the "King of Dharma", there must have been something regal and majestic reflected in him, something that gave his disciples the notion that he was the "King of Dharma." This might sound curious, but in the context of his authority in the community the point becomes credible. An interpretation of the "four gates" story connected with his Great Renunciation (*mahātyāga*) in which he saw the four signs—the old man, the sick man, the dead man and the monk—is required to clarify this point, for it seems highly unlikely that Śākya would not have known about old age, sick men, death or asceticism until he was twenty-nine years old. There is, then, some special reason for the story.

In his time, as a young man born in a respectable family, he would have been governed by two lofty goals : either to be the ideal king (*cakravartin*) who would unite the world or to live a homeless life and become a saint in order to control the spiritual world.[3] However, the concept of being the ideal king apparently seemed unpracticable to him since he was just the son of a wealthy landowner. This is so even if it is accepted

1. Oldenberg, *op. cit.*, p. 99.
2. Watanabe, *op. cit.*, pp. 90-91.
3. Matzutani, *op. cit.* : "In that time, Kings and new thinkers, appeared as great figures, so that young people were evidently impressed by them." p. 257. Cf., *Chang-pu-Ching Tien* (*Digha-Nikāya*), vol. 26, (Chuan Lun Sheng Wang Tzu Hou Ching); *Nanten* 8, pp. 73-96.

that he was the son of the elected chief of the small Śākya clan,[1] for, at that time, small kingdoms or tribes were fighting and amalgamating one another, and the Śākya tribe, being small, had little power. As the king's son, he would have had little chance of becoming a *cakravartin*. In fact, his tribe was destroyed during his own lifetime. Buddha states that one who is born in a Kṣatriya family of scanty means, but who has an excessive desire to seek the position of King of This World would bring ruin upon himself.[2] It could be argued that this is a judgement reflective of the Śākya's predicament.

There is no record that Gotama attempted to expand the Śākya's earthly kingdom which was already declining at that time. He sought the goal of the eternal, spiritual kingdom. He, therefore, chose a homeless life.[3] The alternatives of his predicament are expressed in the story of his birth : "If he chooses a worldly life, he will become the Buddha."[4] Sato makes the following observation on this point : "Here is embodied the prophetic idea of Buddha as King of Dharma, and it may constitute a basis for the traditional comparison of Buddha with a secular king, and Buddha's teaching as the mighty "wheel of *dharma* (which will) crush all evil in its path."[5] According to some Buddhologists, the *dharma-cakra* represents, symbolically, the sphere of power of universal rule or the spiritual reign of the King of Dharma.[6] This may account for

1. N. Dutt, *op. cit.*, p. 31.
2. Matzutani, *op. cit.*, p. 357. cf., *Hsio-pu Ching Tien, Ching Chi* 6, "Pai Wang Ching", 24 Chieh (*Chuan* 24, p. 4).
3. Sato, *Bukkyo Kyodan no Seiritsu to Tenkai, op. cit.*, p. 31.
4. Oldenberg, *op. cit.*, pp. 82-83; cf., Thomas, *op. cit.*, p. 4; cf., Shastri, *op. cit.* : He says, "They furnish the list of thirty-two major and eight minor marks (*anuvyañjana*) which, according to popular belief, indicated that the individual would either become a universal ruler (*cakravartin*) or a Buddha. The attribution of these marks to the Buddha is probably due to the borrowing of the popular belief in their efficacy." p. 24. cf., Conze, *Buddhism, Its essence and Development*, says : "A list of 32 'marks of a superman' often supplemented by a list of 80 'subsidiary marks', described the most salient features of the Buddha's 'glorious body.' The list of the 32 marks is common to all schools, and it must be fairly old." pp. 36-37.
5. Sato, *Bukkyo Kyodan no Seiritsu to Tenkai, op. cit.*, p. 32.
6. Thomas, *op. cit.*, pp. 221-222.

the claim that in Buddha's funeral proceedings the Emperor saluted him.[1]

All this indicates that the "spiritual" kingdom of Buddha was established as a better alternative to an earthly kingdom. Buddha himself was said to have descended from a royal lineage which he renounced in order to become a different kind of king. He said : "They are Adikkas by family, Sakiyas by birth, from that family I have wandered out, not longing for sensual pressures.[2]

The term "śākya" means "Sun-Family descended." It expresses the pride of his family as descendants of the Sun. The Sun or heaven symbolized a king or emperor in ancient India, Greece and even Japan. Thus the Buddha has been acclaimed as the "Sun-hero."[3]

Thus Buddha would have been royalty-conscious; whether a secular king or King of Dharma, the assumption of regal authority would have been inevitable. Like a secular king, who occupies the highest position in the human hierarchy, he would have had the ruling function in the kingdom of his community (*saṁgha*).

Furthermore, the monks were called "sons of the spiritual Śākya kingdom," and lost their narrow caste position as soon as they entered his community. The relationship of Buddha, as the King of Dharma, to the disciples as his people was like that of a father to his sons and daughters.[4]

A father, like a king, has authority over his people and protects them from their enemies. Buddha called his monks

1. Sato, *Bukkyo Kyotan no Seiritsu to Tenkai, op. cit.*, p. 32.

2. *Sutta-nipāta* (*A Collection of Discourses*) tr. V. Fausboll, *Sacred Books of the East*, Ed. F. M. Müller, Vol. X, Part II, Cf., Matzutani, *op. cit.*, p. 253; cf., Watsaji, *op. cit.* ; "In the Vinaya of four divisions, ten lines of mystical kings were said to constitute Buddha's lineage." p. 44.

3. Oldenberg, *op. cit.*, pp. 72-73.

4. Cf., Nakamura, "Keisei Tojo no Kyodan" (*Bukkyo Kyodan no Kenkyu*), *op. cit.*, pp. 2-9 (a) Monks as Buddhas; Son of Buddha (*Therag* 536; 889; *Therag* 63; 385). (b) Buddha's real son; Putto Buddhassa Oraso (*Therag*, 174; 348). (c) Nuns; Buddha's real daughter : Orasā Dhītā Buddhassa (*Therag* 46) cf., 385. (d) Monks; Buddha's 'Successor' or 'My Son', cf., *Therag* 1168; 1169; 1248), dāyāduka (*Therag* 1142).

"my people" (*māmaka*), and would address one as "my son" which meant "successor", just as a son is his father's successor. Buddha's disciples are all frequently called Buddha's true or genuine sons, *putta orasā*, 'sons of the breast.'[1] The *Saṁyutta-Nikāya* states :

The Exalted one said 'Be it revealed to thee, Vangisa.' Then the venerable Vangisa extolled the Exalted One in his presence with suitable verses :
To-day on feast-day, for full purity,
Five hundred brethren are together come,
Such as have cut their fetters, but their bonds,
Seers who are free from rebirth, and from ill,
And as a king who ruleth all the world,
Surrounded by his empire everywhere,
Driving throughout this earth that ends in sea,
So him, who is our victor in the war,
The peerless Master of our caravan,
We followers attend and wait upon,
Who hold the triple lore, slayers of death,
All we are sons of the Exalted One,
No sterile chaff may amongst us be found,
I worship him who strikes down craving's dart,
I greet the offspring of the sun's great line.[2]

At that time, a king was required to be a teacher through moral example, a teacher of *dharma*, like Buddha. Because of Buddha's relationship to the Śākya family tradition, he saw his disciples as his sons. The disciples on their part trusted

1. Thomas, *op. cit.*, p. 59, cf., *Therag* 295; 41; 348; 536; cf., *Samy.* iii 83,

Who understand the Khandhas five,
in the good doctrine live their life,
worthy of praises, righteous men,
These are the Buddha's genuine sons.

So Kasyapa the Great describes himself, *Samy.* ii, 221, and Buddha tells his disciples, when asked who they are, to say that they are true sons of the Lord (*Digha.* iii, 84).

2. *Saṁyutta-Nikāya*, (*Kindred Sayings*) Part I, tr. by Mrs. R. Davids, pp. 243-244.

him as their father; he had the authority of a king in presenting *dharma* and they were pleased to be called the sons of Śākya. Buddha was the king of *dharma*, and the disciples happily accepted the spiritual status of sons in the community (*saṁgha*).

According to early Buddhist scriptures, it was essential for the monk to leave his home and give up everything. But Buddha seems to have been an exception to this rule when it came to his family relations. After an absence of twelve years, he visited his father at Kapilavastu, where he performed several miracles and converted many Śākyas to his Path.[1] He visited his home town several times. The Śākya people considered it a great honour that their tribe had produced Buddha, and they respected him very much. When the Śākya people were celebrating the completion of their new assembly hall, they invited Buddha to be the first to enter the hall and bless them for the eternal happiness of the castle of Kapilavastu. Buddha entered first accompanied by his disciples and did what his relatives requested him to do.[2] This procession was similar to one wherein a king, surrounded by his people, entered his new government house.

In the community, Śākya's people played a very important role, especially when the monks edited the *dharma-vinaya*, and gave it authority. At that time *dharma* was authorized by Ānanda, Buddha's life-long secretary and cousin, and *vinaya* was authorized by Upāli. Both Ānanda and Upāli held positions

1. M. Müller, "Buddha and Buddhism", ed. M Müller, *Studies in Buddhism*, p. 6; cf., N. Dutt, *op. cit.*, : "Śuddhodana: The king with a large retinue proceeded towards the Nyagrodha hill to welcome the prince, now a recluse. He was then thinking within himself what a great son he had, endowed with all the auspicious signs which prognosticated his sovereignty over the whole of Jambudvīpa, but alas! He was now living on alms collected from door to door. Buddha could easily read his thoughts and then in order to convince the king that he was far greater than a sovereign ruler, he rose up in the sky and walked; there to and fro as if he was entering into the river water. The exhibition of miracles produced the desired effect on the mind of the king and the Śākyans accompanying him." p. 104.

2. M. Anesaki, *Kompon Bukkyo* (*Primitive Buddhism*), p. 111.

of significance in relation to doctrinal authority, and both had come from the Śākya family. Devadatta who rebelled against Buddha and founded his own community, which suggests that he was a person of considerable importance, was also his cousin.

His son, Rāhula, also had a special status as Buddha's son, even though a story recounts that he was so disrespectful to the great disciple Sāriputta and that Buddha criticized his manner. Buddha's father was also converted.[1]

As noted previously, at first Buddha did not allow nuns to enter the Buddhist community, but, finally, permitted them to do so. Even though he did not deny that men and women were equally able to become enlightened, he did not accept this in the practical sense. He seemed to believe that women presented a threat to the purity of the community, and he stated that if nuns entered the *saṁgha*, the longevity of the Buddhist *dharma* would be reduced from a thousand years to five hundred years. Most religious orders of that time did not admit women to a homeless way of life, because, except in the larger cities, police power had not developed to the extent that it was possible for women to lead a homeless life. A homeless life was especially hazardous for women in mountainous areas under the conditions prevailing at that time, as some recorded cases of injuries to nuns show.[2] Buddha accepted nuns because his step-mother, his own wife, and many Śākya women wanted to be nuns. His step-mother was the head of the nuns' community. These points indicate that Buddha subconsciously viewed his ideal kingdom as Śākya-family-oriented. This orientation was accepted by his disciples, who became members of the spiritual kingdom of Śākya.

Buddha's disciples regarded him as the "King of Kings" occupying the highest position among men over whom he had control through *dharma*. The duty of this ruler was to teach people the principles of good conduct and to conquer the

1. Nakamura, *Genshi Bukkyo Sono Shiso to Seikatsu* (*The Thought and Life in Early Buddhism*), p. 149.

2. Watanabe, *Bukkyo no Ayumi* (*Steps of Buddhism*), p. 33.

earth, not through the use of force, but through *dharma*, and to build his spiritual kingdom which was oriented toward peace and unity.[1]

Evidently, Buddha did not accept the divinely oriented authority of the *Vedas*, the Brahmans, or the caste division.[2] He believed that only his experience of universal *dharma* was authoritative. His *dharma-vinaya* was fundamentally different from the caste-*dharma*, the metaphysico-social basis of Hindu holy community,[3] which emphasized that each person must perform the duties assigned to him by his caste as the only route to liberation.

Buddha's disciples believed their master to be an omniscient teacher who was well grounded in *dharma*. They believed that Buddha's personality had balanced both his teachings and his actions, and they desired to follow his teachings and model in their attempts to attain *nirvāṇa*. Lay followers especially trusted Buddha's teaching because of his personality and his way of life. As a teacher Buddha occupied a dominant position in the life of the people who loved and worshipped him. Scriptural study meant nothing to the lay people who were only attracted by the example of the teacher, Buddha. Only through their faith in and dependence on him would they make progress.[4] Long after Buddha's death, the *stūpa* worship was developed because of lay people's deep faith in and reverence for Buddha himself.

1. Warder, *op. cit.*, p. 175.
2. M. Müller says : "Buddha refused to allow the *Vedas* any independent authority whatever and this constituted the fundamental difference between the two philosophies." Cf., Mizuno, *op. cit.*, p. 242 : "Such were the three important principles of Brahmanism since the days of Brahmanas and which were the thoughts of (divine dispensation of the *Vedas*, 'all-in-all ritualism', and the 'absolutism of the Brahmins.' "The Brahmins looked up to the *Vedas* as absolute truth and recognized its authority; they made it that rituals and prayers could dominate over all fates of man, and that the Brahmins were by birth the highest and gods of the earth. Buddhism negated the authority of all these. Because of this, Buddhism was badly hated by Brahmanism and this was one of the chief reasons why Buddhism had lost its own place in India." *op. cit.*, p. 11.
3. Kitagawa, *op. cit.*, p. 169.
4. B. Sangharakshita, *Three Jewels*, p. 154.

Dharma and the example set by Buddha's impersonal nature were understood to be identical as far as their authority over the people was concerned. Buddha as the king of *Dharma* acted much like a secular king as defined by the Hindu understanding of *dharma* but without any divine or metaphysical sanction. A king in Hinduism should be ruled by *dharma*, caste-*dharma* rather than by relying on his own judgement alone. Thus caste-*dharma* was primary, and the king as the guardian and executor of *dharma* was unique. Likewise, as King of *Dharma*, Buddha had the authority to rule over his people through *dharma*. He was the transmitter of *dharma-vinaya* and the disciples trusted him and followed his *dharma*.

The Mahāyāna concept of *dharma-kāya* over which Buddha ruled as king may not have been there from the very earliest days. Even at the earliest stages, however, there were some similar links between Buddha and *dharma*. As an omniscient teacher he presented a living example of *dharma* in his teaching and character. There was no clear separation between these two even in his time. Without the great personal authority of the teacher's person and example, his doctrine could scarcely have succeeded in its world-mission. Irving Babbitt was right when he observed:

> The fact is that one cannot read long in the Pali records without getting the impression of a definite doctrine and a definite personality. For the personality of Buddha, which seems to many even more impressive than the doctrine, one needs to turn from the *Dhammapada* to other portions of the canon, especially to certain Suttas of the *Dīgha-nikāya*.[1]

Buddha was superior to men, Brahmans, or gods, and therefore became a teacher, a dynamic supreme authority. In Buddhism, however, the authority exercised by the founder was different from that in Christianity, for the authority was never absolute, nor did it bring in the instrumentality of any divine being like the Holy Spirit, so central a notion in Christianity. The disciples of Buddha understood the master's authority as

1. *The Dhammapada*, tr. I. Babbitt, pp. viii, 1.

that of the omniscient teacher and of the king of *dharma* who ruled his community through *dharma* and could not separate Buddha's doctrinal authority from the personal example of his life. Buddha asked for wisdom rather than for the faith of his disciples, and the impersonal authority grounded in the *dharma* continued in that same form and that form only.

CHAPTER II

THE NATURE OF THE SAṀGHA
(The Buddhist Community)

INTRODUCTION

In this chapter the nature of the Buddhist community as reflected in the understanding of the early Buddhist disciples is discussed.

In order to discuss the subject it would legitimately be presented in four parts centred around the following four questions: (1) Did the *saṁgha* become a 'church' or an esoteric community? (2) Did the early Buddhist community possess the character of religious unity? (3) What was the nature of the original discipline in the *saṁgha*? These are the three aspects of a single coherent topic and appear to be most important for one discussing the nature of the community. (4) In what sense was Buddha a source of unity?

By way of introduction, the following topics have been examined: (1) Importance of the subject; (2) Definition of the community; and, (3) Religious discipline.

1. IMPORTANCE OF THE SUBJECT

E. J. Thomas sheds light on and accentuates the importance of studying the *saṁgha* when he states:

> ... the Buddha-word includes also the rules of the community which was founded for the purpose of practicing the new life. To begin by analysing the Doctrine without first examining the community and the circumstances in which it originated would be likely to lead to quite arbitrary results. The movement began not with a body of doctrine but with formation of a society bound by certain rules.[1]

1. E. J. Thomas, *The History of Buddhist Thought*, p. 14.

Buddhism did not start with religious teaching only: the formation of the religious community was central to it from the beginning. Without a knowledge of the religious community, one could not fully comprehend the Buddhist doctrines. Early Buddhism seems to consist of a balance between knowledge of the doctrines and their practice within the community. When one speaks of doctrines, they are not to be separated from practical training, ascetic practices, or life in the *saṁgha.*

Many scholars study Buddhism only as a philosophy. S. Dutt considers this an erroneous approach. He says:

> Hence it is that the ancient Buddhist Saṁgha, through which Buddhism as an organized religion actually developed, has received far less than its due share of attention. But the history of Buddhism cannot be viewed apart from the growth and development of the Buddhist Saṁgha, and, apart from the organization of monastic life and community, ancient Buddhism is at best an abstraction. ... The tendency to comprehensive treatment and the adoption of the philosopher's stand-point, that prevail among writers on Buddhism, ... On reading, for instance, the meagre accounts of the Buddhist Saṁgha, out of all proportion to the importance of the subject, in the popular pages of Rhys Davids, Oldenberg, Kern and other writers ....[1]

This methodological clarification is necessary in order to understand the essence of Buddhism. Theory should inevitably be balanced with a consideration of the practical aspects, such as the community and discipline, which seem to be much less studied than the philosophical doctrines.[2]

It seems important to study the original pattern of the Buddhist community not only in its relationship to discipline, but also in relation to the question as to whether the early Buddhist community constituted a "church" or an esoteric community. (I use the term "church" in a very tentative sense. In the west the term involves the questions of institution and

1. S. Dutt, *Early Buddhist Monachism*, pp. 6-7.
2. *Ibid.* pp. 6-7.

authority, the very questions which the first portion of this work endeavors to explicate with regard to "early" Buddhism). Different scholars express different opinions on this matter.

H. Oldenberg says: "But if the order (Buddhist) be regarded as the ideal unit of believing monks over the whole face of the earth, . . . yet in actual life the order never appears in this universal sense. There is really not one order, but only orders, communities of the monks sojourning in the same diocese."[1] With a slightly different emphasis J. H. Kern states, "Buddhism is properly a monastic institution, and the laity is but accessory."[2] In opposition to Kern's position, S. Dutt maintains that there was no difference between monks and lay people.[3] H. Nakamura supports Dutt, but adds a qualification. He states that the earliest Buddhist community consisted both of monks and lay people, because everyone who gathered to admire Buddha had the same status, but when the community was developing, there was a division between monks and lay people.[4]

The *saṁgha*, the Buddhist community, was called "unity of monks (or assembly)."[5] Unity was inherent in the nature of the community. The Buddhist community, being one of the oldest religious communities, has, therefore, stood as an example of unity for religio-sociological studies.[6] Hayazima has observed that a major problem in modern times is the conflict between society and the individual, for which modern social services

1. H. Oldenberg, *Buddha : His Life, His Doctrine, His Order*, p. 340.

2. J. H. Kern, *Manual of Indian Buddhism*, p. 72.

3. S. Dutt, *Monachism, op. cit.*, pp. 63-65.

4. H. Nakamura, *Gotama Buddha*, p. 251.

5. *Vinaya Texts*, Part II, tr. by T. W. Rhys Davids and Oldenberg, *Mahāvagga*, X. 4. 4, p. 310. Cf., *Ssu Fen Lu Hsing-Shih Chao*, *Taisho Taizokyo* : "Saṁgha means, 'A community gathered together.' If some members are present in the assembled community, while others absent from the community, then it is impossible to achieve the great result through the Law." Vol. 40, p. 6.

6. A. Hirakawa states that the ways adopted by Buddha for achieving peace, would be important for the study of religious sociology, *Ritsuzo no Kenkyu* (A Study of the *Vinaya-Piṭaka*), p. 1.

have found no permanent satisfactory solution.[1] Study of the Buddhist community as an ideal of unity could perhaps help modern pluralistic societies, torn by selfish pursuits of individual interests, in their search for unity and peaceful coexistence.

2. Definition of the Community (*saṁgha*)

First let us discuss the meaning of the word *saṁgha*, which occurs in Pāli, Sanskrit, and is translated into Chinese. In Pāli the meaning is not so precise : literally it means "comprising" ; hence "multitude, the order, the priesthood, the clergy, the Buddhist church or community."[2] In Sanskrit, *saṁgha* is defined as "close contact or combination, and collection or assemblage ... multitude ; any member of people living together for a certain purpose ; society, association, company, community, church, the whole community or collective body of monks."[3] In Chinese, it is translated as "multitude" (衆) and "unity" (和 和合).[4] It also means "assembly, society or church or monastic order."[5]

Now, let us examine some Buddhist texts. The *Mahāvagga* states : "In this way, Lord, do we live in unity and concord, without quarrels, like milk and water (mixed together) and looking at each other with friendly eyes."[6] In *Dhammapada* we read :

1. K. Hayjima, *Shoki Bukkyo to Shakai Seikatsu* (*Early Buddhism and Social Life*) pp. 1 ff.

2. T. W. Rhys Davids, and William, *Pāli-English Dictionary*, p. 667.

3. M. Monier-Williams, *A Sanskrit-English Dictionary*, p. 1129.

4. S. Mochizuki, *Mochizuki Bukkyo Daijiten*, (*Mochizuki Buddhist Great Dictionary*), vol. 4, pp. 3017-3018. Cf., H. Ui, *Indo Tetsugaku Kenkyu* (*A Study in Indian Philosophy*) V. 4, p. 5.

5. W. E. Soothill and L. Hodous, *A Dictionary of Chinese Buddhist* Terms, : "... Saṁgha, an assembly, Collection, company, society. The corporate assembly of at least three (formerly, four) monks under a chairman, empowered to hear confession, grant absolution, and ordain. The church or monastic order, the third member of the Triratna. The term (衆) used alone has come to mean a monk, or monks in general." p. 420.

6. *Vinaya Texts*, Part II, *Mahāvagga, op. cit.*, X. 4, 4.

"Happy is the arising of the awakened, happy is the teaching of the true Law, happy is harmony in the Order, happy is the devotion of those who dwell in harmony."[1] The *Ta Chih Tu Lun* says : "*Saṁgha* is called an assembly (of Buddhist monks); when many *bikkhus* were together in one place, saṁgha."[2] According to the *Ssu Fen Lu* : "United, the monks held firmly to the *Dharma*, never neglecting to follow it. They were in harmony, joyful, free from disputes, learning under the same teacher, becoming like the sum of milk and water, living within the Buddhist law. Thus they advanced, living in physical comfort and spiritual joy."[3]

In the light of the above statements, we see that the term *saṁgha* is used not only to refer to the Buddhist community of monks, but also, in a broad sense, to the assembly of Buddhist monks, nuns, laymen, and laywomen. Also, *saṁgha*, as a community of people living together for a certain purpose, means that these people came together through Buddha, joining together with one another for the purpose of practising his teachings, attaining freedom from suffering, and the attainment of *nirvāṇa*.

In Buddha's time, the term *saṁgha* was applied not only to the Buddhist community but also to the assembly of religious leaders who gathered together with their disciples. However, within the context of Buddhism, *saṁgha* primarily meant the "unity of monks." It had its beginning when Buddha taught his *dharma* to five monks near Benares and they returned to him. The designation *saṁgha* was applied to any Buddhist order[4] or

1. *The Dhammapada*, 194, tr. I. Babbitt, New York, 1936, reprinted 1965, p. 31.

2. *Ta Chih Tu Lun* (*Mahāprajñāpāramitā-sutra*), Vol. 2, *Taisho*, Vol. 25, p. 80 :

云何名 僧伽 奏言衆、多比丘 一處 和是名 僧伽"

3. *Ssu Fen Lu*, Vol. 5, *Taisho*, Vol. 20, p. 595 :

"… 和合僧[法堅持不捨 … 僧和合 歓喜不諍。同一師學 如水乳合於佛法中有増益安楽住…"

4. *Vinaya Texts*, Part II, by T. W. Rhys Davids and H. Oldenberg, *Mahāvagga*, viii. 24, 6 : Cf., *Ssu Fen Lu*, *Taisho Taizokyo*, Vol. 22, p. 595 : "僧者四比丘 若五若十乃至無数"

gathering of three or more monks, and it constituted one of the "three treasures" together with Buddha and the *dharma*. The Chinese character for *saṁgha* incorporated the character for both "individual" and "community."[1] Since *saṁgha* or *gaṇa* means "community", it cannot correctly be applied to one monk. From ancient times, *saṁgha* has been used in China for one monk, but this is not the correct use of this term.

The *saṁgha* was also called *gaṇa*, but while the Buddhists often used the word *saṁgha*, the Jains employed *gaṇa*.[2] This usage may be related to the concept of *gaṇa* which refers to groups of people in the context of *Upaniṣads*. The reference occurs in the *Bṛhadāraṇyaka Upaniṣad* as follows : "Yet he did not flourish. He created the *Viś* (the commonalty), those classes of gods who are designated in groups (*gaṇaśaḥ*). The Vasus, Rudras, Ādityas, Viśvedevas and Maruts."[3] The term *gaṇa* was applied to organized groups comparable to guilds of people in agriculture, industry, commerce, etc. The word *gaṇa* had long been used for a system of political government, comparable to "republic."[4]

Jayaswal conjectures that, "the Buddhist brotherhood, the Saṁgha, was copied out from the political Saṁgha, the republic, in its constitution."[5] In ancient India, some tribes had two kinds of *gaṇas* : one was controlled by one king, the other by two or more rulers or a council known by the name *rājya*. There were several kinds of aristocratic unions and oligarchies. Such communities would be called royal families, and in them the head of the community was the highest in rank.[6] Among the ancient Indians, a father, his children and their husbands and

1. Ui, *op. cit.*, pp. 6-7. Cf., p. 40 fn. 2 above.
2. H. Nakamura, "Keisei tojo no kyotan", (The Formation of the Community), Ed. S. Yoshimura, *Bukkyo Kyodan no Kenkyu*, (*A Study of Buddhist Community*), p. 6.
3. S. Radhakrishnan, Ed. tr., *The Principal Upaniṣads* (*Bṛhadāraṇyaka Upaniṣad* I 4. 12), : "sa naiva vyabhavet, sa viśam asṛjata, yāny etāni devajātāni Gaṇaśa ākhyāyante, vasavo rudrā ādityā viśvedevā maruta iti." p. 169.
4. H. Nakamura, "Keisei Tchuno Kyotan," *op. cit.*, p. 6.
5. K. P. Jayaswal, *Hindu Polity*, p. 103.
6. R. D. Bhandarkar, *Lectures on the Ancient History of India*, p. 169. Cf., K. Tsukamoto, *Shoki Bukkyo Kyodanshi no Kenkyu* (*A History of the Early Buddhist Order*), p. 345.

wives, and their children lived together, constituting the family. Several families made up a tribe, each tribe having a head. A king was elected to serve as head of a community of tribes with his authority limited by the tribal council. Thus political organization had developed in India even in very ancient times. The politically organized community under a king and council was called *saṁgha* or *gaṇa*. During Buddha's time, there existed five monarchies : Kāśi, Videha, Kośala, Magadha, and Mahājanpada; and eight republican nations (*Gaṇa-rājya*) : Śākya, Licchavi, Videha, Malla, Koliya, Moriya, Buli, and Bhagg. It was usual for a republican nation facing collapse to be annexed to an absolute monarchy.[1] S. Dutt states :

> The political constitution of many tribes in the area that first came under the influence of Buddhism and from wherein early times Buddhist Bhikkus were largely recruited was of a republican type. In these small tribal republics, the authority vested in monarchy in a personal ruler was exercised by an assembly, oligarchical or democratic. The people were quite familiar and conversant with free institutions like voting, committee, popular tribunals, and collective legislation. Many of them were transplanted in the Buddhist Saṁgha, when after the decease of the founder, the need arose for a constitution for the Saṁgha.[2]

The terms *gaṇa* and *saṁgha* appear in Vedic literature where they are used to refer to a political union or organization of tribes in which the laws of the tribes were amalgamated, and where the official decisions were then made by an intertribal council (*sabhā*, *samāja* or *samiti*).[3]

The organization of the Buddhist community was patterned after the republican system of political organization rather than the monarchic system. The republican government of the tribes

1. Ui, *op. cit.*, p. 11 : H. C. Raychaudhuri, *Political History of Ancient India*, pp. 184-204. Cf., K. Tsukamoto, *op. cit.*, p. 333.

2. S. Dutt, *Early Buddhist Monachism*, pp. 119-20.

3. R. S. Sharma, *Aspects of Political Ideas and Institutions in Ancient India*, Cf., K. Tsukamoto, *op. cit.*, p. 344.

was the ideal of *bhikhu saṁgha* and its rules formed the basis of the *saṁgha's* rules for religious practice. Sociologists generally interpret the Buddhist *saṁgha* meetings as being organized after the tribal councils' law (*dharma*)-preaching halls (*dharma-samāja*, "law-meetings," *sāmājya*, *mahāsāmājya*, "religious community council").[1]

The official application of the name *saṁgha* to the Buddhist community occurred, according to Nakamura, in Aśoka's time,[2] and prior to that the Buddhist people were frequently called *sākyaputtiya samaṇas*[3] (sons of *Sākyaputta*), indicating a father-and-son relationship between Buddha and his disciples.[4] Buddha called his followers "my followers" (*māmaka*)[5] or "disciples" (*savaka*).[6] The *saṁgha*, as noted above, was organized after the republican form of government, but the Buddhist community was primarily a monk community. During his lifetime Buddha was the head of the community which he controlled as an omniscient teacher and the community's only leader. After his death, his teaching remained the only authority. The Buddhist community, therefore, cannot accurately be described as a truly democratic community, since, as noted above, only Buddha had

1. Cf., H. Nakamura, *Indo Kotaishi* (*Ancient History of India*), Vol. I, pp. 234-236. Cf., K. Tsukamoto, *op. cit.*, p. 344.

2. Cf., H. Nakamura, *Genshi Bukkyo no Seiritzu* (*The Formation of Early Buddhism*), p. 241.

3. T. W. Rhys Davids, *Buddhist India*, p. 143.

4. *Theragāthā* (*Psalms of the Early Buddhist Brethren*) No. 536, tr. by Mrs. Rhys Davids, ". . who that which is insuperable hath o'ercome. And father of my Father art thou, Sakiyan, To me thou, Gotamid, art grandsire in the Norm." P. 251. Cf., Putto Buddhassa oraso "the very Buddha son" *Ibid.*, No. 174. p. 135.

5. *Sutta-nipāta* (*A Collection of Discourses*), Tr. V. Fausboll, Ed. Max Müller, Atthakavagga, Garasutta 6. 3, No. 806, "That even of which a man thinks 'this is mine' is left behind by death : Knowing this, let not the wise (man) turn himself to worldliness (while being my) follower (*makako*)." Cf., *Ibid.*, No. 927, p. 176.

6. *Theragāthā* (*Psalms of the Early Buddhists Brethren*), *op. cit.*, No. 1241 : "And one of these, from meditation come, Full fain his gracious Master to behold—Thy true disciple, mighty Hero, see ! Low at thy feet Vangisa worships thee." P. 404. Cf., B. C. Law, "Early Buddhist Brothers and Sisters," *Journal of the Royal Asiatic Society of Bengal Letters*, Vol. XI, 1945, Calcutta, p. 42.

authority as law-transmitter and judge and as the only source of *dharma*. When changes in the *dharma* became necessary, the community had no authority to enact them. The early Buddhist community, however, consisted of Buddha and his organization centered round his teaching: it combined the democratic *saṁgha* with the leadership of Buddha, who was not the absolute head but rather the teacher of *dharma*.

3. Religious Discipline

Religious discipline consisted of rules for the maintenance of order through restraint of the monks' activities within the *saṁgha*.[1] The *saṁgha* as a group feared that if there were no restraints on the monks' conduct some individuals would yield to external temptations and neglect their monastic responsibilities. Furthermore, since the *saṁgha* had been formed for the common purpose of following the teaching of the Buddha these teachings would not have been respected if the *saṁgha* had not had control over the monks' activities.[2] Discipline also served to distinguish the Buddhist community from other communities. For example, the elegance of the monks' three robes, required by Buddhist discipline, distinguished the Buddhist monks from the Brahmins and the Jains.[3] Furthermore, if neither the *saṁgha* nor the discipline had been formed nor promulgated, then Buddhism could not have perpetuated itself. Without the community, it would have been impossible to maintain discipline, for it was the community which collected and developed the disciplines. This appears to be the reason why the notion of the *saṁgha* was understood together with Buddha and *dharma* as one of the Three Treasures.[4]

1. T. T. Kimura, *Genshi Bukkyo Shisoron* (*The Theory of the Thought of Primitive Buddhism*), p. 384.

2. G. Kyono, tr. *Ritsu Bu. I. Shibunritsu Kaidai*, *Kokuyaku Issai Kyo*, p. 1.

3. *Op. cit.*, *Vinaya Texts*, Part II, *op. cit.*, p. 212. Cf., *Shih Sung Lu*, Vol. 27, *Taisho*, Vol. 23, p. 194. Cf., M. Monier-Williams, *Buddhism*, and S. Dutt, *Early Buddhist Monachism*, p. 17.

4. *Vinaya Texts*, Part I, *Mahāvagga*, *op. cit.*, 1, 12, 4. Cf., *Nanten*, Vol. 3, p. 39.

Whether the *saṁgha* became a "church" or an esoteric community is of obvious importance in relation to religious discipline. It must be established whether or not the practice of religious discipline was largely confined to the community of monks. The unity of the community is also closely related to religious discipline in early Buddhism. Buddha established rules of religious discipline for the sake of unity among his monks, even though they came from different backgrounds and developed separate communities. Discipline also served to preserve the essence of the community as a group gathered for a common purpose, with a congenial, common spirit. If the monks had sought to reach purity and to rectify their mistakes individually, without discipline imposed by the community, the community would have appeared to be disorganized and lacking in unity. In discussing discipline, these two topics, *viz.*, the kind of communities which practised discipline, and unity as the major contribution of discipline, should be considered simultaneously, because *saṁgha* has the inescapable meaning of "unity of monks." For the reasons stated above, the discussion of religious discipline and the *saṁgha* cannot be separated. The discussion of the *saṁgha* is essential to the discussion of discipline. Hence we turn to the question of the *saṁgha*. Also, it seems most important to discuss the nature of the *saṁgha*, or community, and the unity of *saṁgha*, these being two aspects of a single topic related to discipline. We return to the main theme of the chapter.

I. The Nature of the Saṁgha : Three Main Questions

Now, in investigating the nature of the *saṁgha* we must raise the question whether the *saṁgha* became a "church" or an esoteric community. The settlement of the matter seems to be important in relation to religious discipline in early Buddhism. But before we are able to answer that question it must first be established whether or not the practice of religious discipline was largely confined to the communities of monks. Secondly, we must find out whether Buddhist communal unity prevailed chiefly among monks or whether lay people were also included. Only then can we raise the question as to whether the early

Buddhist community constituted a church or an esoteric community.

1. A Monkish Community

Accordingly, therefore, let us first consider why the early Buddhist community has been considered to be a monkish community. The early use of the words *bhikkhu-saṁgha* and *bhikkhunī-saṁgha* indicates that the *saṁgha* consisted of *bhikkhus* (monks) and *bhikkhunīs* (nuns) as regular members. We are, therefore, led to surmise that the early *saṁgha* must have been an ascetic community from which laymen (*upāsaka*) and laywomen (*upāsika*) were excluded.[1]

Although the universal *saṁgha* is now seen as extending to the three worlds, it is evident that the early "Four Quarters *saṁgha*" was fundamentally a monastic association of monks and nuns. According to the *Vinaya Piṭaka*, it did not include lay people.[2]

The *saṁgha* consisted primarily of *bhikkhus* and *bhikkhunīs*. This was also true of the "Four Quarters *saṁgha*," since it was understood to be an extension of the individual *saṁghas*. There were four categories of followers—monks, nuns, laymen, and laywomen—but this does not mean that there were four organized groups. The lay people, who had been selected in the early days of Buddha's life, belonged to the *saṁgha* only as individuals, rather than as part of an organized group such as that of the monks or of the nuns.[3]

According to the *Mahāvagga*,[4] Buddha was undecided after his enlightenment as to whether he should deliver the dharma

1. S. Yoshimura, "Kodan Ken Kyu no Katei," S. Yoshimura, *Bukkyo Kodan no Ken Kyu* (*A Study of Buddhist Community*), p. 96.

2. A. Hirakawa, *Genshi Bukkyo no Kenkyu* (*A Study of Primitive Buddhism*), p. 41. Cf., S. Dutt, *Early Buddhist Monachism*, p. 13.

3. A. Hirakawa, *op. cit.*, p. 13.

4. *Vinaya Texts*, Part 1, *Mahāvagga*, *op. cit.*, 1, 5, 4 : "Blessed One thought : 'Alas ! the world perishes ! Alas ! the world is destroyed ! If the mind of the Tathāgata, of the holy, of the absolute Sambuddha inclines itself to remain in quiet, and not to preach the doctrine.' And Brahma

or not, but, following the advice of the god Brahma, he began to transmit it. The legend of Brahma's advice obviously is a later addition; nevertheless it can be assumed that the Buddha underwent some inner psychological torment as to whether or not he should present the *dharma* to the people.

Why, then, did Buddha hesitate to preach the *dharma*? The *dharma* which he taught was not a kind of hidden truth to be taught to special students only, following the tradition of the Vedas,[1] but it eluded comprehension unless one had superior wisdom. Buddha presumably felt that it might be futile trying to transmit the *dharma* to people who were ignorant.[2] Also he gained the *dharma* through the utmost application of his

Sahampati . . . said to the Blessed One : Lord, may the Blessed One preach the doctrine, may the perfect One preach the doctrine ! there are beings whose mental eyes are darkened by scarcely any dust; but if they do not hear the doctrine, they cannot attain salvation." p. 86. Cf., T. Kimura, *Genshi Bukkyc Shiso Ron* (*A Theory of Thought in Early Buddhism*: "There is a paradoxical aspect in Buddha's thinking in that he employed elements of Brahmanism in presenting Brahman, lord of the Brahman world, a cultural deity. Because Buddha related to people in Brahman society, it would not have been possible to disregard the faith of this society. Therefore, Brahman was presented as praising and supporting Buddha and as asking Buddha to teach the Dharma to the people. Ideally, however, to those who accepted and understood Buddha's teaching, Buddha expressed skepticism about Brahman existed, instead of being an imaginary being comparable to a young girl's dream lover who did not really exists." pp. 25-26.

1. *Buddhist Suttas*, tr. T. W. Rhys Davids, *The Sacred Books of the East*, Vol. XI, *Mahā-Parinibbāna-Sutta* (*The Book of Great Decease*) : "I (Buddha) have preached the truth without making any distinction between exoteric and esoteric doctrine : for in representation of the truths, Ānanda, the Tathagata has no such thing as the closed fist of a teacher, who keeps some things back." p. 36. Cf., Radhakrishnan, *The Principal Upaniṣads*, "The face of truth is covered with a golden disc (*hiranmayena pātreṇa satyasyāpihitam mukham*)," p. 577. Cf., *B. U.* V. 15 : 1.

2. *Vinaya Texts*, *Mahāvagga op. cit.*, 1, 5, 2 : "I (Buddha) have penetrated this doctrine which is profound, difficult to perceive and to understand which brings quietude of heart, which is exalted, which is unattainable by reasoning, abstruse, intelligible (only) to the wise . . . Now if I proclaim the doctrine, and other men are not to understand my preaching, there would result but weariness and annoyance to me."

strength in mental and physical cultivation.[1] Those who were unable to apply themselves, because of their ties to worldly desires and pleasures, and the limitations imposed by secular conditions at the time, would find it extremely difficult to attain *dharma.*

When the Buddha did decide to present the *dharma* he wanted primarily to teach monks rather than laymen. This does not mean that he was uninterested in laymen,[2] but that he believed that laymen were unprepared to receive the *dharma.* He apparently believed that monks were prepared to receive it because they had renounced their homes for a homeless life practising asceticism to free themselves from all mundane, material ties and were searching for a higher way of life and cultivating this objective. The *Mahāvagga,* for example, states that Buddha decided to teach the monks, rather than the teachers[3] themselves, and when he learned that they had gone away, he selected five of his former companions[4] and preached the *dharma* to them as they covered the long distance to Benares on foot. Thus Buddha preached the *dharma-cakra* (the Wheel of the Law) to five monks, who had already entered the ascetic life. When one monk understood the *dharma* and expressed his wish to become Buddha's disciple, the latter accepted him along with other monks and, thus, founded the *saṁgha.* He said, "Come, O Bhikkhus,"[5] and ordained them, but he did not say, "Come," to laymen. At that time there were six monks,[6] including Buddha, in his community. Previously, two merchants, Papussa and Bhallika, had become followers of Buddha and of the *dharma* as laymen, but there was then no *saṁgha.* If two members had not been enough to establish a *saṁgha,* then the two of them might have joined the othet six monks and established the *saṁgha.*[7] However, when the *saṁgha* was established, the two laymen were excluded.

1. *Ibid.,* 1, 5, 3, "... with great pains have I (Buddha) acquired it."
2. If he had not been interested in laymen, why would he have sent his disciples on a mission to them ?
3. *Vinaya Texts, Mahāvagga, op. cit.,* 1, 6, 1, 2, 3, 4.
4. *Ibid.,* 1, 6, 5.
5. *Ibid.,* 1, 6, 35.
6. *Ibid.,* 1, 6, 47 ; "At that time there were six Arahats (persons who had reached absolute holiness) in this world." p. 102.
7. *Ibid.,* 1, 4, 5.

Evidently, it was intended that the *saṁgha* should be a community of monks, with laymen excluded from full membership.

Dharma was given (primarily) to monks because since it involved philosophical methods of analysis, it was they who could use it to draw up categories of doctrines, such as the "Four Noble Truths" and the "Noble Eightfold Path," the "Anātman" doctrine, and the doctrine of "Twelve Links," etc. As already noted, some exceptionally well-qualified lay people were also taught by Buddha.[1] Even though one did understand the *dharma*, it (the *dharma*) required a sort of sanctity, such as celibacy and the restricting of one's desires so as to lead a spiritual, disciplined life.[2] This effected a balance between Buddha's teachings and the practical way of life.

The *Sutta-nipāta* states: "A householder's work I will also tell you, how a Sāvaka is to act to be a good one; for that complete Bhikkhu-dhamma cannot be carried out by one who is taken up by (worldly) occupations."[3]

In other words, *dharma*, was based on the ethical grounds of self-denial and self-discipline. Indulgence of one's passions was regarded as a hindrance in the course of training to be an *arahat* in order to attain *nirvāṇa*, the state of bliss and freedom from rebirth. This, the necessity of discipline, seems to constitute the primary difference between monks and laymen.

Hunabashi seems to have observed correctly that:

> The principles of the path of monks and nuns were discipline, meditation, wisdom, the theory of conditional causation and the 'Four Noble Truths.' The path of lay people was *puñña*, which consisted of giving alms to the monks, the theory of lay discipline, and the heavens where those living in this world can be reborn.[4]

1. *Vinaya-Piṭaka* (*The Book of the Discipline*), Vol. V, tr. I. B. Horner, Cullavagga 6, 15 : "Then the Lord thanked the (great) merchant of Rajagaha in these verses :... To these food and drink, raiment and lodgings. He should give, to the upright, with mind purified. (Then) these teach him dhamma dispelling every ill; He, knowing that dhamma, here attains nibbāna, cankerless." p. 206.

2. E. Thomas, *op. cit.*, pp. 12-13.

3. *Sutta-nipāta*, 9, (*A Collection of Discourses*), tr. V. Fausboll, ed. F. Max Müller, *The Sacred Books of East*, p. 65.

4. K. Hunabashi, "Genshi Bukkyo ni-okeru Shutsukado to Zaikado",

Buddha, however, gave other worldly promises than those of *nirvāṇa* for monks and, correspondingly, he spoke of various stages of heaven for lay people. He said that *nirvāṇa* was primarily for monks, but that a few lay people would also reach it[1] although most lay people would go to heaven. Because the lay people should support not only the monks but also the poor through their alms-giving, he encouraged them to work hard to earn money, to conserve their property by avoiding waste.[2] For monks, he prohibited both labour and money and required them to give up all worldly things for the pure life. The *Sutta-nipāta* states: "He who did not go too fast forward, nor was left behind, having seen that all this in the world is false, that Bhikkhu leaves this and the further shore, as a snake (quits its) old worn-out skin."[3] But for layman, *Aṅguttara Nikāya* states:

If one dwells in a fitting dwelling-place,
And friendship makes with Ariyans,
And perfectly applies the self,
And hath aforetime merit done,
There rolls upon him wealth of crops,
Fame, good report and happiness.[4]

However, the encouragement given to the layman to earn money and secular blessings differs from the ascetic attitude fundamental to his *dharma*. If Buddha had really believed that

('Ways of monks and ways of laymen in early Buddhism'), *Indogaku Bukkyogaku Kenkyu*, (*A Study of Indian and Buddhistic Studies*), Vol. 3, No. 1, 1954, p. 34.

1. *Vinaya-piṭaka* (*The Book of the Discipline*), Cullavagga, 6, 9, 2, *op. cit.*, : "Then the Lord thanked the householder Anāthapiṇḍada in these verses. They ward off cold and heat and beasts of prey from there... He, knowing that dhamma here, attains nibbāna, cankerless." p. 230. See *Ibid.*, 6, 15, *Talaka*, 1, 93. Cf., Eliot, *op. cit.*, p. 249. Cf., E. Conze, *Buddhism : its essence and development*, "The Questions of King Milinda, it is true, somewhat grudgingly admit.. that also a layman can win Nirvāṇa, but add at once that he must then either enter the order, or die. In any case, a layman could attain Nirvāṇa in this life only if he had pursued a monastic life in some former existence. pp. 53-54.

2. Hayajima, *op. cit.*, p. 585.

3. *Sutta-nipāta* (*A Collection of Discourses*), No. 392, *op. cit*., p. 2.

4. *Aṅguttara Nikāya* (*The Book of the Gradual Sayings*), Vol. II, VI, 31, tr. F. L. Woodward, p. 35.

laymen should have regular status in the *saṁgha*, why would he not have given the *dharma* equally to monks and laymen, and encouraged both to strive toward the goal of *nirvāṇa* ? Monks who belonged to the *saṁgha* would reach the four *phalas* (stages of sainthood),[1] but laymen could only advance to the stage of the *anāgamin* (non-returner from heaven). Even after reaching the *anāgamin's* stage, they would still retain some illusions which could prevent their attaining the state of *arahathood.*[2] Thus it appears that although Buddha's Path to *nirvāṇa* was not entirely closed to laymen it was primarily for monks.

Let us now consider the disciplines, the Buddhist *vinaya*, which, it is generally believed, were made for monks. Of the ten rules[3] set forth by Buddha, five applied equally to monks and

1. William Edward Soothill, *A Dictionary of Chinese Buddhist Terms*, *op. cit.* : 四果 The four phala, i.e., fruitions, or rewards : *srota-āpanna-phala*, *sakradāgmi phala*, *anāgāmiphala*, *arahat-phala*, i.e., four grades of saintship; See 須陀洹, 斯陀含, 阿那含 and 阿羅漢 The four titles are also applied to four grades of *śramaṇas:* yellow and blue flower *śramaṇas*, lotus *śramaṇas*, meek *śramaṇas*, and ultrameek *śramaṇas*." p. 177.

2. Daito Shuppansha, ed., *Japanese English Dictionary*, p. 60.

3. E. Thomas, *History of Buddhist Thought*, "The rules for novices (*samaneras*) are contained in the ten rules of training.

(1) Refraining from killing living things,
(2) From taking what is not given,
(3) From unchastity (or incontinence),
(4) From falsehood,
(5) From intoxicants,
(6) From eating at unseasonable times,
(7) From seeing displays of dancing, singing, and music,
(8) From the use of Garlands, scents, and unguents,
(9) From the use of a high or a big bed,
(10) From receiving gold and silver." pp. 25-26.

Cf., *Hsiao-Pin Pan-jo-po-lo-mi-to-ching*, *Taisho*, Vol. 6 :

阿惟越致相品 '不殺生，不偸盗，不邪婬，不妄語，不両舌，不悪口，不無義語　不貪愛，不瞋恚，不邪見，十善道'

Taisho, Vol .8, p. 564, *Khuddakapāṭha*, 2, Vinaya, i. 83.

laymen, with the exception that a layman is permitted a sexual life with his wife only. If a monk did not obey these five rules, then, according to *parājika* rules, he would be deprived of all the rights of a monk and be expelled from the *saṁgha.* For a monk, this would be like a sentence of death,[1] for he would be forbidden to reenter the *saṁgha* and would be deprived of the context most conducive to the attainment of *nirvāṇa.* For a layman, however, there was generally no punishment if he did not obey these rules. Buddha's other five rules applied to the monks only, not to the lay people. Monks, for example, were forbidden to eat in the afternoon, to sleep in a comfortable bed, and to have money, while lay people, in contrast, were permitted to enjoy such things. These rules for monks were based on practical considerations for life in the *saṁgha.* Eating in the afternoon, for example, would interfere with meditation, for which this period was reserved. The required three robes afforded protection from cold winter nights, since the monks did not live in houses. Money might tempt them to go astray from their ascetic lives. Lay people, however, could eat in the afternoon, so as to have more energy for more work, through which they could earn more money to support the monks. Since they lived in houses, they needed no restrictions as to their clothing. Such activities as taking a meal at the "wrong time," i.e., afternoon, or drinking wine, or sexual acts (with one's wife), although impure for monks, were innocent enough for laymen.[2] Monks, who gave up everything secular, put on *kāṣāya,* the three required robes of a monk, brown in colour, while laymen who lived secular lives with only the five rules of *upāli,* put on white garments. Also, begging for food, wearing rags, sleeping at the foot of a tree, and using only decomposed urine as medicine applied only to monks, and not to laymen.

Monks obeyed the rules of discipline which led them to liberation, to *nirvāṇa.*[3] They received the *saṁgha's* ceremony of *upasampāda.* Accordingly, the expedient method of giving the whole rules by stages is very important, and makes the differ-

1. Hirakawa, *Ritsuzo no Kenkyu, op. cit.*, p. 442.
2. A. Hirakawa, *Ritsuzo no Kenkyu, op. cit.*, p. 675.
3. H. Nakamura, *Genshi Bukkyo* (*Early Buddhism*), p. 154.

ence between monks and secular men.[1] The precepts that the Buddhist monks and nuns were expected to follow consisted of 227 rules for monks and 311 for nuns.[2] Receiving *upasampāda* meant receiving the requisite qualification for becoming a monk (*bhikkhu-bhava*). The spiritual power of precept-observance was communicated to a monk during this ceremony. If one who had not received *upasampāda* was found to be living in the *saṁgha* and acting as a monk, he would be called an enemy and would lose the right to receive *upasampāda* forever.[3]

Therefore, Buddhist discipline was primarily for monks. They were dependent on lay people and had to behave so that lay people would respect them and give them alms. It seems significant that there is no record in the *sūtras* of any lay people's having participated with the monks in the compilation of Buddha's *dharmavinaya*, even though some of them might have heard Buddha's *dharma*.

Furthermore, if Buddha seriously considered the lay people to be part of the *saṁgha*, why did he not frame rules for their basic life-events, such as births, marriages, funerals, and offerings to the dead ? Why did he let them continue to follow Brāhmanism in their religious ceremonies, which would qualify them for heaven, after death ? This total lack of rules for the ordinary events of life in the early Buddhist *saṁgha* would show that the *saṁgha* as originally conceived by the founder was meant only for the monks. A community of ascetic celibacy, of monks and nuns alike, could not have been a community in the wider or ordinary sense.

Regarding the notion of heaven, *Aṅguttara-Nikāya* states, "... who never takes life, nor speaketh lies, Nor goes to another's

1. Cf., Watanabe *op. cit.*, p. 130. Cf., Thomas *op, cit.*, p. 21.

2. M. Sato, *Genshi Bukkyo Kyodan no Kenkyu* (*A Study of the Early Buddhist Order in the Vinaya Piṭaka*), pp. 6-9. Cf. Hirakawa, *Ritsuzo no Kenkyu, op. cit.* : "Moreover, the term *'pratimokṣavibhaṅga'* is found in the *Taisho* No. 143, Vol. 23, p. 176 b, c, and the *Mahāsaṁghika-vinaya, Taisho* No. 1425, vol. 22, pp. 412 b, 544 c, Refer. p. 302, while the term 解二百五十戒経 *Vibhaṅga of the* 250 *Precepts* appears in the 大智度論 Mahāprajñāpāramitā-śāstra." p. 11.

3. Hirakawa, *Ritsuzo no Kenkyu, op. cit.*, p. 521.

wife, takes things not given, Nor drinks strong drink, is not addict of these Hate-breeding things — moral is he, 'tis said : At death that wise man will arise in heaven."[1] The Hindu ideas of the *dharma* still controlled much of lay life. *Ssu Fen Lu* also states : "Buddha taught that the law for layman required him to preach his discipline and doctrine and the law of rebirth in heaven."[2] Still on the question of the layman Monier Williams says :

> "... he (the layman) was already bound to do so by the rules of Hindu caste and family-religion. The chief test of his Buddhism was his readiness to serve the monks. It was for this reason, I think, that lay-adherents were not called, as might have been expected, Śrāvakas, 'Hearers', but simply Upāsakas, 'Servers,' and in the case of women Upāsikās. They could not be called disciples of Buddha in the truest sense, unless they entered his monastic order."[3]

Jaini also claims that, "A Buddhist layman might worship the Buddhas and support the monks with food and shelter, yet he was dependent on the Brahman priests for ceremonies at birth, marriage, and death, and was guided by them according to the lawbooks of Manu."[4]

Buddha prohibited monks from becoming involved in secular matters relating to birth, commerce, death ceremonies, or incanta-

1. *Aṅguttara-Nikāya,* V, XVIII, 174, *op. cit.*, p. 151. Cf., p. 50 fn. 3 above. Cf., *Kaṭha Upaniṣad,* I, 1, 18 : "*trināciketas trayem etad viditvā ya evaṁ vidvāṁs cinute nāciketam, mṛtyu-pāśān purataḥ praṇodya śokātigo modate svarga-loke.*" "The wise man who has sacrificed thrice to Naciketas and who knows this three, and so knowing, performs meditation on fire throwing off first the bonds of death and overcoming sorrow, rejoices in the world of heaven." Radhakrishnan, *The Principal Upaniṣads,* p. 602.
2. *Ssu Fen Lu,* 18, *Taisho* vol. 22, p. 69 :
   世尊曰謂法者， 説施，説戒説，生天之法
3. M. Monier Williams, *Buddhism, op. cit.*, p. 89.
4. P.S. Jaini, "ŚRAMAṆAS"-their conflict with Brahmanical Society," *Chapters in Indian Civilization,* Vol. I, *Classical and Medieval India,* Joseph W. Elder, ed. A. K. Narain, p. 78.

tions. Thus he made a distinction between monks and the lay people who served them, since he wanted the monks to be devoted only to spiritual life. He saw funerals as secular matters with which monks should not concern themselves; he therefore enjoined before his death that his own funeral be conducted by lay people and not by monks.

The *Mahā-Parinibbāna-Sutta* narrates the following :

"(Ānanda asked) what are we to do, Lord, with the remains of the Tathāgata ? Hinder not yourselves, Ānanda, by honouring the remains of the Tathāgata. Be zealous, I beseech you, Ānanda, in your own behalf ! Devote yourselves to your own good ! Be earnest, be zealous, be intent on your own good ! There are wise men, Ānanda, among the nobles, among the Brāhmans, among the heads of houses, who are firm believers in the Tathāgata; and they will do honour to the remains of the Tathāgata."[1]

This indicates further how Buddha distinguished between monks and laymen. That he did not concern himself deeply with family and secular life may be one of the reasons that Buddhism declined in India. It was perhaps ignored by the lay people who continued to follow Hinduism which considered these matters. Although many early Buddhist monks lived near large cities and contacted the royal families and rich merchants, such contacts were not because of a positive attitude toward secular life. In fact, they maintained their negative attitude toward it and were devoted to the ascetic monasticism which they practiced.

2. The Layman's Position

What exactly, then, was the layman's position in the *saṁgha* ? If monks and lay people were followers of the same three treasures, of Buddha, of the *dharma*, and of the *saṁgha*, it would have been very difficult for lay people to have been completely excluded from the *saṁgha*. A scriptural text explains

1. *Mahā-Parinibbāna-Sutta*, V. 24, *op. cit.*, p. 91.

it as follows : "Whoever had learned Buddha's scriptures and truth, all were Buddha's disciples."[1] Where this scripture mentions the holy disciples (*āryasāvaka*), it includes not only monks but also lay people in this category.[2] Also lay people of exceptionally high quality could learn not only Buddha's teachings as it applied to lay people but could also study the theory of causation and the Four Noble Truths, just like the monks.[3]

A. Nakamura also supports the view that all those people who respected Buddha and gathered together, monks and lay people, had at first the same status, but he adds that, as the community expanded, the distinction was made between monks and lay people. He states that early Buddhism consisted simply of a community of people who gathered from different places because of their attraction to Buddha's personality. Gotama called the people who gathered "my people" (*māmaka*). Those who returned and became dependent upon him were called "disciples" (*sāvaka*). The original meaning of this word may have been "to hear the teaching" (meaning the same as the Sanskrit term (*śrāvaka*). Gotama's disciples were called "disciples of Buddha" (*buddha-sāvaka*) or (*buddhassa sāvaka*), meaning the hearers of Buddha (*samma-sambuddha-sāvaka*) of "Gotama's disciples" (*gotama-sāvaka*). The term "*sāvaka*" was applied not only to monks but also to lay people. This application of "*sāvaka*" to lay people is found in many places in old Buddhist scriptures. The term "holy disciples" (*ariya sāvaka*) was also applied to pious lay Buddhists. This was found also in Jainism. Monks and lay people appear to have had the same status as the people who heard his teaching (*sāvaka*). In this sense, they were equal, and

1. Cf., *Fo Ban Nee Huan Ching*, *Taisho*, Vol. I. pp. 164-166. *Vinayapiṭaka (Book of the Discipline)*, Vol. I, *op. cit.*, (Translator's Introduction) : "A common designation of the monastic followers of Gautama was *samana Sakyaputtiya*, recluses (lit. sons of the) Śākyans, or Śākyan recluses. This was also used of them by the laity (e.g., Vin. iii, 43, 136, 172=pp. 67, 234, 299 below), including these occasions where the monks had given them cause for complaint (vin. iii, 44, 73, 119=pp. 70, 125, 200 below)." p. iii.

2. Nakamura, *Genshi Bukkyo no Seiritzu*, *op. cit*, pp. 227-228.

3. *Vinaya Texts* : *Mahāvagga*, 7, 10, 11, *op. cit.*, pp. 24-25; cf., Hunabashi, *op. cit.*, p. 35.

there was no difference between monks and lay people. However, as the *saṁgha* developed and gained in importance, monks were considered to be higher than lay people (or, lay people to be lower than monks). Some time later, lay people were designated "serving men" (*upāsaka*), which means that lay people served monks.[1] In the early days, it appears that laymen and monks participated together in meetings of purity in the Buddhist monasteries, although later these meetings were restricted to monks only.[2] Without the lay men's alms, monks could not engage in spiritual cultivation.[3] Monks provided spiritual leadership and were respected by the laymen. Buddha gave rules for the lay people as well as for the monks, although some of the lay people's rules were not the same as those for the monks. Also there were eight punishments, applicable when monks did wrong to laymen and, conversely, when laymen did wrong to monks.[4]

The goal of the lay people was heaven where those living in this world could be reborn — quite the same thing as popular Hindu notion of heaven. This, however, does not seem to have been their ultimate goal. In the *Aṅguttara-Nikāya* the Lay Disciple states :

Seeing hell's fearfulness, shun wickedness;
Wise men shun that, firm set in Aryan Dhamma,
Not harming aught that breathes where progress is;
Lie not, not knowingly touch things ungiven;
Live gladly with thine own, leave others' wives;
No man should drink strong drink that dulls the thought;...
Who serve the good — wise men and by wise men,
Held wise — go to the deva-realm, or here
Are born within some clan: and as wise men
In gradual course attain Nirvāṇa's bliss.[5]

1. Nakamura, *Genshi Bukkyo no Sei Ritsu*, *op. cit.*, pp. 227-228.
2. S. Watanabe, *Bukkyo*, p. 129.
3. Oldenberg, *Buddha*, *op. cit.*, p. 382.
4. *Vinayapītaka* (*The Book of the Discipline*), vol. V, tr. I. B. Horner, *Cullavagga*, 1, 5, pp. 18-19, *Ibid.*, 20, 3-6.
5. *Aṅguttara-Nikāya* (*The Book of the Gradual Sayings*), vol. III, V, XVIII, IX, tr. E. M. Hare, pp. 156-157.

Lay people were taught that the heaven of rebirth was not the only goal open to them, and that if they sought wisdom and practised liberation of the mind they might seek the ultimate liberation of *nirvāṇa*.[1] Although rebirth in heaven was the primary aim of lay people, *nirvāṇa* was not closed to them. They had both possible goals, the heaven of rebirth and also *nirvāṇa*, although *nirvāṇa* does not appear to have been their primary objective.

Through the Middle Path, Buddha rejected both extremes of pleasure-seeking in secular life and extremes of asceticism in monastic life. He required that one, even though a layman, should give alms to monks and to the poor so that one might restrain one's own desires. Monks were told that, although they were leading a homeless life, they should not accede to the adoption of extreme asceticism as a means of reaching *nirvāṇa*. Thus, through the law of revision as the Middle Path, Buddha established a pluralistic order, with monks being primary and the laity being secondary. This made it possible for monks and lay people to coexist.

For both monks and laymen, what was most important appears to have been the correct and sincere following of Buddha's teachings. Whether one was a monk or a layman, if one practised Buddha's teachings correctly, one would reach *nirvāṇa*. Buddha established separate rules for monks' and laymen's lives, because of the differences in their modes of living, but the foundation of the rules for both monks and laymen was the similar ultimate good leading to *nirvāṇa* or to heaven. Rules for lay people dealt with almsgiving, family ethics, economics, and the layman's moral code. For example, the *Kulavagga* states : "Let him dutifully maintain his parents, and practise an honourable trade; the householder who observes

82. Hayajima, *op. cit.* : "The idea of heavens was not taught in early Buddhism. The concept of heaven in early Buddhism was similar to that in Vedic literature generally. A single heaven for lay people (Aśoka-the sorrowless), was, also mentioned in the context of almsgiving, discipline, and reborn heaven. This was one ideal realm of heaven, not heavens, in the plural. In this connection, it could be supposed that Buddha used the word "heaven" for a state preparatory for the absolute state of Nirvaṇa," p. 701.

this strenuously goes to the gods by name Saeyampabhas."[1] According to *The Mo-ho-sêng-chih-lu* :

> Buddha said that a layman could provide a good well along a heavily travelled road, where travellers could drink; or plant fruit trees, or a cool, refreshing forest by the road; or build a bridge or provide a boat where a road comes to a river; and give alms, especially to a monk or a community of monks. He should cultivate pure discipline, and seek to attain wisdom so that he could give up feelings of petulance and greed. The reward of such virtue would be his advancing through rebirth in the heavens or the world of men.[2]

Buddhist social practice is fundamentally different from "social work" in the secular Western sense of the term. It is derived from the ideal of the Bodhisattva. One's real life in Buddhist social practice involves both the spiritual and the material; the Bodhisattva's compassion and selflessness were the grounds for altruism.[3] The *Saṁyutta-Nikāya* states :

> On a 'certain occasion the Exalted One was staying near Kapilavatthu in Banyan Park.' Now Mahānāma the Śākyan went to see the Exalted One ... and said this : 'Pray, lord, how far is one a disciple?' 'By going for refuge to the Buddha, Mahānāma (Saṁgha), to the Norm (Dharma) and to the Order, one is a disciple.' 'But lord, how far is a disciple virtuous?' 'From the time when a disciple abstains from killing, from stealing, from wrong conduct in sensual lusts, from falsehood and from addiction to the neglect caused by intoxicants,— thus far Mahānāma, a disciple is virtuous.' 'But, lord, how far is a disciple a believer?' 'Herein, Mahā-

1. *Sutta-nipāta*, *op. cit.*, No. 403, Kulavagga 29, p. 66.
2. *Mo-ho-sêng-chih-lu*, vol. 4, 34 T, *Taisho-Taizo Kyo*, vol. 22, pp. 260-261 :

   世尊(以偈答天子)曰曠路作好井 穜植園果施樹林施清凉

   橋般波人民 布施修净戒 智慧捨慳貪
3. Hayajima, *op. cit.*, pp. 733-734.

nāma, a disciple believes in the wisdom of the Tathāgata, thus: He it is, the Exalted One ... teacher of Devas and mankind, a Buddha, an Exalted One. Thus far, Mahānāma, a disciple is a believer.' 'But lord, how far is a disciple given to generosity?' 'Herein, Mahānāma, a disciple dwells at home with a heart freed from the taint of stinginess. He is open-handed, pure-handed, delighting in self-surrender, one to ask a favour of, one who rejoices in the dispensing of charitable gifts. Thus far, Mahānāma, a disciple is given to generosity.' 'Pray, lord, how far is a disciple blessed with insight?' 'Herein, Mahānāma, a disciple is a sage, blessed with insight into the rise and fall of things, insight which is Ariyan, penetrating, going on to the utter destruction of ill. Thus far, Mahānāma, a disciple is possessed of insight.[1]

There were, however, common rules for both laymen and monks : to study the *dharma* and to believe that the Buddha, the *saṁgha*, and the *dharma* were one. There were different practices to be followed, but the objective of enlightenment was one and the same.

Historically, the *saṁgha* seems to have been primarily a monkish community. Thus it might seem that Buddha had primarily no concern about secular matters. Ultimately, however, monks and laymen alike belonged to Buddha's realm (*saṁgha*), through the *dharma*, even though the teachings given to monks and laymen were different, and had different aims. The alms-giving of laymen as a love-experience corresponded to the religious discipline and wisdom of the monks. Both had vision of a reality beyond *dukkha,* whether toward heaven or *nirvāṇa.* Although Buddha was primarily concerned with monks, these monks were an inner, elite group whose purpose was to lead the people and to build the kingdom of Buddha. Buddha taught the *dharma* to all through this inner, elite group—the monks. If Buddha had not been interested in lay people, why did he require his monks to be missionaries and why did he live like a missionary throughout his life? He rejected no one who wanted to join his lay disciples. He ordained them, visited the places

1. *Saṁyutta-Nikāya*, Part 5, LV. XI. IV, vii, *op. cit*., pp. 338-339.

where they lived, and gave them rules. Historically, lay people were not full members of the *saṁgha*, although they were included in the concept of the *saṁgha*. In Buddha's kingdom monks and lay people had different functions, the monks being the inner group, the laymen the outer group, but fundamentally they were all sons of the Śākya kingdom through universal *dharma*.

However, the *saṁgha* was primarily a monkish community. The laity were secondary rather than equal participants, but they were not completely excluded from the *saṁgha*. Although not regular members of the organized *saṁgha*, the lay people individually belonged to the *saṁgha* in the fuller sense. They remained part of the Hindu community as far as secular matters were concerned, but they belonged to Buddha's "spiritual" kingdom which centered on him as the king of *Dharma*.

II. Religious unity in early Buddhist community

In this section, the nature of of the early Buddhist community as a "unity" is discussed. It was previously emhasized that although each of the early Buddhist communities was organized as a separate body it was independent and autonomous. Ever mutually dependent, Buddha's teaching and the discipline of *Dharma* were essentially united in an ideal relationship.[1] It can, therefore be asked: How did each community perpetuate the founder's teachings and thoughts? How did members live together obediently in a particular way, with common adherence to Buddha and the *Dharma* as a guiding factor?

This is illustrated in "*saṁgha*" which generally means "unity of community." According to the Pali-English Dictionary, *samagga* (from *sam-agga*) means being in unity, harmonious.[2] Also, the Chinese characters 和合 mean "to blend, unite, be of one mind, harmonize"[3] What these definitions indicate in common is that Buddha and his disciples apparently wanted to make the *saṁgha* a realization of the ideal, unified, orderly community.

1. Cf., S. Dutt, *Early Buddhist Monachism*, *op. cit.*, pp. 19, 64; cf., Hirakawa, *Genshi Bukkyo no Kenkyu*, *op. cit*, p. 307.
2. T. W. Rhys Davids, and William Stede (*The Pali Text Society Pali-English Dictionary*), *op. cit.*, p. 681.
3. Soothill, *op. cit.*, p. 253.

The monks seemed to hold the same belief as their teacher, i.e., that *dharma* and *vinaya* were not only the same but also held up the same goal for men—to be *arahats* and to attain *nirvāṇa.* Their aim to be as one, however, was not easily achieved; even in early Buddhism, there were seeds of disunity. Before examining the major topic i.e., religious unity of the community, it seems necessary to discuss the factors of disunity in early Buddhism.

1. *Factors of Disunity*

(A) *Cakrabheda* (破法輪僧) Devadatta's episode[1]

Devadatta asked Buddha to transfer the leadership of the *saṁgha* to him. As already noted, Buddha refused to do so. Devadatta also suggested five restrictive rules of conduct to Buddha, which he did not entirely accept. He suggested instead that monks should be free to choose whether or not they would follow these restrictions. Consequently, with five hundred other monks, Devadatta founded a new community which the record reveals as having lasted several hundred years. This new community separated from the Buddhist community. Devadatta challenged Buddha's leadership, and the new community changed from the *saṁgha* to another sect, known as the *Cakrabheda*, which means "the split circle" the broken *saṁgha* or "schismatic *saṁgha.*" This not only disrupted the religious order of Buddhism but also caused a dogmatic separation from *dharma*, which resulted in the destruction of Buddhist *dharma*. This is the earliest schism. In fact, it was not really Buddhist at all as it constituted a challenge to Buddhism and to Buddha himself. It was a parallel religious community.

(B) *Karmabheda* (破羯磨僧)[2]

The term "*karmabheda*" indicated a varied interpretation within one *saṁgha*, wherein such division was not accompanied by

1. Hirakawa, *Shoki Daijo Bukkyo no Kenkyu* (*A Study of Early Mahayana Buddhism*), p. 678. Cf., V. V. Gokhala, *Abhidharmakośa Kārikā*, p. 89; *Ta-p'i-p'o-sha-lun*, Vol. 116, *Taisho Taizokyo* vol. 27, p. 602; *Chu-she-lun*, vol. 18, vol 29, p. 93.

2. *Ibid.*

the neglect of Buddha's teaching and the notion of *karma* (duty). These sects or groups were divided from the main stream of Buddhism but still claimed to be Buddhist in essence.

About one hundred years after the *parinirvāṇa* of Buddha, there was a conflict between the Sthaviravādins and Mahāsaṁghikins. The elders claimed that the ten rules should be strictly followed, whereas the "innovative" monks (recognizing certain exceptions) claimed that some of these rules need not be strictly adhered to.

(C) *Conflict between dharma and vinaya*

(a) The two groups, *vinaya-dharma* and the *dhamma-kathika*, quarrelled. Even though the two factions later became reconciled, this quarrel emphasized the difference between *vinaya* and *dharma*.[1]

(b) When Buddha was living at Kosambi in Ghosita Park, Bhikkhu Bahiya, who lived with the elder Anuruddha, wanted to break up the community. Thereto, the *Aṅguttara-Nikāya* cites four reasons:. . . immorality (a wicked nature), impurity, a suspicious behaviour, and covert deeds.[2]

(D) *Differences of opinion among monks*

The *Kosāmbīya-sutta* states that at Kosāmbiya many monks argued so that there was no harmony or peace. A Chinese translation of the same material picture these disputes as follows: Monks had become deeply committed to their own opinions and were given to fighting and making accusations and to committing offences. Sometimes confrontations between monks led not only to vehement arguments in support of their respective views, but even to attacks upon each other with sticks or swords.[3]

1. E. Kanekura, *Indo Chusei Sei shin shi*, vol. II, (*A Spiritual History of Medieval India*), pp. 198-199.

2. *Aṅguttara Nikāya* (*The Gradual Sayings*), *op. cit.*, Vol. II, IV, XXIV, 239, p. 244 : Cf., *Nanten Daizokyo*, 18, p. 418.

3. *Majjhima Nikāya*, vol. 1 : "... If, monks, a monk, disputatious, quarrelsome, contentious, lives, wounding with the weapons of his tongue, to this extent is his mind obsessed." P. 323. Also, Kaya, Nanten Daizokyo vol. 10, p. 54 :"

"拘深比丘 恒好 鬪訟犯 諸悪行 面行 面相談説 或時刀 相加

In the foregoing paragraphs we have some of the main factors of disunity. However, during the Buddha's lifetime, excluding Devadatta's revolt, the community appears generally to have been united under his leadership and teaching.[1] After his death, they appear to have undergone a crisis of disunity.[2]

At the meeting of the First Council, a monk who said that members of the community were free to do whatever they wished, seems to have expressed the opinions of many of those present. Furthermore, problems had arisen and would arise in the future because of differences of opinion about religious matters.[3] The council was, therefore, convened in order to determine the correct views, and for the purpose of promoting unity the disciples recited in unison the teachings left behind by Buddha. Also, they made *dharma-vinaya* the authority for the whole Buddhist community. At this point let us return to the main topic.

p. 626; and E. Frauwallner, *The Earliest Vinaya and the Beginnings of Buddhist Literature*, pp. 3, 103 ff.

1. Kanekura, *op. cit.*, p. 6.

2. In *Dīgha Nikāya* (Dialogues of the Buddha), Part III, 117, (XXIX, Pasadika suttanta), tr. T. W. Rhys Davids, we read that "... at his (Buddha's) death the Niganthas became disunited and divided into two parties, in mutual strife and conflict, quarreling and wounding each other with wordy weapons :—Thou dost not understand this doctrine and discipline; but I do understand it. Thou art in the wrong; I am in the right ... " p. 111. Cf., S. Miyamoto, *Chudo-shiso oyoby Sono Hatdatz* (*The Thought of Middle Path and Its Development*), "We are informed that when another innovative teacher, Nigantha Nathaputta, died, his followers became divided into two groups, who clashed with each other because of different opinions about his teachings, discipline, and practices. This indicates what is likely to happen in new movements generally after the death of the founder; there is always the possibility of division, as happened in Buddhism very much like the way it has happened in other movements. According to the *Pasadika-Suttanta* the relationship between Buddha and his disciples involved inherent elements of disunity as well as of unity." p. 65.

3. For an example, *Vinayapiṭaka*, vol. V, *Cullavagga*, XI, I, II, states *op. cit.* : "Reverent Purana, dhamma and discipline have been chanted by Monks who are elders, submit yourself (upehi, as at V, IX, 3, 3, towards the end) to this chanting." "Your reverences, well chanted by the elders

2. *Religious unity of the community*

First let us discuss the teachings of Buddha (*dharma*), the discipline of Buddha the (*Śīla-vinaya*), and the person of the Enlightened One, all of which were employed for the sake of promoting the unity of the community.

(A) *The Dharma-unity*

One of the most important expressions of unity within the Buddhist community was given by Ānanda, as recorded in the *Majjhima Nikāya*, (*Gopaka-Moggallana-Sutta*), where we read : "...as you are thus without a support good Ānanda, what is the cause of your unity ?" "We, brahman, are not without support; we have a support, brahman. Dharma is the support."[1] This passage seems to be grounded in Buddha's remark to Ānanda which was one of his last commands : "...the truths and the rules of the order which I have set forth and laid down for you all, let them, after I am gone, be the Teacher to you."[2]

The above passages seem to indicate that for the sake of unity after Buddha's death, *dharma-vinaya* was instituted as the guide to the community, in the place left vacant by Buddha. It appears, therefore, that the *dharma* was the principal means of achieving this unity. Having said this, it is now useful to examine the specific ways, in which the *dharma* (the Middle Path) contributed to the unity of the Buddhist community.

(i) *The Middle Path*

'The Middle Path' implies avoidance of the two extremes. The idea is expressed with great lucidity by the following

are dhamma and discipline, but in that way that I heard it in the Lord's presence, that I received it in his presence, in that same way will I hear it in mind." p. 402. Cf., S. Dutt, *op. cit.*, pp. 18-19; and Kanekura, *op. cit.*, pp. 196-197.

1. *Majjhima-Nikāya* (*Middle Length Sayings*), vol. III, by I. B Horner, Pali Text Society tr. No. 31, 108 Gopakamoggallana—sutta III, p. 60.

2. T. W. Rhys Davids, tr., *Buddhist Suttas*, *Mahā-Parinibbāna-Sutta*, Chapt. VI. I, *The Sacred Books of the East*, ed. Max Muller, vol. XI, 1881 p. 112.

statements made, as the tradition believes, by Buddha himself. They concern both practical living on the one hand and theoretical belief on the other :

(a) Monks, these two extremes should not be followed by one who has gone forth as a wanderer. What two? Devotion to the pleasures of sense, . . . and (on the other) devotion to self-motivation,...By avoiding these two extremes the Tathāgata has gained knowledge of that middle path. Cohid giveth vision, which giveth knowledge, which causeth calm, special knowledge, enlightenment, Nibbāna.[1]

(b) Thus far, Kaccaya, he has the right view. Everything exists :—this is one extreme. Nothing exists :—this is the other extreme. No approaching either extreme the Tathāgata teaches you a doctrine by the middle (way).[2]

The practical formula of the Middle Path expressed in the first statement recommended avoidance of the extremes of asceticism and hedonism. The theoretical formula expressed in the second likewise counsels avoidance of the extremes of belief in being and belief in non-being—both of these are inconsistent with the Middle Path. The doctrine of the Middle Path is grounded in the theory of dependent origination (*pratītya-Samutpāda*, or *paṭicca-Samuppāda*).[3] Buddha called his teaching 'doctrine by the middle' (*dhammo majjhena*) as all things are "causally continuous (or collective) uprising."[4] Secondly, it leads to the positive practice of the Noble Eight-Fold Path which leads to *nirvāṇa.*

How, then, did one follow the Middle Path? It cannot be held that Buddhism as conceived by its founder was not really

1. *Saṁyutta-Nikāya* (The Book of the *Kindred Sayings*), Part V by F. L. Woodward, Pali Text Society tr. No. 16, *Mahāvagga,* LVI, *Sacca-Saṁyutta, op. cit.*, pp. 356-357.

2. *Saṁyutta-Nikāya* (*The Book of the Kindred Sayings*), Part II, tr. Mrs. Rhys Davids, XII, 2, 15, p. 13.

3. H. Matzutani, *Bukkyo Kairon* (*Introduction to Buddhism*), pp. 141-142.

4. *Saṁyutta-Nikāya* (*The Book of the Kindred Sayings*), *Notes, op. cit.*, vol. II, p. V.

ascetic at all. It was ascetic in a moderate way, and hence avoided the extremes of hardship and physical self-denial practised by some other contemporary movements such as Jainism. Jainism emphasized the principle of non-possession, believing that this led one to spiritual development. Buddhism avoided this, because it was felt that undergoing great physical hardship might hinder the development of wisdom. Likewise, it was held that a life of pleasure disturbed the holy life required of monks. Therefore, moderate asceticism in life and non-adherence to any view of being, as well as of non-being in doctrine were considered the only safe rules. Evidently, it called for an understanding which was essentially dialectical; as the dialectic was pursued further the Middle Path came better into view.[1]

Buddha also saw the Middle Path as the logical principle of unity in the community. When problems of disunity arose in the *saṁgha* he wanted unity within the community, not as a matter of right *vs.* wrong but in a manner which paradoxically transcended right and wrong.[2] The following is worth noting: The Kosambi monks were divided into two disputing groups. Buddha did not say which group was right or which was wrong. Rather, he suggested that, for the sake of unity within the community, it would be justifiable to say that one faction was right even though it appeared to be wrong, or that one was wrong even though it appeared to be right.[3] Also, in the story of Devadatta mentioned earlier Buddha neither accepted the five rules suggested by Devadatta nor did he entirely reject them; instead, he said that the monks should be free to choose whether or not to follow these rules.[4] This appears to

1. *Op. cit.*, p. viii.
2. Hayajima, *op. cit.*, p. 58.
3. Hirakawa, *op. cit.*, p. 601; Genshi Bukkyo, *op. cit.*, p. 133. Cf., *Vinaya-piṭaka*, vol. I, *Saṁghādisesa*, XII. 1, 2, *op. cit.*, pp. 310-312. Cf., *Vinayapiṭaka*, vol. I, X, 2, *op. cit.* : "The order, harmonious, on friendly terms, not quarrelsome, dwells comfortably under a single rule." "A second time they should say . . . A third time they should say . . . If he gives it up, this is good. If he does not give it up, it is an offence of wrong-doing." p. 301.
4. Cf., *Vinaya-piṭaka* (*The Book of the Discipline*), Vol. I, *op. cit.*, *Saṁghādisesa*, X, I-III, pp. 296-300.

indicate his concern for peaceful coexistence in Buddhism. He applied the principle of the Middle Path to promote unity and coexistence among the different Buddhist factions. He had supreme concern for the unity of the community to which the ethical aspects of his teachings naturally led.

He always took into consideration the time, the place, and the people inasmuch as the causes were always related to problems arising from the factors of time and place.[1] For example: After the Buddhist community expanded, harmony and discipline in the community could not have existed if Devadatta's suggestions had been adopted. Also nuns were prohibited from living in the forest, for there was the question of their safety and the problem of creating temptation for the monks. This emphasis on minute practical matters does not mean, however, that there was any lack of universally significant laws.[2] Also, before his death, Buddha even suggested that minor rules[3] might be abolished to avoid such controversy.

In considering the Middle Path, it is important to note that Buddha chose a balanced, pragmatic standard for this community in the interests of unity, rather than the imposition of a transcendent moral judgement.

1. *Dīgha Nikāya* (*Dialogues of the Buddha*), Part III, tr. T. W. and C.A.F. Rhys Davids, pasadikasuttanta XXIX, iii, 134 : "... If the past meant what is true, what is fact, and what does redound to your good, concerning that the Tathāgata knows well the time when to reveal it." p. 28. For example : It seems that for collective living and the maintenance of order in the *saṁgha*, they needed rules for food, clothing and life generally. If each person had followed his own inclinations, communal life would have been impossible. Regarding the hour of rising, the times for eating, the kind of clothing, and the use of the common property of the *saṁgha*, rules were needed which did not relate to concepts of good and evil, but merely enforced the pragmatic requirements of communal living.

2. E. Conze, *Buddhist Thought in India*, "Dharma is the order of law of the universe, . . . dharma means the moral law . . .," p. 93.

3. *Buddhist Suttas*, *op. cit.* Cf., *Mahā-parinibbāna-sutta*, *op. cit.* : "When I am gone, Ānanda, let the Order, if it should so wish abolish all the letter and minor precepts." p. 112.

(ii) The Theory of Dependent Origination

As it has already been said, the notion of the Middle Path rested on the theory of dependent origination, *pratītya-samutpāda* or *paṭicca-samuppāda*,[1] let us now turn to it. Briefly it is expressed as follows: 'this' being, 'that' becomes; from this arising of this; this not being that becomes not; from the ceasing of this, that ceases.[2]

The sūtra also states:

Conditioned by ignorance activities come to pass, conditioned by activities consciousness; thus conditioned (arises) name and shape; and sense arises, contact, feeling, craving, grasping, becoming, birth, decay-and-death, grief, suffering, . . . even such is the uprising of this entire mass of ill. But from the utter fading away and ceasing of ignorance (arises) ceasing of activities, and thus comes ceasing of this entire mass of ill.[3]

This concept of dependent origination was not a special feature of Buddhism, but had been an ideal common to many others before Buddha.[4] What was unique in the Buddhist view was that the doctrine of production by causation, leading to the Middle Path, was concerned not with metaphysics but with practical considerations.[5] This concept of the Middle Path promotes cooperation among individuals and groups. It holds that if one takes an extreme partisan position, one can lose one's self-control and with it one's sense of direction in life. It

1. *Majjhima-Nikāya* (*The Middle Length Sayings*), Vol. I, *op. cit.*, 28 *Mahāhatthipadopamasutta*, 1, 191 : "This was said by the Lord ; Whoever sees conditioned genesis (the dependent origination) sees dhamma, whoever sees dhamma sees conditioned genesis." p. 237.

2. *Saṁyutta-Nikāya*, Vol. II, XII, 3, 21, p. 23.

3. *Op. cit.*, p. 13.

4. For the presence of the theory in Sāṁkhy-yoga see, H. Jacobi, *Der Ursprung des Buddhismus aus dem Sāṅkhy-yoga*, pp. 1 ff. Rhys Davids, *Early Buddhism* pp. 85-86. For its presence in Jainism see, Nakamura, *Genshi Bukkyo no Shiso*, II (*Thought of Early Buddhism*), pp. 77-84.

5. Cf., *Saṁyutta-Nikāya* (*The Book of the Kindred Sayings*), Vol. II, XII, 5, 48, p. 53; Miyamoto, *op. cit.*, p. 56.

exhorts one, therefore, to eschew all extreme positions and to follow the Middle Path, which presents the coalition between opposing sides and a high degree of mutual cooperation and continuous identity as the norm and essence of life. Thus, by following the Middle Path, minor factions should be drawn toward middle positions. This is the principle of unity and harmony. The doctrine of production by causation as expressed in the Middle Path unifies all the followers in Buddhism.

(*iii*) *The Eight-fold Path*

This theory of the Middle Path must be grounded in the practice of the Noble Eight-fold Path. The *Sacca-saṁyutta* says as follows: " . . . What, monks, is that middle path which giveth vision . . . Nibbāna? Verily it is this Aryan eightfold way, to wit: Right view, right aim, right speech, right action, right living, right effort, right mindfulness, right concentration . . ."[1] The Noble Eight-fold Path oriented to the right view[2] examining both sides led ultimately to the good (right) view. The Middle Path, therefore, is set-forth in the following verse: "To refrain from all evil, to achieve the good, to purify one's own heart—this is the teaching of the Awakened."[3]

When a controversy arose over the interpretation of *dharma* it, was not to be dealt with by arguments and strife,[4] but through openminded discussion, so that the truth might be discovered in a spirit of inquiry, without the loss of the spirit of peace. By following the Middle Path, one should be able to develop the ability to discriminate between good and bad, right and wrong.[5] By following it, one would be aware of how and when one could serve the cause of justice.

Therefore, the *Dhammapada* says, "A man is not just if he carries a matter of violence; no, he who distinguishes both right and wrong, who is learned and leads others, not by violence but

1. *Saṁyutta-Nikāya* (*The Book of the Kindred Sayings*), Part V, *sacca-samyutta*, p. 357.
2. Thomas, *op. cit.*, p. 192.
3. *The Dhammapada* (*A Collection of Verses*), No. 183, p. 30.
4. Cf., *Suttanipāta* (*A Collection of Discourses*), No. 907, p. 173.
5. Hayajima, *op. cit.*, p. 216.

justly and righteously, and who is guarded by the Law and intelligent, he is called just."[1]

(*iv*) *Nirvāṇa*

The aim of the Middle Path was to attain *nirvāṇa*. *Nirvāṇa*, therefore, can be equated with the Middle Path which led its followers io avoid the two extremes of either self-mortification or self-indulgence.[2]

Although *nirvāṇa* is beyond description, it can be interpreted as follows: First, through physical (*śīla*), mental (*citta* or *samādhi*), and intellectual (*paññā*) efforts one would reach a state of individual liberation, and attain arahatship,[3] as Buddha had, yet be able to retain his individual status in the community. As one who was enlightened, the individual would renounce self-interest, and progress toward purity of mind.

The *Ākaiṅkheyya sutta* states: " . . . attain to Arahatship to emancipation of heart, and emancipation of mind, let him then fulfill all righteousness, let him be devoted to that quietude of heart which springs from within . . ."[4]

Also, there is the concept *nirvāṇa* as a perfect life in arahatship. One entered the Noble Path with concern for each of

1. *The Dhammapada* (*A Collection of Verses*), op. cit., p. 41. Cf., C. V. Joshi, "Life and Teaching," P. V. Bapat, ed., 2500 *Years of Buddhism*, p. 26. Speaking of this Noble Eightfold Path, Dr. Rhys Davids says : "If this Buddhist ideal of perfect life is remarkable when compared with the thought of India at that time, it is equally instructive when looked at from the comparative point of view." *American Lecture*, p. 139; cf., Miyamoto, *op. cit.*, p. 49. The teachings of Buddha, as King of Dharma, were primarily presented as the war-cry which would fight for justice and destory evil. It was summoned to turn the *dharma-cakra*, or wheel of *dharma*, to build the new moral social order. *Dharma's* universal applicability and its availability to all not only contributed to equality within the Buddhist community but also led to a common goal for all its members.

2. Narada, "Nibbāṇa," B. C. Law, *Buddhistic Studies*, p. 573.

3. Thomas, *op. cit.*, pp. 190-191; S. Dutt, *op. cit.*, p. 139. Cf. T. W. Rhys Davids, "Introduction to the Maha-Sudassana Sutta."*Buddhist Suttas*, pp. 243-244. Cf., *Saṁyutta-Nikāya* (*The Book of the Kindred Sayings*), Part II, XI, 2, 16, p. 14.

4. *Buddhist Suttas : Ākaiṅkeyya Sutta*, 19, *op. cit*, p. 218.

one's fellow men, and had pity for his ignorance, sympathy for his weakness, equanimity and an all-pervading feeling of deep and lasting love.[1] The life of such an individual would, therefore, constitute an ideal pattern for other monks to follow in living peacefully together. Secondly, *nirvāṇa* could be compared to the sea, to which all rivers flow: *The Aṅguttara-Nikāya* states: "... All the great rivers: the Gaṅgā, the Yamunā, the Airavatī, the Sarabhū and the Mahī, on reaching the mighty ocean, lose their former names and identities and are reckoned simply as the ocean ... the mighty ocean has one (unmixed taste), the taste of salt."[2] Thus *nirvāṇa* may appear monistic.[3] In this "sea," all would be parts of *nirvāṇa*, without the particularisms of "I" and "you." It would not be necessary to struggle wi h self-exaltation; ideal unity in mutual support would be possible.

The *Saṁyutta-Nikāya* states: "This, too, is a matter hard to discern, to wit, the renunciation of all substrates of rebirth, the destruction of natural cravings, passionlessness, cessation, Nirvāṇa."[4] This means that *nirvāṇa* would eliminate all actions related to hatred, delusion, and the like. While attempting to describe *nirvāṇa* people call it a state in which there is a cessation of suffering and disease in which the pure mind is liberated and the heart is set at rest.[5] There would be no seeking after self-interest; for in Buddha's great harmonious spirit, everybody would be one through ethical perfection. *Nirvāṇa* solved the problems of old age, sickness, and death by treating them as objective conditions; it reached states of non-old-age, non-sickness, and non-

1. Cf., T. W. Rhys Davids, *Early Buddhism*, pp. 59-64.

2. *Aṅguttara-Nikāya*, Vol. IV, 2, 19, pp. 136-137. Cf., Sato (*Genshi Bukkyo no Kyodan Rinen*), *op. cit.*, p. 83.

3. N. Dutt, *op. cit.*, Vol. I, p. 292, In Pali Texts therefore the problems of non-duality is not mentioned. *Nibbāṇa* is described as one and only one and that it is of one taste (*ekarasa*). *Nirvāṇa*, according to the Buddhists of all times, is absolutely different from everything which is worldly or is constituted causally.

4. *Saṁyutta-Nikāya* (*Kindred Sayings*), *op. cit.* Part I, 1, 136, p. 172.

5. A. T. Bahm, *Philosophy of the Buddha*, pp. 80-81.

death deductively and achieved unity through welding harmony with complete perfection in impermanency and non-self.[1] Through Buddha's teachings one could experience liberation and reach *nirvāṇa* through *dharma*. Thus *nirvāṇa* consists of an indivisible and eternal peace,[2] which is communicated to the Buddhist community, called to "unity" through the monks called "peace monks."

III. THE NATURE OF THE ORIGINAL DISCIPLINE IN THE SAṀGHA

In the ideal sense, *dharma* was important as a source of unity within the *saṁgha*. From a practical viewpoint, religious discipline (*sīla-vinaya*) was necessary as a basis of unity in the daily life of the monks in the *saṁgha*.

Although saṁgha included the *arahats*, most of its members were ordinary monks and nuns. Therefore, if the Buddhist community was to be unified with a definite purpose, rather than allowed to turn into a heterogeneous group or disintegrate, religious discipline was necessary for the unity of the Buddhist community.

Reasons for the necessity of discipline included the following: The Buddhist community included not only those who had chose to become monks for purely religious reasons but also many who had joined purely for secular reasons,[3] such as their dislike for the rulers of other communities. Many uneducated and young people were present in the community, many members of which had come from other sects, and did not, therefore, know how to behave as Buddhists; they did not, for instance, know how to dress acceptably and often argued, vociferously in the dining room. When Sāriputta met Asvajit he was attracted to Buddhism because of Asvajit's "respect-inspiring" appearance. This illustrates a positive value of discipline

1. G. Watanabe, *Buddha no Kyosetzu* (*Teachings o, Buddha*), pp. 479-480

2. *Saṁyutta-Nikāya* (*Kindred Sayings*), I, 1, 2 : "Let him aspire after the final peace (The final peace (*accanta-santi*) termed Nirvāṇa). *Ibid.*, I, 20 : "Happy the mastery of them and the peace : ("Vūpasamo" expresses both 'mastery' and 'peace.' A Synonym for *Nibbāṇa*.)"

3. Cf., Hirakawa, *Ritsuzo no Kenkyu*, pp. 658-659.

and also indicates that in the earliest days of the Buddhist community, an effort was made to maintain the purity and unity of the community through discipline. Had there been no such attempt at purity and respect for the public, including the lay people who gave alms, how could it have attracted new followers and developed so rapidly?

Since the *saṁgha* rejected thieves, slaves, sick people, young people, *et al.*, it may be asked how Buddha himself did not accept them and make good monks of them.[1] He appears to have rejected such people for the sake of the unity and purity of the *saṁgha*, for they constituted a potential source of disorder and disunity which could have led to the dissolution of the *saṁgha*.

How then did the Buddha exercise his discipline of the first ten rules[2] for the purpose of harmony in the community?

1. *The Ten Rules*

The ten rules for monks not only enabled them to progress in their cultivation of the higher life but also constituted the basis of unity in the *saṁgha.* For example, "Do not Kill" was an expression of compassion toward men and animals.[3] This was a very important aspect of the unity of brotherhood as it inculcated loving reverence for one another. The admonition "Do not tell lies" built up trust among the members of the community since lying would always involve danger of division in the life of the community. "Do not claim superiority" prohibits that which would destroy the necessary feeling of equality in other members of the community. These rules seem to have

1. *Vinaya-pitaka (Book of the Discipline)*, Vol. 4, *Mahāvagga* 1, 76, 1, p. 120; cf., *Nanten Daizokyo*, Vol. 3, pp. 159-160; cf., Nakamura, *Keisei tochu no Kyotan*, p. 13.

2. See supra p. 52 fn. 6.

3. *Dīgha Nikāya (Dialogues of the Buddha)*, Vol. 1, II, *Sāmañña-phala*, 62:43: "And how, O King, is his conduct good? In this, O King, that the Bhikshu, putting away the killing of living things, holds aloof from the destruction of life. The cudgel and the sword he has laid aside, and ashamed of roughness, and full of mercy, he dwells compassionate and kind to all creatures that have life." p. 79., *Nanten Taizokyo*, vol. 6, p. 95.

been the ground of harmony in the community. Some of these applied only to monks, rather than to the lay people, because they were very important to monastic communal life, but not to the lives of laymen. If a monk violated one of these special rules, he was banished from the community; and this penalty meant his spiritual death. It was inflicted because of the importance of unity through purity in the community.

2. *Seven Rules Governing Disputes (saṁgha-kammas)*

When disputes arose among the monks threatening the unity of the *saṁgha*, the disciplinary court passed judgments concerning right and wrong. Seven disciplinary laws (*saṁgha-kammas*, or provisions for allaying disputes) were therefore introduced and certain punishments for transgressions were imposed for preserving unity.

In connection with the seven provisions, it should be noted that four of them arose out of a 'formal dispute' (*adhikaraṇa*), *viz.*, (1) *vivādādhikaraṇa*: a dispute on a point of *dharma* or *vinaya* (the Second Council 'ten dispute law'); (ii) *anuvādādhikaraṇa*, or a dispute relating to the state of a *bhikkhu's* opinions, morals, character, conduct or manner of life; (iii) *āpattadhikaraṇa* or a dispute bearing upon the kind or category of offence alleged against a *bhikkhu*, and (iv) *kiccādhikaraṇa*, a dispute regarding the validity of an act.[1]

We may discuss the seven rules governing disputes (*saṁgha-kammas*) as follows:

(A) *Sammukhā-vinaya* (現前毘尼)

The court which considered offences demanded the following: (i) the presence of the party concerned; (ii) the lawfully constituted assembly; (iii) that it should be based on knowledge of *vinaya*, i.e., the rules of process proper to the case; and (iv) the *dhamma*, i. e., the doctrines. However, no settlement of a dispute nor the application of discipline, could be carried out in camera;

1. S. Dutt, *Buddha and Five After Centuries*, p. 89.
2. Cf., S. Dutt, *Ibid.*, pp, 113-124; cf., Sato, *Genshi Bukkyo Kyodan no Kenkyu*, pp. 330-340; cf., Tsukamoto, *op. cit.*, pp. 348-352.

the settlement or the trial must be open, and the law, both procedural and substantive, must be followed and applied.[1] This is very important because after Buddha's death, *dhamma vinaya* had to be the central authority to unite the *saṁgha*. If there could be different opinions and interpretations, without the founder's own authoritative standards, there would be a serious threat to unity in the community. *Sammukhā-vinaya* was, therefore, most essential to the solution of problems of disunity.

(B) *Sati-vinaya* (憶念毘尼)

When a person, who had been falsely accused, asked to be acquitted of charges against him, he would be examined by the *saṁgha*. If he was to be found innocent, certain specified conditions would have to be met.

The *Cullavagga* states:

> Monks, there are these five legally valid properties in giving a verdict of innocence: If the monk is pure and without offences; and if they reproach him; and if he asks; if the Order gives him a verdict of innocence; if it is by rule, the assembly being complete. These, monks, are the five legally valid properties in giving a verdict of innocence.[139]

(C) *Patiññākaraṇa* (自言治法)

Unless one confessed his guilt, it was assumed that any judgment against him by the *saṁgha* could be erroneous. The *Kullavagga* (Cullavagga) says: "No official act, O Bhikkhus is to be carried out against Bhikkhus who have not confessed themselves guilty. Whosoever does so, shall be guilty of a dukkata offence."[3]

1. S. Dutt, *op. cit.*, p. 91; cf., Sato, pp. 343-383.
2. *Vinaya-Piṭaka* (*The Book af the Discipline*), tr. I.B. Horner, Vol. V, *Cullavagga*, IV, 4, p. 105.
3. *Vinaya Texts*, Part III, trs. T. W. Rhys Davids and H. Oldenberg, *Kullavagga*, IV, 7, 1, p. 23.

(D) *Amūlha-vinaya* (不痴毘尼)

When one had committed a sin when one was not in one's right mind, but was believed by others to have been sane at the time of the offence, he would be acquitted if he could demonstrate that he had in fact not been in full possession of his faculties at the time. He would do this in several ways: (i) if he could say, "I do not remember"; (ii) if he could say, "I remember it, sirs, but as if in a dream"; or (iii) if he had a dispensation to the effect from the *saṁgha.*[1]

(E) *Yebhuyyasikā* (多覓毘尼)

When they were unable to settle a disputed question, the *saṁgha* would decide by majority vote. The *Kullavagga* states . . . Blessed One, I allow you, O Bhikkhus, to settle such a dispute by the vote of majority. . . ."[2] Also, the following conditions were required: Again the Kullavagga states:

> Which are the ten in which the taking of votes is invalid? When the matter in dispute is trivial—when the case has not run its course that is, when the necessary preliminaries of submission to arbitration have not been carried out—when regarding the matter in dispute the Bhikkhus have not formally remembered, or been formally called upon to remember, the offence—when the taker of votes knows that those whose opinions are not in accordance with the law will be in the majority, or probably may be in the majority—when he knows that the voting will result in a schism in the saṁgha—when he is in doubt whether the voting will result in a schism in the saṁgha—when the votes are irregularly given—when all do not vote equally—and when they do not vote in accordance with the view which they really hold. These are the ten cases in which voting is invalid.[3]

1. *op. cit.*, IV. 6, 1, pp. 20-21.
2. *op. cit.*, IV. 9, 1, p. 25.
3. *op. cit.*, IV, 10, 1, pp. 26-27.

(*F*) *Tassapārpiyyasika* (覓罪相法)

When there was confusion as to a monk's guilt or innocence as a result of his having confessed a sin and later retracted his confession, his guilt would be determined by a majority vote. Five aspects of the attitude of the monk and three questions about the sin of which he was accused, had to be determined. These are given by the *Kullavaga* as follows: "To wit—he is impure he is shameless—a censure has been set on foot against him—the Saṁgha carries out the Kamma—it carries it out lawfully, and in full quorum , . . three things . . . is characterized, it is against the Dhamma, and against the Vinaya, and difficult to settle."[1]

(*G*) *Tinavatthāraka* (草覆地法)

When disputes among monks at court became prolonged, with complex and conflicting testimonies, it was suggested that the disputing factions themselves resolve their differences amicably, rather than by resorting to force, or by having a judgment imposed upon them from without. The *Kullavagga* expresses it this way: " . . . Blessed One . . . I enjoin upon you, O Bhikkhus, to settle a matter of this kind by Tinavatthāraka the covering over as with grass . . . And this, O Bhikkhus, is it to be settled. All are to meet together in one spot."[2]

3. *Upavasathā* (*general meeting of the monks*)

All monks were required to attend an *upavasathā*, or general meeting of monks, which they could reach within a day's

1. *op. cit.*, IV, 12, 1, p. 30; cf., *op. cit.*, IV, 11, 2: "Let the venerable Saṁgha hear me. This Bhikkhu Uvala, being examined in the midst of the Saṁgha with an offence, when he has denied it then confesses it, when he has confessed it then denies it, makes countercharges, and speaks lies which he knows to be such. If the times seem meet to the Saṁgha, carry out the Tassapārpiyyasikā-Kamma against the Bhikkhu Uvala. This is the motion." p. 29.

2. *Op. cit.*, IV., 13, 1-2, pp. 31-32.

journey.[1] If any monk was prevented from attending due to illness, he was to send a report on the purity of his deeds and agree to abide by any decisions, which the Council might make. Decisions made at these meetings were by unanimous vote, or if a unanimous vote did not materialize, by the decision of the majority. These decisions were to be followed by all in accordance with some prior agreement. This principle was established to avoid disunity. When disagreements ensued, there were public institutions, such as *saṁgha-karma*, which existed to mediate and restore amity. If a number of monks abandoned one *saṁgha* and started another, because of differences of opinion, the two communities were permitted to coexist in the same district, with neither being expelled.[2] The *Upavasathā*, which brought together monks of different individual *saṁghas* within a district, was established to promote the ideal of unity in the Buddhist community as a whole.

4. *The Monk Teachers*

According to the *Mahāvagga*, the Buddha said:

> Monks, I allow a teacher. The teacher, monks, should arouse in his pupil the attitude of a son; the pupil should arouse in his teacher the attitude of father. Thus these, living with reverence, with deference, with courtesy towards one another, will come to growth, increase, maturity in this dhamma and discipline . . .[3]

Junior monks would have a monk-teacher who instructed them in the *dharma* and trained them in the *vinaya*, so that they would properly perform the duties of monastic life. A monk-teacher was generally one who had followed the monastic life for at least ten years.[4] The relationship between the

1. Cf., *Vinaya-Pitaka*, Part I, *Saṁghādisesa*, X. 2: "Harmonious means: an order belonging to the same community is established within the same boundary." p. 300. Cf., Sato, *op. cit.*, pp. 198-199.
2. See Chukamoto, *op. cit.*, p. 147; see also Sato, *op. cit.*, p. 199.
3. *Vinaya-Pitaka* (*Book of the Discipline*), tr. I.B. Horner, Part 4, *Mahāvagga*, 1, 32, 1, p. 79.
4. *Op. cit.*, *Mahāvāgga*, 1, 35, 1.

monk-teacher and his students was like that between a father and his sons. The junior monks were required to obey the instructions of the monk-teacher. Sāriputta and other great disciples of Buddha came from the ranks of these monk-teachers. They became leaders of the community and advanced the cause of unity among its members.

Theoretically, there were no class distinctions in the Buddhist community. In practice, however, it was found that the *saṁgha*, being a social community, required the recognition of classes among its members for the purpose of maintaining order. An "inner group" of five classes was established in the *saṁgha*, consisting of the *bhikkhus* (monks), *bhikkhunīs* (nuns), and three classes of candidates : the *samanera*, *samanerī*, and *sikkhamana*. These latter groups were *bhikku* and *bhikkunī* centered, and were of primary importance in the *saṁgha*. In addition, two lay classes constituting an "outer group," were established — the *upāsaka* and the *upāsikā*.[1] The *bhikkhunīs* had five more strict rules to obey than did the *bhikkhus*. Thus, although the nuns were part of the monastic community, the order was monk-centered.

5. *The 'Four-quarters Saṁgha'* (*catuddesa saṁgha*)

Let us now discuss the individual *saṁgha* and the 'Four-quarters *saṁgha*' in relation to unity. These two levels of the *saṁgha* were organized by the Buddha, in order to create an organic unity of the part and the whole.[2] The individual *saṁgha* consisted of those members gathered within a specific, limited district. Each of these individual *saṁghas* developed independently, under the common influence of Buddha's teaching. Because the monks were spread over a large area and means of travel were slow, it was not possible for all the monks to meet together. In the universal 'Four-quarters *saṁgha*', there could easily have been no unity among the individual *saṁghas*.

1. H. Ui, *Indo Tetsugaku Kenkyu*, Vol. 4, (*A Study in Indian Philosophy*), p. 45.
2. Hirakawa, *op. cit.*, p. 684.

Therefore, the "Four-quarters *saṁgha*" included all the monks and constituted the ideal foundation for all of the district *saṁghas*. It did not, however, exist as a central political organization. *Dharma-vinaya* belonged to the 'Four-quarters *saṁgha*'.[1] and, therefore, no individual *saṁgha* could change it. Thus, ideally, every *saṁgha* practised the same *dharma-vinaya*. Also, it was intended that the 'Four-quarters *saṁgha*' should possess all the property of the *saṁgha* as a principle of universal ownership of property.

Therefore, according to the *Mahāvagga*, Buddha said: "... whatever many goods, many requisites are there, these are for the Order of the four quarters (*catuddesa-saṁgha*)—those who have come in, those who have not come in—they are not to be divided up."[2]

Such property as buildings and furniture were decreed to belong to the 'Four-quarters *saṁgha*', with every monk having an equal right to use any part of it. Hence, no monk or individual community would be dominated by possessions. Because the *dharma-vinaya* belonged to it, and because it held all property, the 'Four-quarters *saṁgha*' was very important for both ideal and practical unity among the individual *saṁghas*.

IV. In What Sense Was Buddha a Source of Unity?

Buddha should now be discussed as a source of unity, for the simple reason that the unity of the Buddhist community appears to have been based fundamentally on his personal authority.[3] Having been the founder of the community, he was its leader and his disciples were dependent upon him as the basis of the *dharma-vinaya*. He said: "Hush, Vakkali! What is there in seeing this vile body of mine? He who seeth the Norm (dharma), Vakkali, he seeth me : he who seeth me, Vakkali, he seeth the

1. Sato, *op. cit.*, pp. 89-91.
2. *Vinaya-Piṭaka* (*Book of the Discipline*), tr., I.B. Horner, Vol. IV. Mahāvagga, VIII, 27, 5, pp. 435-436.
3. This is discussed in Chapter I; cf., M. Anesaki, *Kompon Bukkyo* (*Primitive Buddhism*), p. 377.

Norm (dharma). Verily, seeing the Norm (dharma), Vakkali, one sees me : seeing me one sees the Norm (dharma)."[1]

Buddha had desired that after his death there would be unity in the community through the *dhamma-vinaya*. His teachings became the center of the community, because his disciples longed to continue to belong to the field of excellence exemplified by him. His personality was the foundation of the *saṁgha*, not only during his lifetime but also after his death, because the *dharma-vinaya* was not claimed by the disciples to have been made by them but by the Master himself.[2] In fact, they viewed the *dharma-vinaya* as being the collected words of Buddha, which they had no authority to change.[3] Since they believed that no one could change the *dharma-vinaya* but Buddha himself, no council was established to enact changes in the law, even though there might have been different interpretations and understanding of his teachings, and even though it became very difficult to follow all the laws as the social conditions changed after his death.[4]

Although the *saṁgha* had developed as a universal community, different interpretations of Buddha's teachings arose, and communities in different districts developed independently.[5] Buddha's disciples respected their Master's personality[6] and

1. *Saṁyutta-Nikāya* (*Kindred Sayings*), Part III (XXII, 87), tr. F. L. Woodward, p. 103; see also Hayajima, *op. cit.*, p. 454.

2. See, p. 65 fn. 3. Cf., S. Dutt, *Buddhist Monks and Monasteries of India*; Dutt relates that the *pātimokkha* formula is: "If a Bhikkhu did such-and-such an act, he was guilty of (a named offence); the Vinaya formula, posting the Buddha as the Law-giver (Sattha), is: 'I allow you, Bhikkhus, to do or refrain from doing such-and-such an act.' p. 74.

3. Y. Takahashi, "Kai to sono kiban," (Śila and it's foundation), ed. Nihon Bukkyo Gakukai, *Bukkyo ni okeru kai no Kenkyu* [*A Study of Śila in Buddhism*], p. 2.

4. *Ibid.*, p. 2.

5. See the previous Chapter on, "Section of unity," p. 108-109. Cf., Oldenberg, *op. cit.*, pp. 340-343.

6. *Theragātha*, *op. cit.*, No. 510:

"When first I saw the blessed Master, Him
For whom no fear can anywhere arise,
A wave of deep emotion filled my soul
At sight of Him, the peerless man of Men." p. 243.

had faith in the *dharma* as right teaching; they practised his discipline in search of truth. However, Buddha was the origin of the *dharma-vinaya,* which was the basis of Buddhism. The *dharma-vinaya* was understood to be the practical expression of Buddha's vision which seemed to be the only possible basis for the existence of the *saṁgha.*

Although Buddha's *dharma-vinaya* became the foundation of ideal unity in the *saṁgha,* without him, the *dharma-vinaya* was inadequate as the basis for unity. The *dharma* itself and the life of the *saṁgha* had been grounded in his personality because it could be said that the *dharma* was his wisdom and the *saṁgha* was his compassion, the expression of his love.[1]

It is important to note that the *dharma-vinaya* had arisen from the historical Buddha, whose personality had always been at the center of the community. It should also be noted that his people gathered because they were attracted to him personally, and that they wanted to obey the *dharma* which he taught and to become his disciples with the sole objective of attaining *nirvāṇa.* Like members of other ascetic groups, they returned to their teacher, the Buddha and his teaching, and started a community. This original community, which was centered on the teacher, the Buddha and his disciples, was the model after which other Buddhist communities were patterned.

In brief, Buddha's leadership, as head of the community, was the primary basis of unity in the early Buddhist community. A balance developed between *dharma* and *vinaya* as the spiritual successors of Buddha's personal authority. Buddha, as noted above, used the *dharma-vinaya* as a means of developing unity in the *saṁgha.* First, *dharma,* as the formula of the Middle Path, appears to have constituted the ideal basis of unity in the *saṁgha.* From a practical viewpoint, the Middle Path, instead of imposing decisions as to right and wrong upon the different opinions in the community, transcended these differing opinions and balanced them for the sake of peaceful coexistence. Thus Buddha's ethics were exercised relatively, rather than absolutely. The concept of the Middle Path gave rise to the "doctrine of

1. H. Ui, *op. cit.,* p. 57.

dependent origin," which held that everything is related to everything else.

Also, the doctrine of *anātman* ('no soul' or 'soullessness') seems to provide the ethical basis for self-denial, for the sake of cooperation among the members of the community. However, in the ideal sense, the Middle Path was right-view oriented, even though on the practical level good and bad were transcended and allowed to coexist for the sake of unity. Ultimately, right should be the goal of the community, because Buddha was the "King of *dharma*" and he would destroy evil through good in order to build up the moral order. Further more, *nirvāṇa* provided a monastic all-embracing ideal of unity in the *saṁgha*. The understanding of *nirvāṇa*, as the essence of peace, was the ground for the monks being called "peace monks." It is noteworthy that the voluntary practices followed by these monks were oriented not only toward individual perfection but also toward a unified community.

For the sake of unity in the *saṁgha*, Buddha also used religious discipline to maintain order in the community. This discipline, which, as *vinaya*, included rules enforced by punishments, was balanced with *śīla*, which, as spiritual cultivation, was also designed to promote unity within the community.

The unity of the community was also promoted by the following aspects of Buddhist community organization : the "Four-quarters *saṁgha*" as the ideal foundation of the universal *saṁgha*; the *upavasatha* ("general meetings of monks"), at which all the monks in attendance made decisions democratically; and the leadership in the *dharma-vinaya* provided by the monk-teachers for their disciples.

However, the *saṁgha* respected the disciplines which it claimed had been made by Buddha. This was so because the community itself desired unity. Discipline not only led to unity through ethical cultivation, i.e., being subservient to discipline for personal perfection, but it was also held to be the means of attaining *nirvāṇa*. Furthermore, it should be noted that Buddha's discipline appears to have been based primarily on the concept of the Middle Path.[1]

1. Cf., Drekmeier, *Kingship and Community in Early India*: "The Buddha is the most famous of these who questioned the old ways, and the

In the first place, Buddha's discipline appears to have been a collection of his judgments made in response to problems arising from specific, actual situations. Therefore, the Buddhist community did not claim to have a divinely originated absolute, monistic model of ethics such as the one claimed by the Judaeo-Christian tradition in, for example, the Ten Commandments, which had to be obeyed because they were given by God. Buddha wanted a transcendent concept of right and wrong in the spirit of the Middle Path. He used a pluralistic model of ethics for the sake of the unity of the community.

Similarly, a community decision that a monk was guilty of a sin was not made in an absolute sense. If a monk, for example, believed that he had committed an offence, he was supposed to expiate it voluntarily; the rules were not primarily enforced by others. If a monk found it difficult to decide whether his actions had constituted an offence or not, he was required to trust the decision of others, and if others said that he had sinned, he accepted their judgment and confessed, as required by *vinaya*. This was required for peace in the community, lest dissension

answer he proposed was in essence psychological. It involved a discipline that aimed at no less than the transcendence of the dichotomy of subject and object." 283. For example, see B.G. Gokhale, "Buddhist Social Ideal," ed. N. N. Law, *Gautama Buddha, 25th Centenary Volume*, 1956: "The five commandments for the laymen, namely, abstinence from violence, stealing, falsehood, immorality and drinking intoxicating liquors, were a simple formalization of the four pillars of society and became the basis of Buddhist social ethics. When to these were added Faith in the Buddha, Dhamma and Samgha, respect for elders and women (Cf., the seven conditions of stability as preached to the Vajjis by the Buddha, *Mahāparinibbāna Sutta, Dīgha Nikāya, S.B.E.*, XI, pp. 3-5), disciplining of the mind in the way of righteousness, the formulation of the Buddhist social ethics was completed. These ideals were postulated as a middle way between the two extremes of aggressiveness resulting in constant preoccupation with acquisitiveness to the exclusion of all other considerations and indulgence leading to dissipation and degradation. Reason, moderation, harmony, a constant awareness of primacy of righteousness, the ennobling nature of charity as a way of life, compassion and wisdom were the norms which were now constantly put before society. This society was conceived of as universal." pp. 38-39.

should arise within the community when some monks claimed that they had not sinned and others claimed that they had.[1]

The unity of the *saṁgha* was primarily based on Buddha's personal authority, with the *dharma-vinaya* being the means of unity. Buddha, not only during his lifetime but after his death, led the *saṁgha* towards unity through the *dharma-vinaya.* Without the unifying force of his personality, the *dharma-vinaya* could not have constituted the basis for unity after his death and the *saṁgha* would have become a disorganized community.

The community was the place where one could learn Buddha's teaching and practise one's discipline, purge oneself of impurity, and strive for liberation in *nirvāṇa*. It was centered on Buddha as the external origin of the *dharma-vinaya,* and it was dependent on him as head of the community.

Objectively, the *saṁgha* wanted to unify itself through the *dharma-vinaya.* Actually, however, the life in the monastic community was focused on Buddha's personality and his teaching. Therefore, a Buddha-centered religious community was desired not only for monks but for all human beings everywhere. Buddha's personality and teaching were the foundation of his kingdom, although the unity of the community discipline and community organization were the means of attaining this kingdom. His ethics were the means by which the community was unified. It appears significant that, although his teaching consisted fundamentally of moral discipline for individual perfection, its true orientation was towards a unified community in which moral authority would be respected.

It was not only in the early Buddhist community but for all generations that Buddha would be head of the community and that his personality, through the influence of his example, would be a unifying force along with the *dharma-vinaya.* Thus Buddha's great personality and influence in the early Buddhist community became the universal basis of unity for Buddhism.

1. See, Hirakawa, *op. cit.*, p. 133.

CHAPTER III

DISCIPLINE IN THE EARLY BUDDHIST COMMUNITY

INTRODUCTION

We now turn to discipline in the early Buddhist community and introduce an important opinion which argues against the view that we were developing in the previous chapter, according to which *dharma* and *vinaya* along with Buddha were sources of unity in the community. We argued that *vinaya* had its source in Buddha's teaching and that Buddha himself, after his death, lived through *dharma* and *vinaya* in the *saṁgha.* The opinions of Watsuji are different. He particularly disputes the view that *vinaya* originated from Buddha himself. Thus he observes:

> The community does not actually appear to have received its laws directly from so great a personality as Buddha during his lifetime. Instead, the law appears to have been produced by the community itself, at a time when its leaders who were comparatively incompetent and lacked the power to influence many people significantly. Evidence for this view exists in the emphasis in the law on the exclusion of persons from the community. It is not conceivable that a great religious leader would have rejected sinners, cripples, public servants, or young people. Because of Buddha's stature as a great and honorable leader, I cannot accept this attitude as representing his own beliefs. To the best of my knowledge there is no evidence in the *Sūtra-Vinaya* that the law came from Buddha.[1]

The argument implies that discipline, especially in its *vinaya* aspect, was not important—first, because it had not come from Buddha, secondly, because the influence of Buddha's great personality on the community would have eliminated any need for formal rules, and, thirdly, because the rules were mostly of

1. Watsuji, *Genshi Bukkyo no Jissen Tetsugaku* (*Practical Philosophies in Primitive Buddhism*) p. 65.

later origin and had been devised by relatively insignificant leaders. Watsuji, however, would not entirely deny that Buddha's leadership had contained some disciplinary elements; he notes, for instance, that "he (Buddha) would preach to the people that they should overcome lust."[1]

Watsuji bases his argument on two grounds, namely, that Buddha's personality was so great that he could not have made such rules; and, that there is no evidence that the disciplinary rules were given by Buddha—instead, Watsuji suggests that his followers appear to have attributed the rules to him.

The author is not primarily concerned with the historical question of whether the rules of discipline were entirely Buddha's or whether they were the creation of his disciples.[2] Watsuji appears to have been correct to a degree in stating that Buddha's personality was so great that the early Buddhist community would not have needed such rigid and detailed rules as those given in the *vinaya*. The making of so many rules appears to be inconsistent with Buddha's emphasis on noble attitudes, practised in self-cultivation, which would cause his monks to be well-disciplined. A *sūtra*, in fact, states that during the first fifteen years of Buddha's mission there were no disciplinary rules, so well did his disciples behave.[3] This does not mean, however, that one can accept Watsuji's conclusions that the rules were not attributable to Buddha and were, therefore, unimportant.

Theragāthā's version appears to be more acceptable: "What the training doth prescribe (was) revealed to us by glorious Gotama."[4] Discipline is important primarily because it was based on Buddha's personal authority. Tradition claims that it originated with Buddha, who not only gave it[5] but also practised

1. *Ibid.*, p. 60.
2. Cf., S. Dutt, *Early Buddhist Monachism*, p. 29.
3. Cf., H. Ui, *Indo Tetsugaku Kenkyu* (A Study in Indian Philosophy), p. 34.
4. *Theragātha* (*Psalms of the Early Buddhist Brethren*), tr. Mrs. Rhys Davids, p. 236.
5. *Digha Nikāya* (*Dialogues of the Buddha*), Part II, trs. T.W. and C.A.F. Rhys Davids, 154, "Buddha says . . . Ānanda, . . . The Truths, and the *Rules* of the Order, (which) I have set forth and laid down for you all." p. 171. *Vinaya-Piṭaka* (The Book of the Discipline) Vol. V by

and exemplified it. Without his authority, it would not have been obeyed by the monks of the *saṁgha*; they respected it because it had been given by Buddha rather than being mere moral laws.[1] Furthermore, Buddha's teachings were not merely philosophical; practice of moral discipline was required. They together formed the basis of all Buddhist systems.[2] Also, discipline was the great guide that led to the cultivation of ascetic life.[3] Therefore, physical and moral discipline as a means of rectifying mistakes and as a means of making pure monks was the quintessence of the Buddhist Way.[4] To become an *arahat* and to attain *nirvāṇa* required individual effort in spiritual awakening and called for the practice of discipline as the cultivation of the *dharma* preached by Buddha. Without the spiritual authority of Buddha, there would have been no ground whatever for obeying his discipline.

Buddha's mission lasted for more than forty years, during which his followers lived in monastic communities. Had these communities been so long without rules, disorder would likely

I.B. Horner, *The Sacred Books of the Buddhists*, Vol. II, *Cullavagga* XI, 1, 9, has this to say: "Then the venerable Ānanda spoke thus to me at the time of his attaining nibbāna: 'If the Orders, Ānanda, after my death is willing, the leader and minor rules of training may be abolished'." p. 398. Cf., B.C. Law, *Early Buddhist Brothers and Sisters* p. 42.

1. Cf., T. Kimura, *Genshī Bukkyo Shiso Ron* (*A Study of the Thought in Early Buddhism*), p. 13; cf., Kitagawa, *Religions of the East*, p. 175.

2. Cf., H. Beck, *Buddhismus*; Buddha und seine Lehre 1, p. 125; cf., M. Walleser, *Die Philosophische Grundlage des altern Buddhismus*, cf., H. Oldenberg, *Buddha*, pp. 230 f. The scholars named above apparently did not consider Buddha's teaching to have been philosophical. The Buddha seems to have been unwilling to discuss such philosophical problems as self, soul, and life after death. This does not mean, however, that the Buddha's thought was not philosophical. His concepts of no-self, the five *skandhas*, dependent origination, the Four Noble Truths, etc., were certainly philosophical although the Buddha does not seem to have been interested in a system of philosophy. His not providing answers to questions on philosophical matters indicates a deeper philosophical approach to these questions.

3. S. Watanabe, *Bukkyo Buddhism*, p. 88.

4. Kimura, *op. cit.*, p. 384.

have arisen and the survival of the communities would have been jeopardized. For the communities to endure as "united" and "purely moral-oriented" communities, discipline was therefore, not only important but essential.[1] Although Buddha's spiritual authority was indeed great, how could he have controlled so many people who were spread over so large a territory without formal discipline? In his time, with means of transportation being primitive, he could not bring his personal influence to bear on all the communities at all times.

Watsuji, therefore, not only appears to have failed to realize the importance of the Buddhist discipline but also seems to have erroneously stated that there is no ground for believing that it originated with Buddha. Certainly the major elements of this discipline came from Buddha himself. The author, however, does not deny that some of the rules were of later origin.[2]

The above discussion not only demonstrates the importance of the subject of discipline but also indirectly, why religious discipline should be discussed in connection with "the authority of the founder" and "the unity of the community".

1. Discipline, combined with the Buddha's teachings, was very important for the unity of the Buddha's early community. Krestser, however, does not seem to be entirely in agreement with this view, in the following statements from his book, *Man in Buddhism and Christianity* : "The problem of the neighbour therefore, even within the Saṁgha itself, is not taken seriously. The Saṁgha is not a community, which is bound together by bonds of interior necessity, it is a collection of individuals, who help each other to attain Nibbāna. The structure of the saṁgha is atomistic. In any case, the anatta doctrine,which is the fundamental postulate of Buddhism, makes community life impossible." p. 106. Although having correctly perceived the individualistic aspect of the Buddhist community, Krestser seems to have missed the aspect of unity; the Buddha's desire to establish an ideal society is expressed not only in his discipline but also through his compassion. It is not true that the *anātman* doctrine made the formation of a true community impossible, as Krestser has maintained. On the contrary, *anātman,* non-desire and the self sacrificial aspects seem to be conducive to unity. Also the Buddha's spiritual authority, on which his teaching and discipline were based, constituted a basis for unity in the community.

2. S. Dutt, *op. cit.*, p. 13.

DEFINITION OF THE BUDDHIST DISCIPLINE

In the early writings of the Buddhist tradition, discipline was usually referred to as both *śīla* and *vinaya*. *Sikkāpada*, *upasampadā*, and *pratimokṣa* were also used.[1]

In the Pali language, the word *śīla* means "nature," "character," "moral practice," "Buddhist ethics," etc. *Vinaya*[2] means "driving out" or "rule" (" . . . judging"). In Sanskrit, *vinaya* means "removing" or "training", "discipline", "education."[3] In Chinese, discipline is called *sīla-vinaya*, the two terms being used together, but this compound word cannot be traced in the *Tripiṭaka*.[4] *Śīla* could be translated by 戒 or 尸羅, meaning "precept," "command," "prohibition," "rule," "discipline," or "morality;" "*vinaya*" could be translated into 毘尼, 毘奈耶 "discipline under control."[5] Because the rlues were supposed to extinguish all evil they were called *vinaya*.[6]

According to *Pyi-Ni-Mo-Ching*, the term "vinaya" has also five meanings: 1. confession, 2. obedience, following, 3. extinguishing, destruction, 4. resolution, judgment, and 5. abandonment.[7] Because of this combination of several elements, the term appears similar in meaning to the Pāli meaning of the term.

The term "śīla" as used in *Dhammapada* also means the inner spiritual aspect of moral nature in relation to autonomous practice: "To refrain, from all evil, to achieve the good, to purify one's own heart . . ."[8] "*śīla*" however, is related pri-

1. A. Hirakawa, "Kairitsu vori mitaru Bukkyo no Shinrikawn" ("A Buddhist view of truth in the light of discipline"). ed. S. Miyamoto, *Bukkyo no Kompon Shinri* (*A Foundational Truth of Buddhism*), p. 261.
2. T. W. Rhys Davids, and M. P. William, *Pāli-English Dictionary*, p. 623.
3. A. A. Macdonell, *A Practical Sanskrit Dictionary*, p. 284.
4. Cf., A. Hirakawa, *op. cit.*, p. 262.
5. W. E. Soothill and L. Hodous, *A Dictionary of Chinese Buddhist Terms*, p. 444.
6. *Pyi-ni-Mo-Ching*. Taisho, Vol. 24, p. 801.
7. *Op. cit.* Vol. 7, Taisho, Vol. 24, p. 842.
8. *The Dhammapada*, No. 183, tr. I. Babbitt, p. 30.

marily to spiritual attitudes and self-discipline rather than to rigid rules and prescribed punishments; *vinaya*, in contrast, as "rules" or "judge," regulated the external aspects of the lives of monks and nuns.[1] It was heteronomous in nature and required specific punishments in certain cases.

It does not seem correct, therefore, to equate "*śīla*" with "*vinaya*", because the former deals with moral nature, autonomous self-discipline, and inner spiritual development, whereas the latter is obligatory in nature and pertains more to legalistic matters affecting the community. Also, *vinaya* originated as a result of misconduct by monks in the *saṁgha*. The origin of *śīla* is related to the general disciplinary rules for monks among other sects of the time.[2]

Śīla and *vinaya* did, however, have many rules in common. Taking a broader view, it can be said that, primarily, *śīla*, and, secondarily, *vinaya*, supplement each other in fulfilling the spirit of Buddha. Without *vinaya*, it would have been difficult for *śīla* alone to bring about moral order and unity in the community; the *saṁgha* needed the law and correspondent punishments in order to maintain order. Without *śīla*, the individual effort of the moral mind could not by itself have developed to achieve the true spirit of discipline. Both *śīla* and *vinaya* were, however, claimed to have been given by Buddha and were to be evenly balanced in order to provide adequate direction to the example of Buddha's enlightenment and to follow his way of life. But *śila* was of necessity primary, because, if there were no strong spiritual attitude of self-discipline, it would be very difficult to practice *vinaya*. Buddha, therefore, appears to have emphasized the inner moral attitude, and to

21. *Vinaya-Piṭaka* (*Book of the Discipline*) Vol. I : . . . governing and regulating the outward life of monks and nuns in monastic orders founded by Buddha." P. vii. Cf., *Dīgha-Nikāya* part 1. 2. (p. 63). 42 : "When he has thus become a recluse he lives self-restrained by that restraint that should be binding on a recluse." p. 79. Cf., S. Dutt, *op. cit.*: "We have so far considered Vinaya in its purely external aspect vis-à-vis state and society at large. In this aspect, the Vinaya is a body of conventional laws (Samaya) of a Saṁgha or 'association-group'." p. 82.

22. L. Masunagai, *Kompon Bukkyo no Kenkyu* (*A Study of Primitive Buddhism*), p. 370.

have considered rules to be of secondary necessity for the purposes of communal life.

Contents of the Disciplines

a. *Śīla (individual discipline)*

The *Brahma-Gala Sutta* in the *Dīgha-Nikāya* describes moral discipline (*śīla*) as consisting of three aspects : *kūla* (minor), *majjhima* (middle), and *mahā* (major). The three are enlarged upon as follows :

1. The *kūla-śīla*[1] enjoins that one must refrain from the following :

(1) killing of living things;
(2) taking of what has not been given;
(3) unchastity;
(4) lying words;
(5) slander;
(6) rudeness of speech;
(7) frivolous talk;
(8) causing injury to seeds or plants;
(9) taking more than one meal per day, attending shows and fairs;
(10) adorning, or ornamenting oneself with garlands, scents, and unguents;
(11) accepting large and lofty beds;
(12) silver or gold;
(13) accepting uncooked grain;
(14) accepting raw meat;
(15) accepting women or girls;
(16) accepting sheep or goats;
(17) accepting fowls or swine;
(18) accepting elephants, cattle, horses, and mares;
(19) accepting cultivated fields or waste;
(20) acting as go-between or messenger;
(21) buying and selling;

1. *Dīgha-Nikāya* (*Dialogues of the Buddha*) Part I, Vol. II, tr., T.W. Rhys Davids, Pali Texts Society, *Brahmagala Sutta* No. 1, 1, 7-10, pp. 3-6.

(22) cheating with scales or bronzes or measures;
(23) crooked ways of bribery, cheating, and fraud; and,
(24) maiming, murdering, putting a creature in bonds, highway robbery, dacoity, and violence.

2. The *majjhima-śīla*[1] requires one to avoid the following :
(1) causing injury to seedlings and growing plants;
(2) use of things stored up;
(3) visiting shows;
(4) participation in games and recreations;
(5) use of high and large couches;
(6) adorning and beautifying the person;
(7) low conversation;
(8) wrangling phrases;
(9) acting as go-between; and
(10) deception and patter.

3. The *mahā-śīla*[2] stipulates :

Whereas some recluses and Brahmans, while living on food provided by the faithful, earn their living by wrong means of livelihood, by low arts, ...recluse holds aloof from such low arts."

And, in the same context, it asks one to avoid the following :
(1) palmistry, auguries, prognostication, thirst;
(2) knowledge of the signs of good and bad qualities;
(3) soothsaying of the victory or the defeat of chiefs;
(4) foretelling through the moon, the sun, or a star, etc.;
(5) foretelling good harvest, peace or disturbance;
(6) foretelling the lucky day for marriages; and,
(7) offering gifts to a god if a certain benefit is to be desired.

Although the first five prohibitions, in the *kūla śīla* which consisted of general rules for moral living, were applicable to laymen and monks, the *kūla śīla* was otherwise a discipline specifically meant for monks. The prohibition of more than one meal per day and of recreational activities and worldly possessions were rules by which monks led their ascetic lives.

1. *Op. cit.*, No. 5: 11-20. pp. 6-16
2. *Op. cit.*, No. 5: 21-27. pp. 16-26.

The *majjhima śīla* are similar and repeat some of the provisions of the *kūla śila*, such as the prohibitions of recreation, imprudent acts and speech, etc. More emphasis is placed on achieving material possessions.

Primarily, the *mahā śīla* prohibited such activities as palmistry and foretelling the future. At that time, these practices were being indulged in by Brahmanic priests, especially in the Atharva-vedic rituals in which magical charms and incantations were used and astronomical and astrological prognostications were made.[1]

In essence, these three aspects of *śīla* concerned individual moral disciplines for the self-cultivation of monks. All emphasized "giving up" and "leaving behind" those things and acts which were against the rules. These rules were not externally imposed, but were provided so that they might be voluntarily accepted by the monks who would thereby be able to imitate the ideal life and personality of Buddha. The three sets of rules supplemented one another as means for achieving the ideal monastic life.

The discipline presented in the *Sāmañña-phala Sutta* is the same in content. In this scripture, the collections of disciplinary rules are called *ariya-śīla-khandhā*. Here it is said that if one practised these rules, he would acquire the "confidence of heart, absence of fear, resulting from the consciousness of right doing."[2]

The *Dhammapada* also states: "To refrain from all evil, to achieve the good, to purify one's own heart—this is the teaching of the Awakened."[3]

In all of these writings, *śīla* is presented as "right moral discipline," which lies in doing good, and avoiding evil, purifying oneself, and achieving confidence of heart. The first four rules of the *kūla-śīla* are universal moral principles; the remainder were adopted by Buddha from other religions, such as Brahmanism and Jainism, and reorganized to provide individual spiritual and moral discipline for his disciples. The first four rules of the

1. N. Dutt, *Early Monastic Buddhism*, p. 149.
2. *Dīgha-Nikāya* (*Dialogues of the Buddha*), Part II, Vol. 1, tr., F. Max Muller 63, p. 58.
3. *The Dhammapada*, *op. cit.*, p. 30.

kūla-sīla, for example, are similar to rules in Jainism[1] and in the *Chāndogya Upanishad.*[2] *Śila*, therefore, seems to represent the common aspects of monk discipline of the time. What appears to be a unique aspect of Buddhism is that *śīla* was grounded in Buddha's enlightenment experience. "For wisdom, oh Gotama, is purified by uprightness, (*śīla*) and uprightness is purified by wisdom."[3]

Wisdom, the goal of all discipline, was not just knowledge acquired through experience or reasoning but a transcendent experience of enlightenment. It was achieved through moral discipline, and proper meditation. Therefore, the *Sāmaññā-Phala Sutta* states:

> With his heart thus serene, made pure, translucent, cultured, devoid of evil, supple, ready to act, firm and imperturbable, he applies and bends down his mind to the modes of the wondrous Gift.[4]

The *Saṁyutta-Nikāya* also states :

> Whose doth wrong the man that hath no guile:—
> The pure in heart and from all error free —
> On him poor fool, his wicked act recoils,
> Like fine dust that is thrown against the wind,
>
> The man discrete, on virtue planted firm,
> In intellect and intuition trained,
> The broth ardent and discriminant,
> 'Tis he may from this tangle disembroil.[5]

Meditation, in Buddhism as in other sects, was not a sleep-like state but a process of mental concentration. In Buddhism,

1. Cf., Nakamura, *op. cit.*, pp. 123-124. Cf., *Dīgha-Nikāya* Part 3, 48, p. 43.

2. Cf., *The Principal Upaniṣads*, ed., S. Radhakrishnan, III, 17.4: "And austerity (*tapas*), almsgiving (*dāna*), uprightness (*ārjava*), non-violence (*ahiṁsā*), truthfulness (*satyavacana*), these are the gifts for the priests." p. 396.

3. *Dīgha-Nikāya* (*Dialogues of the Buddha*), Part II, Vol. 1, p. 156.

4. *Dīgha-Nikāya* (*Dialogues of the Buddha*), Part II, Vol. 1, p. 88.

5. *Saṁyutta-Nikāya* (*The Book of the Kindred Sayings*), Part I, tr. Mrs. Rhys Davids, p. 20.

however, meditation was oriented toward developing a pure mind and a holy life. This relationship between meditation and ethical discipline was very important in Buddhism, but such a relationship did not exist in all other sects.

Thus Buddha's great example was both the foundation and the exemplification of discipline. Although in outward appearance the rules were similar to those of other sects of the time, the spiritual aspect of discipline is different. Because Buddhism saw wisdom as the "Middle Path", it accepted neither the severe asceticism of Jainism nor the metaphysical pursuits of Brahmanism such as were centered around the *Brahman-Ātman* debates. A balance of "right speech", "right action," and "right livelihood"—all determined in the light of the "Middle Path"—were central to the concept of the Eight-Fold Path as Buddha's way.

The teachings of Buddhism and those of *Ta-Chu-Chy-Lo-Ching* seem to have certain striking similarities in this respect. As for the latter, wisdom involves the realization of the weariness of existence, the realization of non-desire, and the realization of seeing the truth.[1] We can see how Buddhism's emphasis on the disciplinary value of moral behavior and the motive of an action rather than the result, etc., appear very similar.

The *Wu Fen Lu* states: "If one has no intention of stealing, he will not offend the law against stealing; if one has no intention of killing, he will not offend the law against killing."[2] It should be noted that the Buddhist inner moral discipline, as demonstrated by Buddha's enlightenment experience, led, through meditation, to the truth (*dhamma*) of Buddha.

1. *Chung-A-Han-Ching* (*Ta-Chu-Chy-Lo-Ching*), Vol. 58, *Taisho* Vol. 1: p. 780. Cf., *Majjihima-Nikaya*, Vol. 1, 43. 292, pp. 350-351.

2. *Wu Fen Lu, Taisho*, Vol. 22: "佛言 … 非盗心不犯 … 無殺心 不犯" p. 184. Cf., *Shan-Chien-Pi-Pu-Sha* A Chinese version by Sanghabhacira, tr., P.V. Bapat, A. Hirakawa, "The Vinaya-master said: 'If you have not taken it with the intention of stealing it, you should have been guilty of no offence'." p. 236.

Vinaya

Let us next discuss the *vinaya* aspect of discipline, which was oriented toward life in the *saṁgha* rather than being concerned strictly with the individual. The *pātimokkha* consisted of 227 rules for monks and 311 for nuns.[1] These rules, in contrast to those of *śīla*, provided specific punishments for infractions. In general, these rules emphasized prohibitions, having been designed to prevent evil acts in the community. The encouragement of good behaviour, however, was a secondary component of these rules; receiving discipline, *upasatha*, and *vārṣika*, for example, were specifically recommended.[2]

The *pātimokkha* consisted of eight parts. The first, *pārājika*[3] (波羅夷法), was related to several kinds of sins such as the following: 1. carnal sins, with women or with animals; 2. theft, i.e., taking anything not given; 3. despising any form of life, ranging from deliberate killing to the very thought of killing: and 4. claiming extraordinary qualities or powers. If any of these sins were committed by a monk, he was never again allowed to reside among the *bhikkhus*. These sins were not forgivable, even if confessed to, and so this banishment was a capital sentence for a monk. Therefore these rules determined

1. Cf., H. Hirakawa, A Study of the *Vinaya-Piṭaka*, pp. 15-18; pp. 434-478.

2. H. Ui, *Bukkyo Kyoten Shi* (*A History of Buddhist Scriptures*), "Upasatha was observed every fifteen days, the monks then repeating the Pātimokkha, confessing their sins, expounding doctrine and precepts, thus purifying their lives. Also during the rainy season from April 15th to July 15th, the monks curtailed their usual activities, such as wandering about and collecting alms, and remained in the Saṁgha for a period of mental training involving meditation, attendance at lectures, and study of the Buddhist Sūtras, etc. At this time they also confessed their sins." p. 75. Cf., *Wu Fen Lu*, *Taisho* Vol. 22 :

彌沙塞部 和 五分律 "是中波羅提木叉者，以此戒防護諸根增長善法於諸善法最為初門故名為波羅提木叉" p.122.

3. Cf., *Vinaya-Piṭaka* (The Book of the Discipline), Part 1, Vol. III. 11-109, pp. 21-191, Cf., *Ssu-Fe-nLu* Vol. 1. *Taisho* Vol. 25, pp. 571 ff.

whether or not one could be a *bhikkhu* and thus implied the deeper significance of sin.

The second, *saṁghādiśeṣa*[1] (僧殘法), dealt with sins of sexual thoughts and touching girls, verbal expression, greed, false accusations, dissension, blaming others, leading a dissolute life, hindering the unity of the *saṁgha*, etc. If a monk wanted to attain purity, he should confess to the *saṁgha* any sins he committed, even if they were not detected by others. If one confessed later, the prescribed period of banishment would be equivalent to the length of time he had concealed the sin. When one of the rules of the *saṁghādiśeṣa* was violated, the *saṁgha* had the power to decide whether or not the monk should be forgiven. These sins were less serious than those covered by the *pārājikā*, and one who violated these rules could be permitted to remain in the *saṁgha*, or, if banished, could be readmitted by a vote of at least twenty monks. Therefore, these rules were called *saṁghādiśeṣa*.

The third, *aniyatā*[2] (不定法), dealt with allegations by a lay woman that a monk had committed a sexual sin, but which were not supported by adequate evidence, or when it was difficult to determine whether a sexual sin violated the *pārājikā* or *samghādiśeṣa*. In such a situation, it was decreed, that, if a monk did not confess, he should accept the judgment of the community.

The fourth, *nissaggiyā-pāciitiyā*[3] (捨堕法) prohibited possession of material goods other than those required to satisfy one's basic necessities, goods like the cassock and the alms bowl. Gold, silver and money, and the buying and exchange of material possessions were forbidden. Any monk who had acquired such possessions was to offer these goods to the *saṁgha*, thereby divesting himself of all such possessions, and confess his guilt to at least four monks. If he gave the

1. *Op. cit.*, Vol. III. 110-186, pp. 192-329. Cf., *Chi-Jiau-Ta Nanten*, Vol. 4, pp. 62-63.
2. *Op. cit.*, Vol. III, 187-193, pp. 330-339.
3. Cf., *Vinaya-Pitaka* (*The Book of the Discipline*), Part II, tr. I.B. Horner, Vol. III, pp. 195-266; pp. 1-163.

prohibited possessions to the *saṁgha*, he might then be permitted by the *saṁgha* to continue using these articles. Money, however, was strictly prohibited for monks and could not be returned by the *saṁgha*.

The fifth, *pācittiyā*[1] (波逸提法), forbade careless actions, lies, duplicity, abusive language, drinking, staying with women, etc. Such sins should be confessed to four or more monks in one's *saṁgha*.

The sixth, *pāṭidesaniyā*[2] (波羅提提舎尼法), prohibited the monks from receiving any food from nuns which they had received as alms or which they had been given at the home of lay people. Monks who might face dangers in their journeys undertaken with a view to gathering alms could not attempt to avoid the dangers by asking laymen to bring the alms to the monastery. Violations of these sins were to be confessed to one monk.

The seventh, *sekhiyā*[3] (衆学法), consisted of rules for the wearing of clothes, table manners, receiving laymen, and entering cities and towns. If he so wished, he who had violated these rules could confess to his elders and ask forgiveness. Otherwise, he could repent privately, because no objective punishment was prescribed for these offences.

The eighth, *adhikaraṇa-samatha-dhamma*[4] (滅諍法), provided for the quelling and settlement of disputes which arose in the *saṁgha*.

In summary, the *pātimokkha* seems to reflect other Buddhist rules. The predominance of sexual prohibitions is evidently due to the importance of the monks renouncing the world. Buddhist prohibitions seem to have developed as a result of Buddha's

1. *Op. cit.*, Vol. IV, 1-74, pp. 164-314.

2. *Op. cit.*, Vol. IV, 75-184, pp. 315-416; cf., *Vinaya-Piṭaka (The Book of the Discipline)*, Part III, tr. I.B. Horner, pp. 1-102.

3. Cf., *Vinaya-Piṭaka*, (*The Book of the Discipline*) Part III, Vol. IV, 185-206, pp. 120-152.

4. See Chapter II. Cf., *Vinaya-Piṭaka* (*The Book of the Discipline*) Part V. Cullavagga VII, 5.4: "Having split an harmonious order, (Saṁgha) he boils for an aeon in hell." p. 288. Cf., *Nanten* Vol. 4, p. 313.

own observations of unfortunate incidents among his followers. The rules were designed to be practised in the light of Buddha's example, to enable his followers to emulate his moral example. The individual decisions of the monks to follow these rules for self-cultivation made their minds pure and thus receptive to enlightenment. A balance between *sīla* and *vinaya* was the objective; with this balance one might be led to experience enlightenment. The positive aspects of establishing goodness of character in the monks is important. Likewise, the banning of thievery and the prohibition against contempt for life, and the prohibition against self-exaltation, reflected norms of conduct followed throughout civilized society. Buddha imposed these rules not only to promote good behavior within the community of his followers, but, also, in order that his monks might be respected by persons of other sects. Adherence to these rules by all of the monks would result in the development of a unified, pure community. The *pātimokkha* was also designed to prevent luxuries, carelessness, etc., and to ensure that the monks' spiritual discipline was not hindered. Finally, the rules were meant to enable the monks to better relate themselves to laymen as well as to promote harmonious life within the *saṁgha*. The pervading interest was the maintenance of unity in the *saṁgha*.

The basic difference between *vinaya* and *śīla* is that punishments, ranging from light to severe, were imposed by *vinaya*. These punishments were required primarily because the *saṁgha* as a community, desiring unity in moral purity, required rules for the control of misbehaving monks. Secondly, these rules of discipline guided the monks toward moral perfection. Furthermore, if the community did not have punishments as a means of enforcing its rules, its authority could be lost, leading in turn to a loss in the support of the community by the lay public. Punishments were therefore imposed by the *vinaya* although punishments were not its main concern. Sins, except for those in the first category, were forgivable if the monk's intentions were not found to be grossly evil and if confession was made. Moreover, these rules were not absolute; minor rules could be given up if they were found to be unnecessary under conditions other than those which prevailed in India when Buddha gave them.

Oldenberg sees the *pātimokkha* as the basis of the whole body of Buddhist church law.[1] This opinion seems to be correct in part because the *pātimokkha* is indeed church (*saṁgha*) law, but the role of *śīla* in balance with *pātimokkha* as the basis of Buddhist ethics seems to have been missed by Oldenberg. Law is important from the point of view of the result, but morals are important as the motivation. The object of law was control for the sake of social order. Morals, however, were concerned with a higher order, without which law could not be perfect. Therefore, *pātimokkha* provided for the confession of sins of a type which differed from worldly sins.[2] The development of the ideal society envisioned by Buddha was not dependent upon externally enforced law, but upon self-motivation which resulted from self-discipline.

The monks imitated Buddha's great personal example through the balanced discipline of *śīla-vinaya*. Self-cultivation was combined with communal discipline, both positive and negative, to develop moral perfection, and thus to establish an ideal moral society in the *saṁgha*, with *nirvāṇa* as the end in view.

ALMS

In early Buddhism, the term "*bhikkhu*" means "an almsman,"[3] i.e., one who was dependent on alms for maintaining one's life. The monks, however, differed from ordinary beggars seeking material needs in that their begging

1. Oldenberg, *op. cit.*, p. 331.
2. Cf., Hirakawa, *op. cit.*, p. 209. Cf., *Vinaya-Piṭaka* Part I, Vol. III, 19: ". . . Can it be that you, reverend Sudinna, lead the Brahma (monk)-life dissatisfied?" "I do not, your reverences, lead the Brahma-life dissatisfied. I have done an evil deed. I have indulged in sexual intercourse with my former wife. That is why, your reverences, I am remorseful. . . to lead the Brahma-life, complete and purified." p. 34.
3. Sir Charles Eliot, *Hinduism and Buddhism*, Vol. 1, "SK. Bhikshu, beggar or mendicant, because they live on alms." p. 237, n. 1. The term "*bhikṣācaryam*", living by alms, occurs in *Bṛhad-Ār. Up.* III 5, 1.

bowls were of "sacramental character".[1] The begging bowl was, moreover, Buddha's badge of sovereignty, representing his freedom from the secular world and his rejection of the position as an earthly ruler.[2] This distinction is made clearly in several texts. The *Majjhima-Nikāya* states:

Having heard that dhamma, he gains faith in the Tathāgata, and leaves home endowed with this faith that he has acquired, he reflects in this way: The household life is confined and dusty, going forth is in the open; it is not easy for one who lives in a house to fare the Brahma-faring wholly fulfilled, wholly pure, . . . After a time, getting rid of his wealth, . . . getting rid of his circle of relations, . . . having cut off his hair and beard, having put on saffron robes, he goes forth from home into homelessness.[3]

The *Sutta-nipāta* explicitly compares the householder with Buddha's understanding of a virtuous man:

Two whose mode of life and occupation are quite different, are not equal: a householder maintaining a wife, and an unselfish virtuous man. A householder (is intent) upon the destruction of other living creatures, being unrestrained; but a Muni always protects living creatures, being restrained.[4]

A householder's work I (Buddha) will also tell you, how a Sāvaka is to act to be a good one; for that complete Bhikkhu-dhamma cannot be carried out by one who is taken up by (worldly) occupations.[5]

1. S. Dutt observes that like the *muni* the *bhikkhu* is homeless for the sake of "the higher spiritual life" and that his is a sacramental renunciation of home and kin. Attention is also called to *Ṛgveda* X. 136 in support of his concept; *op. cit.*, p. 36.

2. E. Conze, *Buddhism : Its Esssence and Development*, p. 55.

3. *Majjhima-Nikāya* (*The Middle Length Sayings*), Vol. 1, 170, tr. I.B. Horner, p. 224.

4. *Sutta-nipāta* (*A Collection of Discourses*), tr. V. Fausboll, ed. F.M. Müller, *The Sacred Books of the East*, Vol. X, Part II, No. 219, p. 35.

5. *Ibid.*, No. 392, p. 65.

Let him not kill, nor cause to be killed any living being, nor let him approve of other killing, after having refrained from hurting all creatures, both those that are strong and those that tremble in the world.[1]

Because thou sawest my longing, and carriedst me across my doubt, adoration be to thee, O Muni, who hast attained the (highest) gain in the ways of wisdom; O thou who art a true Kinsman of the Adikkas, thou art compassionate.[2]

Let his mind be free from attachment, let him not think much (about worldly affairs), let him be without defilement, independent, and devoted to a religious life.[3]

The *Ambattha Sutta* also states:

For whosoever Ambattha, are in bondage to the notions of birth or of lineage, or to the pride of social position, or so connection by marriage, they are far from the best wisdom and righteousness. It is only by having got rid of all such bondage that one can realize for himself (100) that supreme perfection in wisdom and in conduct.[4]

These passages seem to indicate that in leaving home for a homeless life and in depending on alms, the monk expressed his belief that Buddha's personality, as expressed in his teachings (*dharma-vinaya*), led to enlightenment. Buddha's teachings stressed that unless one renounced selfish desires and worldly competition it would be very difficult to achieve personal liberation or the ideal society of "true peace." The monks, therefore, were required to leave their families, give up personal property, cut their hair, don cheap clothing, and beg for all their genuine needs. A monk should not seek worldly power or pleasures.[5]

1. *Ibid.*, No. 392, p. 65.
2. *Ibid.*, No. 540, p. 93.
3. *Ibid.*, No. 717, p. 130.
4. *Dīgha-Nikāya* (*Dialogues of the Buddha*) Part II, Vol. 1, 3, 2, p. 123.
5. Cf., *The Dhammapada*, *op. cit.*, (No. 186, 187): "There is no satisfying lusts even by a shower of gold-pieces; he who knows that lusts have a short taste and bring suffering in their train is wise. Even in

For their aims of liberation, peace of mind, and virtue, they were enjoined to practise moral discipline in order to attain enlightenment—either individually, or within a monastic community. Manual labour was considered to be unworthy of monks, and it was therefore prohibited[1] so that they could concentrate on spiritual matters. In fact, in early Buddhism, monks were economically unproductive, and were dependent on the lay people for their livelihood.

Alms-seeking did not originate with Buddha; begging monks had existed before his time, as the Four Gates episode indicates. In the *Vedas*, the "world-forsaking almsman" is unknown;[2] in the *Upaniṣads* however, it is significant that mention is made of "world renunciation," in the use of such terms as "*bhikṣu*", "*saṁnyāsin*," "*parivrājaka*," "*avadhūta*," and "*paramahaṁsa*."[3] The conclusion of scholars such as E. J. Thomas that the origin of almsmen is not of the Vedic tradition appears to be acceptable.[4]

Although it is not the author's primary intent to discuss the origin of alms-seeking, which seems to be a development related to the sociological conditions of the time as well as to "spiritual factors," let us briefly consider the historical background. Unlike the Chan monks of China and Japan, monks in India never engaged in manual labour to earn their livelihood. The Chinese appear to have disapproved of begging, and therefore called the monks "alms-teachers" in order to make them more worthy of respect. In India, in contrast, alms-seeking by monks was both traditional and respectable.

Perhaps the institution of alms-seeking monks will become somewhat more understandable if they are put in the proper

heavenly pleasures he finds no delight; the follower of the Supremely Enlightened One (Buddha) delights only in the destruction of every craving." pp. 30-31.

1. Cf., Sato, *op. cit.*, p. 119.
2. S. Dutt, *op. cit.*, p. 36.
3. *Op. cit.*, p. 37.
4. See, E.J. Thomas, *The History of Buddhist Thought*, p. 11.

socio-economic perspective of India in that age. During Buddha's time, India was a vast, fertile land with a good climate; two crops a year were harvested. Generally there was no shortage of food, and conditions were thus good for monks to seek alms.[1] People whose material needs were well satisfied might come to ask whether material concerns alone were sufficient, and therefore leave their material quests in order to find spiritual peace. Such people, therefore, were receptive to the teachings of a leader such as Buddha.

Moreover, agricultural production at that time was shifting from the nomadic herding of animals to the raising of field crops. Under these conditions, the animal sacrifice required in Brahmanism became less feasible and less acceptable to many people. As the concepts of private ownership, an anti-war sentiment, and the morality of not killing or stealing were developing, social justice was increasingly required.[2]

Also, Brahmanism was in a state of disintegration. The Brahmans claimed to be like gods in matters of religious authority,[3] and, moreover, appeared to have become corrupt through their pursuit of worldly ambitions. Therefore, it was necessary to return to the original spirit that the Brahmans as moral and spiritual teachers had possessed. These tendencies could lead to the development of the ascetic movements. Many Brahmanic teachers, most prominently some of those mentioned in the *Upaniṣads*, were themselves turning to a life of renunciation.

Buddha appears to have left his home for a monastic life because of the influence of these Brahmanic teachers. The *Chāndogya Upaniṣad* relates as follows : "There are three branches of duty, sacrifice, study and almsgiving-austerity, . . .[4]

1. Cf. Nakamura, *op. cit.*, p. 215.
2. Cf., Y. Takahashi, "Kal to sono Kiban" "Discipline and its foundation", pp. 3-4. (*Problems in Discipline*) ed. Nihon Bukkyo Gakukai, *Bukkyo niokeru Kai no Mondai* (*Problems in Buddhist Discipline*). pp. 3-4.
3. Cf., H. Matzutani, *Toyo Shiso no Keisei* (*Formation of Eastern Thought*), pp. 98-107; p. 200.
4. Radhakrishnan, *op. cit.*, (*Chāndogya Up.* 11, 23, 1.) p. 374.

Bṛhadāraṇyaka Upaniṣad also commends the life of religious renunciation as follows :

> It is that which transcends hunger and thirst, sorrow and delusion, old age and death. The Brahmans, know that self, having overcome the desire for sons, the desire for wealth, the desire for worlds, live the life of mendicant.[1]

The fourth *āśrama* of Brahmanism has often been connected with this passage. In the Brahman's understanding of *dharma*, *artha*, and *kāma* it was considered more important to remain at home so as to produce descendants for religious service.[2] The fourth stage, that of the *saṁnyāsa* (the mendicant), was to come after the other three had been fulfilled. Buddha, however, felt that the period of leaving home for a monastic life (*saṁnyāsa*) was more important and, therefore, worthy of being undertaken without delay. He thus deviated from the vedic tradition.[3] Among both Brahman and non-Brahman monks, however, worldly desires appear to have been transcended by their desire to achieve liberation (*mokṣa* or *nirvāṇa*) through an ascetic life; their spiritual aims appear to have exceeded their concern for material things. The *Upaniṣads* appear to have been primarily concerned with metaphysical questions such as the *brahman-ātman* equation whereas the Buddhist tradition was more concerned with moral and disciplinary matters.[4] Vedic Brahmanism and the *Upaniṣads* do, however, place some emphasis on moral aspects as well, and Buddha appears to have derived many of his moral disciplines

1. Cf., *Ibid.*, p. 678 (*Muṇḍaka Up.* 1, 2, 11).
2. Takahashi, *op. cit.*, pp. 3-4.
3. Dutt, *op. cit.*, p. 41.
4. Cf., S. Kanekura, *Indo Kotai Seishinshi* (*A Spiritual History of Ancient India*), pp. 408-409. Cf., *The Thirteen Principal Upanishads*, tr., R. E. Hume (*Brihad-Āranyaka Upanishad* 4, 5, 6): "... Lo, verily, it is the Soul (Atman) that should be seen, that should be pondered, be heartened to, that should be thought on, ... that should be pondered on, O Maitreyi." p. 145. Also *Ibid.*, 4, 3, 22: "... a mendicant is not a mendicant; an ascetic is not an ascetic. He is not followed by good, he is not followed by evil, for then he has passed beyond all sorrows of the heart." pp. 136-137.

from these sources.[1] The main difference seems to be in the religious or metaphysical emphasis found in Brahmanism. Brahmanic writings, like those of Buddhism, require that one should not kill, except in the case of ritualistic sacrifice offered to God when killing is justified as being proper and meritorious.[2] The ascetic life was permissible only for members of the twice-born castes, whereas in Buddhism there were no such restrictions based on caste. In Brahmanism, the Kshatriya caste (soldiers) were required by *dharma* to kill other people in wars, but in Buddhism no killing was permitted under any circumstances.

Buddhism placed more emphasis on universal ethics. Asceticism in both the Buddhist and Jain traditions emphasized morality, but differed in that Jain asceticism was extreme, while Buddhism always chose moderate asceticism in the light of the truth of the Middle Path.

Mendicant monks were required to collect alms only in the morning, so that alms-seeking might not hinder their routine meditation in the afternoon. Laymen were to give the monks not only food but also clothing, medicine and lodging. As the *saṁgha* developed, laymen contributed clothing and food to the district *saṁgha*, which divided these gifts equitably among its members. The lay people also donated monastery buildings and other common articles which were held by the universal *saṁgha*.[3]

Monks could accept alms not only from Buddhist laymen but also from the non-believers of any class.[4] The intentions of the alms giver were considered more significant than the value of the gift. When Sīha, a Licchavi general who had been a support of the Jains, was converted, Buddha told him to continue to give support to the Jain Community.[5]

1. H. Kern, *Manual of Indian Buddhism*, p. 68.
2. Cf., N. N. Law, ed., *Gautama Buddha: 25th Centenary Volume*, p. 3.
3. Cf., *Aṅguttara-Nikāya (Gradual Sayings)*, Vol. II, tr., F. L. Woodward, pp. 63-64.
4. Sato, *op. cit.*, p. 124.
5. Cf., *Aṅguttara-Nikāya (Gradual Sayings)*, Vol. 4: ". . . Let the Exalted One accept me as a lay-disciple, . . . 'Your family, Sīha, for many a day has been as a well spring to the Niganthas, wherefore deem it right to

Monks were not required to thank laymen for alms, because, by giving generously to the monks, laymen curtailed their own desire for possessions and thus accumulated meritorius deeds. They increased their chances of going to heaven and, finally, of attaining *nirvāṇa* itself.

According to the *karma* theory, merit was related to individual good or bad, and by giving alms to monks, laymen could aspire to a comfortable future life in a heavenly world. Therefore, if a layman was guilty of "the turning down of the bowl," his punishment would not be light, as Rhys Davids rightly observes.[1] He would be barred from the framework for the salvation of laymen, and thus have a "spiritual death sentence."

Let us consider whether the ascetic life (monastic) lived in self-motivation as Oldenberg has argued.[2] The *Mahāvagga* states: "The recluse Gautama gets along by making (us) widows, the recluse Gautama gets along by breaking up families."[3] Buddha, in taking husbands from wives and sons from parents to lead them to the monastic life, it was argued, took them away from such worldly responsibilities as supporting their families and society. Therefore, their "world-negating" attitude might be interepreted as egoistic and self-centered. In Indian and even more in the Chinese traditions, the family was a central concern, and one who evaded his family responsibilities would be condemned as being selfish. It must be noted, however, that Buddha did not entirely rule out such secular responsibilities as supporting one's family. He prohibited people in the service of the king, as well as children without their parents' permission, from entering the monastic life, purely

give alms to those who approach you.' Monks, there are these four floods of merit, floods of things profitable, bring happiness, giving the best things, whose fruit is happiness, leading to the heaven world, leading to what is dear, delightful and pleasant, to profit and happiness. What are the four? . . . giver of the robe, . . . giver of almsfood, . . . giver of lodging, . . . giver of requisites and medicines for use in sickness . . ." p. 127.

1. Cf., Rhys Davids ("Discipline"), *Encyclopaedia of Religion and Ethics*, ed., J. Hastings, IV, p. 714.

2. H. Oldenberg, *Buddha*, tr., W. Hoey, p. 67. *Op. cit.* , p. 175; p. 355.

3. *Vinaya-Piṭaka* (*Book of the Discipline*), Vol. IV, 24, 5, tr., I.B. Horner, p. 56.

for secular reasons.[1] Evidently he did not want to bring persons who were indispensable to society and necessary for its functioning into his monastic community.

Kern has also commented on Buddha's inconsistencies, noting that at one time he said that, "Those who are wise abandon their children, or a man leaves his poor wife to become a monk," while at another he is said to have maintained that "One's wife is the best friend, and a wife is the most excellent of goods."[2] Although from an objective viewpoint these appear to be inconsistencies, Buddha did actually give different ethics to monks and to lay people. His ethics for monks emphasized the renunciation of worldly interests, while those for lay people emphasized living in society and family, but both ethics had the common factor that they were designed for the purpose of discipline. Because of his vision of *nirvāṇa*, it does seem true that the worldly life received less emphasis, but by the vision the worldly life was not denied. Buddha's monks left home not for the sake of individual liberation, but also, for the reason that they could be taught self-discipline in the *saṁgha* which served as a school of moral training which qualified them to become teachers.[3]

By following Buddha's example and teachings, they developed the ability to remove the this-worldly suffering of others as well as their own.[4] Monks did not by any means live in idleness;

1. Sato, *op. cit.*, p. 100.
2. Kern, *op. cit.*, p. 69.
3. Hayashima, *op. cit.*, pp. 733-734. Cf.. *Digha-Nikāya* (*Dialogues of the Buddha*) Vol. II, 28: "That is what they call a Wanderer, because, my lord, he is one who has gone forth." "What is that, to have gone forth?" "To have gone forth, my lord, means being thorough in the religious life, thorough in the peaceful life, thorough in good actions, thorough in meritorious conduct, thorough in harmlessness, *thorough in kindness to all creatures*." p. 22. See also, the *Majjhima-Nikāya* (*Middle Length Sayings*) Vol. II, 27: "He, being thus one who has gone forth and who is endowed with the training and the way of living of monks abandoning onslaught on creatures, . . . he lives kindly, scrupulous, friendly, and compassionate towards all breathing things and creatures." p. 224.
4. Cf., *Aṅgutatra-Nikāya* (*The Gradual Sayings*), Vol. II: "He, possessed of this Ariyan mass of morals and this Ariyan restraint of the faculties and this Ariyan mindfulness and composure . . . then abandoning the hankering after the world, he abides with heart freed therefrom: having regard for the welfare of everything that lives he purges his heart of the taint of ill-will." p. 224.

in fact, they led a strenuous life, restraining their desires, meditating, and developing moral discipline. Through their humble life of begging they developed dignity of character and set an example which laymen could emulate. They provided laymen with spiritual and moral instruction and helped lay people not only to face temporary earthly problems, but also to develop individual peace, which in turn contributed to a peaceful society. The practice of good moral life would be reflected in the elimination of evil in the individual mind and in the world in general; the world would be changed through the elimination of the suffering of both the individual and society, and the bringing of justice and compassion.[1]

In brief, dependence on alms was fundamentally related to moral discipline. In the fullest sense, monks did not merely escape from the world. Although their primary concerns were not this-worldly, their way of life also constituted a means of serving society through ethical leadership, compassion, and intellectual power. By following Buddha's great example monks were able to lead the people as teachers.

Economics

In early Buddhism, Buddha's disciplinary rules in the area of economics were significantly different for monks from those for lay people. The economic rules for monks were negative whereas those for laity were positive. Let us first consider the rules of economics for monks. The Nissaggiya Pācittiya Dhamma states that,

> Whatsoever Bhikkhu shall receive gold or silver, or get some one to receive it for him, or allow it to be kept in deposit for him—that is a Pācittiya offence involving forfeiture.

We also read,

> Whatsoever Bhikkhu shall engage in anyone of the various

1 Cf., *Ta-Shih-Ching* Vol. 2, 6, 28 *Taisho* Vol. 17, p. 670. Cf., Watsuji, *op. cit.*, p. 255; cf., H. Ui, *op. cit.*, p. 41.

> transactions in which silver is used—that is a Pācittiya offence involving forfeiture.

And, in the same context:

> Whatsoever Bhikkhu shall engage in anyone of the various kinds of buying and selling—that is a Pākittiya offence involving forfeiture.[1]

Buddha prohibited the monks from the possession of money and from "buying and selling." For about one hundred years after *parinirvāṇa* (*parinibbāṇa*), i.e., until the second Council, the monks appear to have generally adhered to these rules and possessed no money.[2] Why did Buddha prohibit the possession of money by his monks, and counsel them to learn to live without it? First, poverty and the renunciation of material possessions were seen as being necessary in order to free the monks from material desires. Secondly, these rules eliminated the possibility of competition in material aspects between the monastic community and secular society. Moreover, the ideal of universal brotherhood in the *saṁgha* required that all property be shared equally by all the members. With the necessities of life divided equally there would be no strife for material goods to jeopardize the peace of the society.

Because of Buddha's concept of the "Middle Path," it was recognized that certain private possessions, such as clothes, bowls, and medicine, were needed by the monks. This moderately ascetic approach was intended to prevent disappointment among the less disciplined monks. It was also believed that extreme asceticism could actually become a hindrance in the quest for liberation.

Some monks in early Buddhism, however, evidently did possess money, despite this prohibition. Upānanda, for example,

1. *Vinaya Texts*, Part I, trs. T. W. Rhys Davids and H. Oldenberg, pp. 26-27. Cf., *Ssu-Fen-Lu Taisho*, Vol. 22:

"沙門釋子販賣錢財持錢來置肆上而去"

"若比丘 自手捉，金銀若錢 教人捉若置地" p. 69.

2. Cf., *Vinaya-Piṭaka* (*Book of the Discipline*), Part 5, XII, p. 407.

is recorded as having accepted gold and silver. Also the *Wu Fen Lü* tells of monks buying and selling.[1] Sir John Marshall observes:

> We must remember, however, that monks and nuns could at any time give up the monastic life and return to the world, if they wished, and, though on entering the order they nominally relinquished all rights over their property, which was regarded as "given away"; in practice their families might look after it during their absence and restore it on their return.[2]

Marshall also noted that archaeologists have found many kinds of coins beneath the floors of monastic cells and in various convenient hiding-places in ancient Buddhist monas-

1. Cf., *Vinaya-Piṭaka*, Vol. II, pp. 100-104; cf., *Ibid.*, Mahāvagga VI, 12, 1: "Now at that time the Khabbaggiya Bhikkhus used to carry about various kinds of boxes for ointments—gold one, and silver ones. People were annoyed, murmured, and became angry, saying, 'like those who still live in the world'." p. 51. Cf., *Wu Fen Lu* Vol. V 29.

"佛在王舍城爾時難陀跋難陀用金銀雜銭買物亦賣物 取之·

見二比丘大以金銀及 銭買物之" 賣物取之 摩訶僧祇律 老十

"時六群 比丘在市中、 買酌油密石密乳酪魚肉種種買食" p. 312.

2. Quoted from M. Shastri, *An Outline of Early Buddhism*, p. 138; cf. Marshall, *Monuments of Sanchi*: "Now at that time a century after the Lord had attained nibbāna, monks who were Jajjis of Vesali promulgated ten points at Vesali saying—The practice concerning a horn for salt is allowable; the practice as to five fingerbreaths is allowable; the practice concerning 'among the villages' is allowable; the practice concerning residences is allowable; the practice concerning assent is allowable; the practice concerning what is customary is allowable; the practice concerning unchurned butter-milk is allowable; it is allowable to drink unfermented today; a piece of cloth to sit upon that has no border is allowable; gold and silver are allowable." Cf., *Ssu-Fen-Lu* 四分律 Vol. 54 *Taisho* Vol. 22, p. 970; cf., *Wu-Fen-Lü* 五分律 Vol. 30 *Taisho*. Vol. 22, p. 194; *Mo He-Seng-Chi-Lu* 摩訶僧柢律 Vol. 33. *Taisho* Vol. 22, p. 493; *Shih-Sung-Lü* 十誦律 Vol. 60 *Taisho* Vol. 23, p. 452. Cf., H. Nakamura (*Genshi Bukkyo no Seiritsu*), p. 325.

teries in India.[1] One scripture states that when Buddha returned to his home town, Rāhula asked him to give him his "heritage" as his mother had suggested.[2] This indicates the possibility that even though Buddha had embarked upon a homeless life, property may still have belonged to him.

Also, there is evidence that many early Buddhist monastic communities became rich, held extensive tracts of land, and received ample financial support from kings, merchants, and other wealthy lay people,[3] although in theory, all property, including money, belonged to the "Four-quarters *saṁgha*" and not to a particular *saṁgha*. The kings received no taxes from monks or monasteries, which, in effect, were extraterritorial of the secular nations. Buddhist monasteries came to be criticized as being luxurious, and, in fact, many people may have entered the *saṁghas* because of the prospect of living in luxury there. Although some monks did possess money or live in luxurious surroundings, most monks continued to respect the rules and lived a simple life in poverty, without money.

Let us next discuss the economic rules for laymen. Although the monks were prohibited from possessing money, the laymen, in contrast, appear to have been encouraged by the Buddha to earn money. For them, money was seen as a blessing by means of which they could contribute to the livelihood of the monks and thereby acquire merit toward getting to heaven.

Also, some of Buddha's teachings, such as his five moral disciplines for laymen, seem to have an ascetic intended to promote the earning of money by lay people. To cite another example, Buddha spoke against dissipation of wealth by lay people.

1. Shastri, *Ibid.*, p. 138.

2. E. Frauwallner, *The Earliest Vinaya and the Beginnings of Buddhist Literature*, "During a visit in Kapilavastu, the former wife of the Buddha sends him his little son Rāhula to claim from him his heritage, whereupon the Buddha charges Sāriputta with admitting Rāhula in the order." p. 76.

3. Cf., *Vinaya-Piṭaka* (The Book of the Discipline), Vol. V, tr., I.B. Horner, *Cullavagga*, VI, 4, 1-10, pp. 217-223; cf., *Nanten Taizokyo* (南伝大蔵経), Vol. 4, pp. 237-244.

The *Sigālovāda Suttanta* states:

> And which are the six channels for dissipating wealth? The being addicated to intoxicating liquors, frequenting the streets at unseemly hours, haunting fairs, the being infatuated by gambling, associating with evil companions, the habit of idleness . . . . .Too cold ! too hot ! too late ! such is the cry. And so past men who shake off work that waits the opportunities for good pass by.[1]

It is also stated in *Mahāparinibbāna Suttanta* that " . . . the wrong-doer devoid of rectitude, falls into great poverty through sloth."[2]

Buddha's encouragement of laymen to control their desires did not mean that they should despise money. On the contrary, he regarded money as being of great importance and wanted the laymen to use it sensibly instead of squandering it on their own personal desires. Also, the *Sigālovāda Suttanta* states:

> Who is virtuous and intelligent, Shines like a fire that blazes (on the hill)
> To him amassing wealth, like roving bee
> Its honey gathering (and huring naught)
> Riches mount up as ant-heap growing high.[3]

Also, it is written in *Aṅguttara Nikāya* that,

> If one dwells in a fitting dwelling-place
> And friendship makes with Ariyans
> And perfectly apply the self
> And hath aforetime merit done
> There rolls upon him wealth of crops
> Fame, good report and happiness.[4]

1. *Dīgha-Nikāya* (*Dialogues of the Buddha*), Part III, 184-185, trs T.W. and C.A.F. Rhys Davids, pp. 176-177. Cf. *Chang-Shih-I-Sheng-Ching*, *Taisho* Vol. 1, p. 70.
2. *Dīgha-Nikāya* (*Dialogues of the Buddha*), Part II, 84, 23, p. 90.
3. *Dīgha-Nikāya* (*Dialogues of the Buddha*), Part III, 189 p. 180.
4. *Aṅguttara-Nikāya* (*Gradual Sayings*), Vol. II. 31, Tr. F.L. Woodward, p. 35.

The text emphasizes that merchants should work hard and earn money: "... (one) possessed of three characteristics of a shop-keeper is incapable of acquiring wealth he had not before, of holding what he gets, or increasing what he holds. What three ? Herein, monks, the shopkeeper at early dawn attends not closely to his work, nor yet at midday, nor again at eventide."[1]

In the Eight-Fold-Path, "right living" has also the meaning of right economic living, as a moralization of livelihood. The *Sutta-Nipāta* exhorts one to "practise an honorable trade."[2] All these teachings indicate that early Buddhists understood that laymen should combine capital-earning practices with moral discipline—that making money while practising the discipline of self-denial constituted the lawful and virtuous way of life. It is important to note that Buddha's approval of capital-earning practice was conditional upon the layman's valuing money neither for its own sake nor as a means of gratifying one's own selfish desires. Specific rules for laymen required them to serve others, including family members, other relatives, guests, recluses, Brahmans, etc. Therefore, the *Sigālovāda Suttanta* states:

> When the good layman wealth has so amassed
> Able is he to benefit his clan.
> In portions four let him divide that wealth.
> So binds he to himself life's friendly things.
> One portion let him spend and taste the fruit.
> His business to conduct let him take two.
> And portion four let him reserve and hoard;
> So there'll be where withal in times of need.[3]

The *Aṅguttara-Nikāya* also declares:

> Now, housefather, that same Ariyan disciple, with the wealth acquired by energetic striving, amassed by strength of arm,

1. *Ibid.*, p. 188; cf., *Chai-Ssu*, *Taisho*, p. 23; p. 353.
2. *Sutta-nipāta* (*A Collection of Discourses*), 403, p. 66; cf., *Aṅguttara-Nikāya* Vol. II: "So, housefather, the same Ariyan disciple, with the wealth acquire by energetic striving . . . lawfully gotten, . . ." p. 97.
3. *Digha-Nikāya* (*Dialogues of the Buddha*), Vol. III, 189, p. 180.

> won by sweat, lawful and lawfully gotten, is the doer of four deeds. . . . the Ariyan disciple makes himself happy and cheerful, he is a contriver of perfect happiness, and makes his mother and father, his children and wife, his servants and workman, his friends and comrades, cheerful and happy, he is a contriver of perfect happiness. . . . maker of the fivefold offering, namely: to relatives, to guests, to departed petas, to the rajah and to the devata. Gift to all such recluses and brahmins as abstain from sloth and negligence, who are bent on kindness and forebearance who tame the one self, calm the one self, cool the one self . . . to such he offers a gift which has highest results, gift heavenly, resulting in happiness and leading to heaven.[1]

Buddha's greatest concern, however, appears to have involved the material assistance given by laymen to monks. He appears to have considered it to be significant that if one had no money, one could not contribute to the monks, and, thus, one would lose opportunities to acquire merit for going to heaven.

The *Vinaya Piṭaka* states that,

> If a monk (not being ill and not invited) accept food from a believing family which is too poor to give alms, he must confess his fault.[2]

Buddha presumably established this rule because of his compassion for the poor, and his concern that they should not be exploited. It is, however, apparent that supporting the monks economically was still a religiously meritorious act for the laity.

The essence of Buddha's economic rules for laymen is that they should acquire money not for its own sake, but as a means of service. They should follow the Middle Path, avoiding the extremes either of luxury or poverty, and imitate the Buddha's compassionate life. He called upon them to support monks and

1. *Aṅguttara Nikāya* (*Gradual Sayings*), Vol. III, pp. 75-76.
2. *Vinaya-Piṭaka* (*Book of the Discipline*), Vol. III, IV, 180, p. 112.

monasteries, as well as their families and relatives, and to contribute to society through such works as building bridges. Material assistance and social works were seen as an external expression of spiritual enlightenment. Spiritual discipline and material service were to be balanced for acquiring merit.

Buddhism was not greatly concerned with economic systems, or plans for secular society. Rulers were advised to prevent poverty, which could be the root of all evil, by such means as grants to the poor, economic assistance to farmers, and capital grants to merchants, as well as through the general encouragement of commerce. A pragmatic view for the sake of spiritual discipline it recommended a kind of monastic communism for the *saṁgha* and prohibited the possession of money by the monks. Its prescription of capital-earning for the lay people, being for the sake of service, was also aimed at spiritual discipline for other-worldly merit—in terms of either heaven or *nirvāṇa*.

LAYMEN

Rhys Davids observes: "Of any formal discipline of laymen in knowledge or faith we hear nothing."[1] If Rhys Davids understands "discipline" as meaning community rules enforced by punishments, comparable to *vinaya* for the *saṁgha* then, except in the matter of "the turning down of the bowl,"[2] there does indeed seem to be no formal discipline for laymen who had no such organization as the *saṁgha*. Therefore, communal rules providing formal discipline and punishment were

1. Rhys Davids, "Discipline (Buddhist)", ed., Hasting, *Encyclopaedia of Religion and Ethics*, Vol. 4, p. 714.

2. Cf., *Vinaya Piṭaka (Book of the Discipline)*, Vol. V, *Cullavagga*, V, 20, 3: "Then the Lord addressed the monks, saying: Because of this monks, let the Order turn the Licchavi vaddha's bowl upside down, let it impose non-eating with the Order. Monks, if a lay-follower is possessed of eight qualities his bowl may be turned upside down: if he tries to non-receiving (of gains) by monks, if he tries for non-profiting by monks, if he tries for non-residence for monks, if he reviles and abuses monks, if he causes monk to break with monk, if he speaks dispraise of the Awakened One, if he speaks dispraise of *dhamma*, if he speaks dispraise of the Order, I allow you, monks, to turn a lay-follower's bowl upside down if he is possessed of these eight qualities." p. 173.

not possible. It may also be that formal discipline for laymen is not provided for in the early Buddhist scripture because the *dharma-vinaya* was compiled by monks, and no reference is made to lay participation.

However, Rhys Davids also says in his "Introduction to the *Sigālovāda Suttanta*" that,

> In this Sutta, he (Buddhaghoṣa) writes, nothing in the duties of housemen is left unmentioned. This Suttanta is called the Vinaya of the Housemen, further. And truly we may say even now of this Vinaya, or code of discipline, so fundamental are the human interests involved, . . .[1]

He does not deny the existence of discipline for laymen even comparable to *vinaya*, although he does not actually equate the discipline for laymen with the formal discipline of *vinaya* for the *saṁgha*. That Buddha did in fact establish religious discipline for laymen appears unquestionable[2] not only from the *Sigālovāda Suttanta* but from other scriptures as well.[3] This discipline was designed not only for individual cultivation but also to provide the necessary wisdom for life in society.

Let us discuss the laymen's ethics. As we indicated earlier, the five ethical principles for laymen were not developed in minor details like the monastic rules. Instead, they were general guidelines for righteous life within the community. Special emphasis is placed on sexual purity for laymen. Buddha says that one should have sexual relations only with one's wife, and that, "... he who is not content with his wife, and plays with other girls,

1. *Dīgha Nikāya* (*Dialogues of the Buddha*), Vol. IV, p. 169.
2. Eliot, *op. cit.*, p. 250.
3. Cf., *Dīgha Nikāya* (*Dialogues of the Buddha*), Vol. II, 86: "Fivefold, O householders, is the gain of the well-doer through his practice of rectitude. In the first place the well-doer, strong in rectitude, acquires great wealth through his industry; in the next place, good reports of him are spread abroad; thirdly, whatever society he enters—whether of nobles, brahmins, heads of houses, or members of a religious order—he enters confident and selfpossessed; fourthly, he dies without anxiety, and lastly, on the dissolution of the body, after death, he is reborn into some happy state in heaven." p. 91.

will be destroyed,"[1] and that, "...One who is rich, but does not support his parents, will be ruined."[2] These passages indicate Buddha's respect for family life and the importance he attached to mutual trust among family members. The Eight-Fold Noble Path seems to apply not only to monks but also to laymen, because it deals with right living in both moral and material aspects.

Now, let us examine the *Sigalovāda Suttanta.* This *sūtra* was given by Buddha to young Sigala, an *upāsaka's* son, who practised daily worship of the *devas* of the earth and sky—to the east, south, west, and north, to the nadir and the zenith—and in so doing, he honored his father's word before his death. Buddha taught his lay disciples better ways to worship. First, he asked them to give up four practices: "destruction of life, the taking what is not given, licentiousness and lying speech"[3] He added: "And how, O young householder, does the Ariyan disciple protect the six quarters: Parents as the east, teachers as the south, wife and children as the west, friends and companions as the north, servants and work people as the nadir, religious teachers and brahmins as the zenith."[4]

A more detailed explanation[5] is given as follows: 1) Children should support their parents and keep the family traditions; 2) parents should love their children, exhort children to follow the ways of virtue, train them for a profession, and guide and protect them: 3) pupils should serve their teachers and be receptive to their instruction, and, reciprocally, teachers should love their pupils and teach them well: 4) a wife should be ministered to by her husband: he should show due respect for her through courtesy and faithfulness, and by entrusting her with responsibility: a wife should love her husband, be faithful to him, and fulfill her duties of hospitality; 5) a man should treat his friends as well as he treats himself, showing them gen-

1. Cf., *She Sutta-nipāta (A Collection of Discourses)*, No. 107, tr., V. Fausboll. *The Sacred Book of the East*, Vol. X, p. 19.
2. *Ibid.*, No. 97, p. 18.
3. *Digha Nikāya (Dialogues of the Buddha)*, Vol. III, 181, p. 174.
4. *Ibid.*, 188-189, p. 180.
5. *Ibid.*, 189-192. pp. 180-183.

erosity, courtesy, and benevolence; he should love and protect a friend, guard his property, and take care of his family in the time of trouble; 6) a master should only require reasonable labour of his servants and employees; he should assist them in their work, provide them with food and wages, tend them in sickness, share unusual delicacies with them, and grant them leave at intervals; 7) servants and employees should love their employer; they should rise before he does and retire later than he; they should be content with what he gives, do their work well and speak well of him among others; 8) one should have affection for recluses and Brahmans in actions, speech and thoughts, and welcome them into one's home and supply their needs of the moment; 9) recluses and Brahmans should love the clansman, lead exemplary lives, exhort the clansman to good, and teach him to do so.

All these disciplines are for laymen. They contained universal moral aspects, and presumably many came from Brahmanism.[1] There is, however, a different emphasis in Buddhism from that in Brahmanism, in that the latter says that one should sacrifice and worship in order that God might bestow material rewards. Buddhist ethics replace this orientation with the requirement of loving service to one's family and fellowmen, not in hope of material blessings from God, but in order to acquire merit for the future. The *Saṁyutta-nikāya* says: "Love and compassion doth the Enlightened feel towards another when he teacheth him."[2] Buddha seems to have replaced the man-God transaction of worship[3] with a man-to-man relationship of loving service and reverence for one another—as if all men are like gods in some way. This discipline for laymen may therefore be viewed as being related to the principle of the Middle Path, with harmony within the family and love for one's fellowmen

1. Kern, *op. cit., Aṅg. N.* II: "In spite of the forementioned dogma, Buddhism has wisely adopted many articles of morality and pious customs flowing from the sources of the Brahmanist code. When the Master command that the pious Buddhist householder, gahapati ariyasāvaka, ought to perform the five Balis: to the family, the guests, the Pitaras, the king, and the gods." p. 68.

2. *Saṁyutta Nikāya* (*Kindred Sayings*), Vol. 1, p. 139.

3. *Op. cit.*, IV, 4, 39, p. 50.

combining to build the ideal family and social relationship through moral discipline.

If Buddha was primarily concerned with the monks in the *saṁgha*, with his discipline being chiefly intended for them and, if his teaching ever emphasized an "other-worldly" vision, it may be asked whether Buddhism contains any social ethics at all. The answer appears to be affirmative, as the foregoing discussions of laymen's ethics in economics, family life, and interpersonal relationships indicate. He gave general instructions, not systematic rules, for princes and for society as a whole. Buddha had good relations with rulers and economic leaders during his lifetime and forbade such men to become monks because they were needed in society.[1] The "Four-Gates, episodes, although literally dealing with individual misery, can be seen as symbolizing the social miseries of the time.[2] Buddha did not spend his whole life in secluded, ascetic, meditation, but, instead was an active missionary and righteous leader of the people.[3] This appears to indicate his social concern. Whether

1. Cf., Frauwallner, *op. cit.*, p. 75.

2. Cf., B.G. Gokhale, "Buddhist Social Ideal," ed., N.N. Law, *Gautama Buddha, 25th Centenary Volume*, "These are significantly described as an old man, an ailing man, a dead body and a recluse. It is possible to interpret these as symbols not only of the different phases of an individual's life but also as those of the changing social scene. The first three may be taken as portents of the sense of anxiety from which the old society now on the verge of a transformation, was suffering while the figure of the Recluse was the traditional answer to the challenge of the times. Siddhārtha himself became a Recluse and practised severe austerities." pp. 31-32. Cf., *Majjhima Nikāya*, 1, pp. 162-163.

3. *Ibid.*, p. 39; cf., Ui, *op. cit.*, pp. 54-58; III, 6, 59: "Now, master Gotama, he who goes forth as a Wanderer from this or that family, from the home to the homeless life, tames only the single self, calms only the single self, leads to Nibbāna only the single self. So what I say is, thus he is, proficient in a practice of merit that affects only one person, as a result of his going forth (as a Wanderer). 'Well, brahmin, as to that I will question you. Do you answer as you think fit. Now what think you, Brahmin?' In this connexion a tathāgata arises in the world, an Arahant who is a Fully Enlightened One, perfect in knowledge and practice, Welfares, World-knower, incomparable Charioteer of men to be tamed, Teacher of devas and mankind, a Buddha, an Exalted One. He says thus: 'Come! this is

he can be considered a social revolutionary may be questioned. Although this is not the subject with which we are concerned in this chapter, it may be said that he was profoundly interested in liberating people from enslavement to material things and that he wanted to provide moral and spiritual guide-lines for the well-being of society.

Buddha also provided directions for political leaders. Five disciplines relate to kings and their ruling over their people. They were called upon to set a moral example for their subjects and to establish peace—not by law but by justice. The rules of non-possession and non-stealing, for example, as applied to kings, can be interpreted as indicating that by giving up their desires for possessions, they could devote their energies to serving the interests of the people.

Buddha's ideal and practice of moral equality among the four castes in the *saṁgha* seem not only to have constituted a challenge to the Brahmans' claim of superiority by birth, but, also, to have presented an ideal of equality in society.[1]

Buddha seems to have emphasized a republican form of government in the *saṁgha*,[2] although his own position of authority seems to have retained the monarchical characteristics of the traditions which preceded him. His application of republican government to the religious community, which appears to be a reflection of his concepts of equality[3] in both

the way, this the practice, proficient in which I make known that incomparable bliss which is steeped in the holy life, by my own powers of comprehension realizing it. Come ye also! practise so that ye too may be proficient therein, so that ye too by your own powers of comprehension may realise it and abide therein.' Thus this teacher teaches dhamma and others to practise to attain that end. Moreover there are many hundreds, many thousands, many hundreds of thousands of sudi. Now what think you, brahmin? Since this is so, is it a practice of merit affecting only one person or many persons; that is, the result of going forth as a Wanderer? 'No, Master Gotama. It affects many persons, this going forth'." pp. 151-152.

1. Cf., Hayajima, *op. cit.*, p. 693; cf., K. Mizuno, *Primitive Buddhism* tr., K. Yamamoto, Ube, pp. 10-11.

2. A. K. Warder, *Indian Buddhism*, pp. 164-165.

3. Cf., *Dhammapada, op. cit.:* "A man does not become a Brahmana by his platted hair, by his family, or by birth; in whom there is truth and righteousness, he is blessed, he is a Brahmana." p. 90. Cf., *Majjhima-Nikāya*,

spiritual and material matters, could be interpreted as providing a model for an ideal political system.

The introduction of moral disciplines into the *saṁgha* may be a Buddhist innovation without precedent in Indian religions. Buddha's monastic rules for the *saṁgha* were designed to make, from the moral point of view, new men of the members and to create an ideally disciplined society which could serve as a model of *dharma* and an inspiration for secular society.

As pointed out earlier, Buddha's efforts to attain peace in the *saṁgha* also had their applicability to society.

He enlisted ten virtues for a king:[1]

1. A king should possess integrity and tolerance.
2. He should accept criticism made by his able ministers.
3. He should give gladly to his people and should be happy when they are happy.
4. He should impose taxes strictly according to law.
5. He should open and close the palace gates at the proper time.
6. He should not becloud his mind with wine.
7. He should avoid laughing with delight or pleasure and maintain his dignity at all times.
8. He should administer justice according to law and not according to his personal whims.
9. He should promote harmony among his ministers and discourage rivalry.
10. He should always be careful about his health.

Buddha's special discipline for kings provided for personal moral virtue which would be reflected in the community through their righteous administration, taxation, judgment, etc. By following these rules, a king would set a moral example for his people. Also when Buddha was in Rajagṛha, the Magadha king Ajātasattu, who wanted to conquer Vajji, sent his minister

(*Middle Length Sayings*) Vol. II, 199: "Therefore I do not speak of 'better' because of birth in a high-class family. But as to this, Brahman, someone from a high class family may refrain from slanderous speech, from harsh speech, from gossiping, and be not covetous, not malevolent in mind, of right." p. 368.

1. *Tseng-i-a-han-Ching* (*Ekottaragāma*), *Taisho*, Vol. II, pp. 777-778.

Vesali to Buddha to inquire about the possibility of this venture. Buddha told Vesali about the highly developed discipline of the Vajjians in which lay their strength.

The *Mahā-Parinibbāna-Suttanta* states:[1]

1. As the Vajjians fore-gather thus often, and frequent the public meetings of their clan; so long may they be expected not to decline, but to prosper.

2. As the Vajjians meet together in concord, and rise in concord, and carry out their undertakings in concord.

3. So long as they enact nothing not already enacted, and in accordance with the ancient instructions of the Vajjians, as established in former days.

4. So long as they honour and esteem and revere and support the Vajjian elders, and hold it a point of duty to hearken to their words.

5. So long as no women or girls belonging to their clans are detained among them by force or abduction.

6. So long as they honour and esteem and revere and support the Vajjian shrines in town or country, and allow not the proper offerings and rites, as formerly given and performed to fall into desuetude.[2]

This indicates that Buddha considered three things to be essential for political strength, namely, that a society should maintain the tradition and have harmony in order to preserve peace[3] and lawful life within it, and that proper laws should be enacted and strictly adhered to; that individuals should be of good moral character; that the integrity of the family should be respected and religious worship practised; and that shrines and *arahats* should be respected and supported. Thus Buddha

1. *Dīgha Nikāya* (*Dialogues of the Buddha*), Part II, p. 78; cf., *Nanten*, Vol. 7, pp. 29-35.

2. *Ibid.*, pp. 29-35.

3. Kimura, *op. cit.*, p. 350.

taught that the strength of a nation depended not on its arms but on ethical discipline as a means toward righteous living in which political, familial, and religious aspects are all properly balanced. He taught that the moral and spiritual values of discipline could be the basis of an ideal society. It was because Buddha's spiritual authority and moral example so greatly influenced the lay people that he was able to provide a spiritual and ethical foundation for society.

PART II

EARLY CHRISTIANITY

Chapter IV

THE AUTHORITY OF JESUS IN THE COMMUNITARIAN SELF-UNDERSTANDING OF THE EARLY CHRISTIANS

In this chapter we will consider the authority of Jesus as an aspect of the communitarian self-understanding of the early Christians. Our approach to the theme of authority is historical; but as we limit out consideration of this theme to early Christian self-understanding, the history in question is not the history of Jesus but the history of the early Christian faith.

It is clear that, on the testimony of the primitive Church itself, the authority of Jesus was the very mandate for the existence of the Chruch. In the Church's consciousness it had itself been called into existence by the authoritative voice of Jesus. The most fundamental and important observation, however, is that Jesus spoke with plenary and decisive authority born of his resurrection from the dead. It was "the paschal experience" of the earliest Christians which accounts for the Church's conviction of being the community of eschatological salvation. In the self-awareness of the Church, Easter is the ground and explanation of Christian existence. Adolf Schlatter put the matter this way:

> First of all the Church did not regard herself as the creation of the Christians, not even as the creation of the apostles. Neither Peter nor Paul claimed to have made her. Since the Event of Easter gave her existence, she knew herself to be the creation of Jesus. That the Christ showed himself to the disciples was his act, vouchsafed to the disciples, not brought about by them. In her own view of herself, the church belonged to Christ because she was fashioned by him.[1]

But once this fundamental point has been clearly made, we must ask whether the pre-paschal Jesus had authority for early

1. A. Schlatter, *The Church in the New Testament Period,* tr. Paul P. Levertoff, p. 4.

Christianity. The answer must be yes. By Easter the pre-Easter Jesus is invested with authority. The Easter event is taken as the validation of the Jesus who proclaimed, argued and taught, and who was rejected and crucified. The "what" of Jesus's authority is his every word and act; the "why" of his authority is the divine vindication of his resurrection from the dead. We might add here that the "how" of the exercise of that authority which the Church itself derived from the risen Christ was given in Jesus's fulfillment of the role of Servant, a matter of basic importance for the Church's self understanding. The resurrection, for early Christianity, did not introduce a cleavage between the Jesus of history and the risen Christ. On the contrary, it established the controlling continuity between them by investing the history of Jesus with the power and authenticity of divine approval.

The structure of our inquiry can, therefore, be described this way: We do not here assume the stance of faith of primitive Christianity. An investigation of this faith made as precisely as possible is our concern as is the consideration of the Jesus of history as one supreme authority for the Church by virtue of his resurrection from the dead. We are dealing historically with the faith-consciousness of primitive Christianity. To pass over the significant role which the public career of Jesus played in the consciousness of the Church would be to ignore data of fundamental significance.

Early Chiristians did not distinguish between Jesus and Christ.[1] Accepting Jesus's vision of things as supremely authoritative, they put their trust in Jesus's teachings (*Acts* 8 : 13-14; *Rom.* 10:17) and were loyal to him as Lord of life and death, King of his kingdom (*Rev.* 19:16). Christ was accepted in and through faith. Christians did not attempt to explain the resurrection, but they left no doubt that they viewed it realistically, as event, as fact. Yet its fact-character was only a base for more probing reflection. These priorities, together with their significance for the authority theme, can be studied in the developed Lukan form of a narrative bearing on the risen Christ: The Disciples *en route* to Emmaus.

1. J.M. Robinson, *A New Quest of the Historical Jesus*, p.78; cf., C.F.D. Moule, *The Phenomenon of the New Testament*, p. 46.

I. The Authority of the Risen One

1. *Emmaus* (*Lk*. 24 : 13-35) : *A Case Study*

Through Luke's story of the two disciples who met the risen Christ on the road to Emmaus we may study the role of the resurrection of Jesus in the early Christians' self-understanding. We will make four points: (1) The resurrection of Jesus shows that in the early Christian consciousness his authority was divine and divinely revealed, and it had, therefore, to be accepted in faith rather than by reason. (2) The resurrection validates and renders authoritative the whole past teaching and total career (including the suffering) of Jesus. (3) Read in the light of faith, the scriptures of Israel testify to the Messiahship and Messianic authority of Jesus. (4) Finally, we will show that the Emmaus narrative is not isolated; it is rather typical of the early Christian consciousness.

Before discussing these points, it is desirable to provide an outline of this narrative: Two disciples were walking to Emmaus, leaving Jerusalem. They were depressed and without hope. Their allegiance to Jesus of Nazareth seemed to them to have been a mistake.[1] Their hope that he was the one who could redeem Israel had led only to disappointment. They were evidently aware of reports of the resurrection of Christ (*Lk*. 24:22-24), but their having left Jerusalem in a state of depression indicates that they were not convinced of the accuracy of these reports.

On the way they encountered an unknown stranger who walked and spoke with them. He talked about the meaning of "suffering" and the "glory" of the Messiah. They invited him to join them at the supper table. When he broke the bread, they recognized him and he disappeared. Then they believed in his resurrection, saying, "The Lord has risen," and returned to Jerusalem to rejoin the other disciples.

This narrative shows that the resurrection of Jesus, in early Christian consciousness, was accepted in faith, as divine revelation, rather than through reason. This story shows that the risen

1. H. Zahrnt, *The Historical Jesus*, tr. J.S. Bouwden, pp. 123-124.

Christ revealed himself to the disciples as a man who could speak and eat with them rather than as a god or angel.[1] It is significant, however, that he appeared to these disciples as a stranger, whom they could not recognize with their natural eyes. His body, in this narrative, was different from that before Easter. A similar lack of recognition appears in other accounts of the resurrection. Since, according to this account "he took the bread and blessed it," and, then, "their eyes were opened, and they recognized him," Christ's body seems to be related to another dimension—as an appearance of glory.

Because the early Christians' belief in the resurrection was based not on reason but on faith it required conviction that Jesus was the risen Christ with the authority of one who was the Lord of all things. Without faith, the resurrection could not be accepted. This point is illustrated in this story, since these disciples doubted the resurrection even though they had heard about it from the women and other disciples. Even when the risen Christ walked with them they could not recognize him. Moreover, there is no record that the risen Christ appeared to his enemies, rather than only to his disciples. It is important that, in this story, the risen Christ revealed himself as the Messiah, who told of the redemptive meaning of his suffering and glory, and that his disciples accepted this in faith.

The risen Christ took the initiative in appearing before his disciples, using both "catechetical" preparation, such as explaining the Scripture, and the liturgical approach of the Eucharist, to reveal himself. It was the risen Christ who "opened their eyes of faith," so that the disciples recognized him.

"Did not our hearts burn within us," they exclaimed— "while He talked to us on the road, while He opened to us the scriptures?" This is how these disciples on the road to Emmaus arrived at the formula for their confession of faith, "The Lord is risen." In the Lukan redaction this faith correlated perfectly with the story of the empty tomb (*Lk* 24:1-7).

Next, the question may be asked whether the resurrection validates as authoritative the whole past teaching and total career

1. P. Benoit, *The Passion and Resurrection of Jesus Christ*, tr. B. Weatherhead, p. 277.

of Jesus, including his suffering. If this question is answered in the affirmative, it may then be asked how, and also whether or not, the pre-resurrection Jesus also had messianic authority in Christian understanding.

The passage in *Luke*, "we had hoped that he was the one to redeem Israel" (*Lk*,24:21a) seems to indicate that the disciples understood that Jesus had messianic authority not only after the resurrection, but also during his earthly life. It should be noted that, according to the *New Testament*, though Jesus refused to accept his messiahship during his lifetime, his disciples and the crowds witnessed his messianic authority. Although he never said, "I am the Messiah," he also did not deny it, especially when Peter, for example, said to him, "you are the Christ" (*Mk*. 8: 29-30).

As understood by early Christians, Jesus was a prophet like Moses who taught the Torah to the people. By feeding the multitudes with bread in the wilderness, he symbolically acted, again, as the new Moses and eschatological redeemer of his people. The early Christians found evidence of Jesus's messianic consciousness in his assuming the authority of judgment (in forgiving sins), in his miracles (cf., esp. *Jn* 7:31), and perhaps most clearly in his cleansing of the Temple (cf., *Zech*.9:9). Indeed, in all his efforts to free the world of Israel from the demonic realm, he appeared to them to accomplish a messianic role.

The disciples' concept of Jesus as the "Savior of Israel," however, seems before Easter to have been based on Jewish "theocracy politics." In this tradition, the Messiah was seen as one who would have worldly authority and would destroy the enemies of his Jewish kingdom. The Messiah, in this concept, would employ pressure in order to exercise authoritarian control. When Jesus died at the hands of his enemies, on the cross, this naturally led to disappointment and a feeling that the expectations of his followers had not been fulfilled. In relation to the traditional Jewish concept of the Messiah as the victorious worldly king, Jesus's suffering on the cross was grossly incongruous.[1] Thus the death of Jesus brought an end to the hope that he was the Messiah. It was the risen Christ who explained the

1. R. Bultmann, *Theology of the New Testament*, tr. K. Grobel, p. 47.

redemptive significance of his death, and opened the minds of the disciples to faith, by saying:

> O foolish men and slow of heart to believe all that the prophets have spoken! Was it not necessary that the Christ should suffer these things and enter into his glory? And beginning with Moses and all the prophets, he interpreted to them in all scriptures the things concerning himself. (*Lk.* 24:25-27)

It was the risen Christ who explained that his suffering and glory constituted the fulfillment of the prophecy of the scriptures.

Through the eyes of faith, the disciples saw Jesus's death in a new light after the resurrection. Then his death was seen as possessing redemptive power, and as being a continuation of his teaching and his self-sacrificial way of life as a servant of mankind. Through the resurrection, in their understanding, Christ began his new rule as Lord, armed not with worldly power but with the authority of love.

Read in the light of the disciples' faith, the scriptures of Israel testified to Christ's Messiahship. *Luke* 24: 25-27 is interpreted by H.C. Kee as follows:

> ...the main force of...Luke is to affirm the real presence of Christ among His people in the interpretation of the Scripture and in the Eucharist. The Threefold Hebrew Canon (Law, Prophets and Psalms) has its fulfillment in Jesus, attesting that he is the One through whom the redemptive purpose of God is being consummated.[1]

In these passages, *Luke* 24: 19-21; 25-27, Cleopas indicates that he had hoped that Jesus would exercise political authority and bring about the release of Israel from oppression. He learns through faith that the glory into which the Messiah entered was other-worldly. Also, Christ's glory is here related to the concept of a king who would be a universal ruler with spiritual authority, as mentioned in *Daniel* 7:14, which says that to the "Son of Man"

6. H. C. Kee, *Jesus in History, An Approach to the Study of the Gospels*, p. 185.

was given "dominion, glory and kingdom," and that "all people, nations, and languages should serve him."

Jesus's suffering on the cross here acquires a new meaning, when related to *Isaiah* 53, where the martyr's death is presented as being the fulfillment of God's purpose, although there is no suffering-Messiah concept in the *Old Testament*. In all these ways, the Emmaus story presents the concept of Jesus as the King as the Suffering Servant, and as the glorious spiritual ruler.

The Emmaus narrative is not something isolated. First, it is evident that the account itself is not an invention of Luke. The tenor of passages such as "Moreover, some women of our company amazed us, they were at the tomb early in the morning and did not find his body" (*Lk*. 24: 22-23), or, "The Lord has risen indeed, and has appeared to Simon !" (*Lk*. 24 : 34), indicates a pre-Lukan tradition.

Secondly, the Emmaus story has substantial parallels which derive from the early days of the Christian community. We will consider three of them.

2. *First Parallel* : 1 *Cor*. 15:3-8

Bornkamm states:

> And so he fans anew the dying flame in their hearts, and they experience his presence at the evening meal. Of course, even the disciples at Emmaus cannot hold him as they might an earthly travel companion. The risen Christ is not like one of them. He vanishes from them again but in the words that he speaks to them and in the supper he eats with them, they have the pledges of his resurrection and presence.[1]

This text deals with Paul as a witness to the resurrection of Jesus. 1 Corinthians 15 : 1-8 is perhaps the oldest extant faith formulation testifying to the risen Jesus.[2] It is contained in a

1. G. Bornkamm, *Jesus af Nazareth*, tr. J.M. Robinson, p. 185.
2. Cf., J. Weiss, *Earliest Christianity : A History of the Period A.D.* 30-150, Vol. I, tr. F.C. Grant, pp. 23-24; cf., Bultman, *op. cit*., p. 82.

letter written about A.D. 56 or 57, about 25 years after the death of Jesus. Paul's conversion had taken place about three years after Jesus's death between A.D. 33 and 35.[1]

Two points should be made, namely, that Paul claimed both to have inherited the tradition or resurrection faith and to be an independent witness to the risen Christ (*Gal.* 1: 11-16; 1 *Cor.*9:1; 2 *Cor.* 5:14-17; 4:6). In saying "I delivered to you as of first importance what I also received (1 *Cor.* : 15:3)," Paul indicated that he had himself inherited this tradition.[2] Apparently, as O.Cullmann has argued,[3] he adopted the earliest creed and further developed it.

It must also be noted, however, that Paul stated that his apostleship and his gospel had been received directly from Christ, rather than having been taught or transmitted to him by man (*Gal.* 1:11-12). His apostleship and gospel, though coherent with Jerusalem, cannot therefore, be regarded simply as part of the Jerusalem tradition or as an extension of the teachings of the Apostles; rather, they represent an independent witness to the risen Christ.

From where or whom could this faith-formula have come ? There are several possibilities. He could have received it when he went to Jerusalem and met Cephas and James (*Galatians* 1:18-19) or it could have come from a Greek-speaking mixed

1. Weiss, *op. cit.*, Vol. I, p. 15; cf., Zahrnt, *op. cit.*, p. 126.

2. J. Jeremias, *The Eucharistic Words of Jesus*, p. 101: "... that the account of the institution of the Lord's Supper did actually circulate as an independent piece of tradition, as we have just suggested in our analysis of the Markan and Lukan accounts of the Supper, is confirmed by 1 Corinthians 11:23-25. Paul here quotes the words: 'For I received of the Lord what I also delivered to you' (1 Cor. 11:23). There should never have been any doubt that 'to receive' (παραλαμβάνειν) and 'to deliver' (παραδιδόναι) represent the rabbinical technical terms *kibbel min* and *masar le* (p. Ab. I, I ff., etc.), so that 1 Corinthians 11:23 says nothing other than that the chain of tradition goes back unbroken to Jesus himself. Immediate proof of this is provided by 1 Corinthians 15: 1 ff., where Paul similarly reminds the Corinthians of an old-established tradition, the kerygma and in so doing uses the same terms 'to deliver' and 'to receive' (v. 3, 'For I delivered ... what I also received'). For it can be established on linguistic grounds that the kerygma here quoted (which runs from 1 Cor. 15:3b 'Christ' to v. 5 and 6) was not formulated by Paul."

3. O. Cullmann, *The Earliest Christian Confession*, pp. 23, 45, 53.

community such as Antioch.[1] Paul in any case was evidently not the originator of this account. This lends support to our contention that faith in the resurrection was central to early Christianity.

Paul's order of witnesses in verses 5-8 is chronological. Weiss writes:

> The fact that Peter was the first to see the risen Lord is the most certain historical fact in this whole obscure history. It is at the same time a fact of the first importance, historically, for upon it rests the new development, and through it we are to understand the historical position of Peter. Peter is without question the first man in the primitive community.[2]

As Peter had been the first of the twelve disciples to confess, "You are the Christ, the Son of the living God" (*Mt.* 16:16), so he is presented in *Acts* (1:15; 2:14ff., etc.) as being the leader of the earliest community; this not only agrees with but explicitly correlates to the Emmaus story: "The Lord has risen indeed, and has appeared to Simon! (*Lk.* 24:34)."

John 20-21: Resurrection and the position of Peter's restoration to the position of leadership is clear in Jesus's farewell charge to Peter: "Feed my sheep" (*Jn.* 21:15-19). Thus it was acceptable that Peter should become the first leader of the earliest community, which was Easter-oriented. Had Peter not been the first to see the risen Jesus, he could not have become the first leader. Also, if this were not true, how could Paul have so written, at a time when many of the first generation of disciples and believers were still living? This, therefore, seems to have been a widely accepted belief rather than merely Paul's opinion. Why, then, is this not recorded in the other gospel records with "the empty tomb" stories, for example ?

Again, the conversion of James and his becoming a leader of

1. E. Kasemann, *Essays on New Testament Themes*, tr. W. J. Montague, p. 49.

2. Weizxacker, *Apostolic Age*, pp. 11 ff; cited in Weiss, *op. cit.*, Vol. I, pp. 24-25.

the Jerusalem Church were probably the fruit of his having experienced the risen Christ.[1]

Paul was witness to an experience of the risen Christ on the road to Damascus. "Have I not seen Jesus our Lord?" he wrote, and "He (God) was pleased to reveal his Son (Christ) to me in order that I might preach him among the gentiles; I did not confer with flesh and blood . . .," (*Gal.* 1:16-17).

All these testimonies (faith formulas) of witnessing the risen Christ were accepted as eyewitness accounts of historical events in the self-understanding of the early church.

It also appears to be significant that individuals — Peter, James, and himself — were named as witnesses to the risen Christ. Because they were leaders of the early Church, this might emphasize that their charismatic authority for the leadership of the community had been given by the risen Christ himself for the sake of unity and discipline within the community.

3. *Second and Third Parallels*: *A Pre-Pauline Hymn* (*Phil.* 2: 6-11) *and the Speeches in Acts*

Philippians 2:6-11, is a Christological hymn emphasizing the universal authority which belongs to Jesus Christ through God's exalting him as Lord. The question remains as to whether the hymn is Pauline or Pre-Pauline.

It would appear from the hymn's reference to "death" and "exaltation", that its *kerygma* is non-Pauline rather than Pauline. Paul's usual terminology in speaking of the above events is "cross" and "resurrection". Although he does refer to the "cross" in the passage under discussion, his reference seems to be an addition of his own, explaining the kind of "death" Christ experienced. Also, although "exaltation', presupposes the resurrection, the hymn does not actually employ the term "resurrection". A further argument supporting the view that *Philippians* 2:6-11 was not original with Paul, can be made

1. H. Campenhausen, *Ecclesiastical Authority and Spiritual Power in the Church of the First Three Centuries*, tr. J. A. Baker, p. 20.

from a linguistic study of the passages in question.[1] Indeed, E. Lohmeyer may be right in thinking that the *Philippians* hymn was written first in a semiti tongue and later translated into Greek.[2]

1. R.P. Martin, *Carmen Christi,* "The evidence of the unusual language may here be assembled. The first writer thoroughly to examine the vocabulary and draw attention to the *hapax legomena* and rare expressions was Lohmeyer, on the Continent, while A.M. Hunter and W.K.L. Clarke did the same thing for English readers. Supplementary studies have followed by L. Cerfaux, P. Henry, J. Jeremias and E. Schweitzer.

(a) Many of the key-terms are *hapax legomena* in the entire New Testament: ἁρπαγμός ia absent from the LXX and quite rare in secular Greek. ὑπερυψοῦν appears in an Old Testament citation in I Clement xiv. 5, which is the only other reference intended in Bauer-Arndt-Gingrich, *Lexicon*, p. 849. The threefold enumeration of the universe in verse 10: ἐπουρανίων καὶ καταχθονίων is unique in the New Testament, while καταχθόνιος is a New Testament *hapax* and is unknown in the LXX.

(b) Some words and expressions are used in an unusual way. Μορφή is found only once elsewhere in the New Testament. This is in the Markan appendix at Mk. xvi. 12. The verb 'he emptied himself', translating ἑαυτὸν ἐκένωσεν presents an interesting problem. The verb κενοῦν is used in four other places in Paul (Rom. iv. 14; 1 Cor. i. 17;ix. 15; 2 Cor. ix. 3), but never with the precise meaning it has in Phil. ii. 7. There it is used absolutely in contrast to the other Pauline usages which are in the passive voice, except 1 Cor. ix. 15 which has the verb in the active voice. But as Lohmeyer acutely observed the other references construe the meaning of the verb *sensu malo*, in contrast to Phil. ii. 7. The phrase ἐν τῷ ὀνόματι Ἰησοῦ is something of a unique specimen in the Pauline writings. His customary term is 'in the name of the Lord Jesus' (1 Cor. i. 2, 10 v. 4, vi. 11; Col. iii. 17; 2 Thess. i. 12, iii. 6). Σχῆμα occurs again in Paul only in 1 Corinthians vii. 31 in reference to 'the appearance' of the world; while ὑπήκοος, 'obedient' has a special meaning in the context of Phil. ii. 8, which is not found elsewhere. In classical Greek it usually connotes political obedience (cf., Liddell-Scott-Jones, *Greek-English Lexicon* (1940), s.v.). In the two other New Testament examples, it is obedience to men (to Moses, Acts vii 39; to Paul himself, 2 Cor. ii. 9) which is in view. In the sense of religious obedience to God its usage in Phil. ii. 8 is unique in canonical literature, while the masculine singular form is only rarely attested (no examples in Liddell-Scott-Jones *ut supra*)." p. 44.

2. *Ibid.*, "Traits of style which are 'impossible' in Greek; phrases which appear to be simply 'translation equivalents' from a Semitic language into Greek; and the use of words and expressions which are drawn directly

Again, there are theological reasons for taking the hymn to be non-Pauline.[1]

Turning now to a discussion of the *Philippian* hymn's emphasis on the universal authority of the risen Christ, we find that this emphasis seems to reflect *Isaiah* 45:23; where it is written, "To me every knee shall bow, every tongue shall swear." The passage in Philippians makes it clear, however, that universal authority has been given to Christ not simply because of his pre-existence with God but precisely because of his obedience to God. This is why "God exalted him." In spite of Paul's use of the hymn to emphasize the ethical requirements of Christianity, i.e., its need for a Christ-like humility, the hymn's own main emphasis is on the exaltation of Christ as the Lord of all things.[2] Therefore the hymn is primarily a confession of faith in the lordship of the risen Christ and a superlative parallel to the Lukan accent on this theme.

The missionary speeches of the *Acts* testify clearly enough to the resurrection of Jesus as the context for and key to his authority. But do they represent an early, pre-Lukan, testimony to the Easter-character of Christian faith and thought?

On this subject there has been considerable debate. Let us examine the *Acts* 2:14-40, 8:32-35, to determine whether or not these passages represent pre-Lukan testimony. The principal argument of those who contend that these passages were freely composed by Luke, rather than being derived by him from

from the Old Testament", he writes, "... all these facts indicate the Semitic provenance of the hymn in its putative original form." p. 27.

1. It is to be noted also that the non-Pauline concepts of Jesus, "equality with God" (cf., 1 *Cor.* 15:28) speaks against Paul's having formulated Philippians 2:6-11. Moreover, as R.H. Fuller remarks concerning the hymn's reference to Christ taking the form of a servant: "Paul never makes use of any of the servant language, except where he is quoting tradition which he has received from Pre-Pauline Christianity." R. H. Fuller, *The Mission and Achievement of Jesus*, p. 57.

2. 1 Peter 3:21 f, states: "... the resurrection of Jesus Christ, who has gone into heaven and is at the right hand of God, with angels, authorities, and powers subject to him."

Both 1 Peter and Philippian hymn are saying that Christ's authority is a cosmic one and He is to be acknowledged as lord and his function is redemptive.

earlier testimony, is that the objectives of the earliest Church did not require or foster the compilation of kerygmatic discourses.[1]

Evans found it difficult to envision a *Sitz im Leben* for the preservation of the speeches of the apostles, and concluded that their words and deeds were not regarded by the early Church as being comparable to the material of the Gospels. He believed that the speeches of the apostles were not regarded as requiring compilation until considerably later. It was only when the apostles were no longer living and preaching, in his view, that the writers resorted to presenting their speeches as models for the preaching of the Gospel.

Conflicting opinions are presented in such works as C. H. Dodd's *The Apostolic Preaching and its Developments*,[2] in which it is contended that the speeches recorded in the *Acts* are derived from pre-Lukan traditions or sources, and do indeed represent first generation Christian preaching.

Let us first examine the passage from one of these speeches, "You crucified (Jesus) . . . but God raised him up" (Acts 2:23-24). The question is whether this passage represents theological archaism or Lukan theology, or whether yet another explanation must be found. This treatment of Christ's death and resurrection differs in any case from that in the Pauline letters, e.g., in *Rom.* 8:1:-4, 2 *Cor*. 5:21. In the public speeches of the *Acts*, Christ's death does not appear as soteriological. The death is the work of men: "You crucified (him)"; God's act is to undo this: "But God raised him up."

Paul, in contrast, attributed a deeper theological significance to the cross when he wrote: "I live by faith in the Son of God, who loved me and gave himself for me" (*Gal.* 2:20), or when he said that (by the crucifixion) God had "condemned sin in the flesh" (*Rom.* 8: 3).

Writers like M.D. Goulder have rightly observed that the speeches are stylistically Lukan'.[3] But is it likely that Luke should have accepted the theme of expiatory death in

1. Cf., Evans, "The Kerygma", *JTS* 7, 1956, 25-41.
2. Cf.. C.H. Dodd, *Apostolic Preaching and Its Developments*, pp. 36, 46.
3. M.D. Goulder, *Type and History in Acts*, p. 82.

Lk. 22: 19c[1] and have consciously omitted it, because he did not really accept it in the speeches of the *Acts*? This seems unlikely. Perhaps, then, the explanation of the missing motif in the speeches of the *Acts* is that, though the early Christians expressed this theme in catechesis for believers (*didaché*) (cf., the formulas such as 1 *Cor.* 15:3-5 and *Rom.* 4:25), they omitted it from public proclamation to unbelievers (*kerygma*).

These two passages from the *Acts*, therefore, are interpreted here as being indicative of pre-Lukan contributions. The developing *kerygma* of the resurrection of Jesus provided the basis of his authority in the earliest understanding of his disciples.

II. The Authority of Jesus as the Founder of Community

1. *The Authority of Teacher and Exorcist*

In early Christianity, Jesus was rightly called a teacher ("*rabbi*": *Mt.* 17:24; 26:18, *Mk.* 5:35, *Jn.*11:28; 20:16c: "*rabboni*" which means "Teacher") because, like the rabbis, he had "disciples" and also because he was sought out by a wider circle of people who wanted to hear his teachings.

According to the account in *Mark*, the people questioned themselves in a way which correlated the power to cure with the authority to teach: "What is this? A new teaching! With Authority he commands even the unclean spirits, and they obey him (*Mk.* 1:27). Again, in *Matthew,* Jesus taught them as one who had authority, and not as their scribes (*Mt.* 7:29)."

His teaching was inseparably related to his person (cf., *Mk.* 5:30; 14:62, *Lk.* 5:17; 6:19, *Jn.* 10:19; 19:10) inasmuch as it was prophetic in character rather than philosophical. It implied the power[2] to carry out a distinctive, God-given mission.

Historically, Jesus's teaching centered on the Kingdom of God (*Mt.* 3:2; 4:23; 6:33; 10:7; 18:3; 19:14; 25:34; 26:29,

1. Cf., J. Jeremias, *The Eucharistic Words of Jesus, op. cit.*, pp. 169, 234-238, 251-255.

2. F. C. Grant, *An Introduction to New Testament Thought*, pp. 211-213.

Mk. 4:43), and this specific prophetic self-understanding was presupposed in the Christian consciousness. Christians saw him (in memory as well as in their own experience) as a divine teacher sent by God. This had two aspects. He was one whose words and deeds were truly his own,[1] and, also, he transmitted the Word of God. He was Truth itself, as the Johannine testimony put it. He did not merely say: "Thus says the Lord." He also said: "It was said to you of old . . . but I say to you" (*Mt.* 5:21 f.; 27 f.; 31 f.; 33 f.; 38 f.; 43 f.).

To the Christian community he was the Christ of the heavenly Kingdom; in the words of Peter, "the Christ, the Son of the living God" (*Mt.* 16:16). As it was God who had made Peter aware of this (*Mt.* 16:17), so it was God who made the Christian fellowship aware of this. And, as Jesus shared the authority of his Kingdom with his disciples (*Mark* 6:12-13), so the Church had no authority whatever apart from him and was therefore dependent on him. In the Lukan form of the promise to the disciples, Jesus says:

> As my Father appointed a Kingdom for me, so do I appoint for you that you may eat and drink at my table in my Kingdom, and sit on thrones judging the twelve tribes of Israel (Lk. 22:29-30).

Jesus exercised his authority, in fulfillment of the messianic promise, in both teaching and action. Moreover, the scope of his power extended to the realm of the devils.[2] In the last analysis, the cures and the casting out of the devils were, in Christian interpretation, the exercise of a power superior to that of a "teacher" or of a "prophet": it was "royal power," the power of the King in his Kingdom. For the *exousia* or power of Christ was that reserved for the Son of Man (cf., *Lk.* 12. 32 or *Mt.*28:18 with *Dn.* 7:14). The exercise of this power,

1. H. Campenhausen, *Ecclesiastical Authority and Spiritual Power in the Church of the First Three Centuries*, p. 4; M. Kahler, *The So-Called Historical Jesus and the Historic Biblical Christ*, tr. C. E. Braaten, "The Counsellor has guided the evangelists into all the truth, which is Jesus Christ himself (*Jn.* 16:13; 14:6; 16)." pp. 93-94.

2. Campenhausen, *op. cit.*, p. 5.

however, was in loving service, modeled on the Servant of Yahweh in the Book of *Isaiah* (42:1-9; 49:1-13; 50:4-9; 52:13; 53:12).

Passages illustrating Jesus's view of how the disciples' share in his (royal) *exousia* was to be exercised are found in *Mk.* 10:45 par. and perhaps best of all in the Johannine account of his washing the feet of his disciples (*Jn.* 13:2-17).

The source of its authority was the risen Lord, but the model of the exercise of authority was the servant. Thus,

> the Son of man came not to be served but to serve, and to give his life as a ransom for many (Mk. 10:45).

As we saw, also, in Paul's citation and expansion of the hymn in *Philippians* 2:6-11, death on the cross was the final symbol of this sacrificial service. When his disciples argued as to who would be the greatest of them, he said:

> You know that the rulers of the Gentiles lord it over them, and their great men exercise authority over them. It shall not be so among you; but whoever would be great among you must be your servant, and whoever would be first among you must be your slave (*Mt.* 20:25-27).

The same ideal is enshrined in the statement, "Whoever humbles himself like this child, he is the greatest in the Kingdom of Heaven" (*Mt.* 18:4, *Mk.* 9:33-37, *Lk.* 9:46-48). Thus, Jesus was taken to embody kingship and service, authority and humility, power and kindness.[1]

Now, we may consider the Christian views of Jesus's authority in relation to the Law of Moses. These views are various, but they tend to belong to two quite different types. We will call them the Matthean and the Pauline. In the Matthean view, Jesus came not to annul the Law but to perfect it (5:17).

F. C. Grant interprets this as follows:

> According to Matthew (5:17-20) Jesus had not the slightest intention of abrogating the law, but meant to deepen and

1. Mckenzie, *Authority in the Church*, p. 31.

widen its application, thus "fulfilling" or completing it. He then preceded to reinforce this deeper interpretation and wider application both with the authority of the original Law giver (God) and with his own messianic authority as well.[1]

J. Jeremias also observes that:

> Jesus, then, is countering the insinuation (*mἧvemιστтє*) that he is an antinomian: his task is not the dissolution of the Torah but its fulfilment. The rendering of *ōsopē* ('add') by πληρῶσαι in Greek aptly expresses the fact that the purpose of the 'fulfilling' is the reaching of the complete measure. We have here the idea of the eschatological measure, which Jesus also uses elsewhere; πληρῶσαι is thus an eschatological technical term. In other words, in Matt. 5:17, Jesus is claiming to be the eschatological messenger of God, the promised prophet like Moses (*Deut*. 18:15; 18), who brings the final revelation and therefore demands absolute obedience. In fact, this claim of Jesus that he brings the concluding revelation is to be found throughout his sayings . . . . Jesus proclaims that the divine will in the basileia stands above the divine will as expressed in the time of the Old Testament (*Mk*. 10:1-12) . . . . The presence of the spirit is a sign of the dawn of the time of salvation. Its return means the end of judgment and the beginning of the time of grace. God is turning towards his people. As bearer of the spirit, Jesus is not only one man among the ranks of the prophets, but God's last and final messenger. His proclamation is an eschatological event. The

1. Grant, *op. cit*., p. 76; cf., Bultmann, *op. cit*.: "According to rabbinic ideas the Messiah, when he comes, will also act *as a Teacher of Torah*, (cf., Seidelin *ZNW* 35 (1930), 194 ff.; Volz, *Die Eschatologie der jud. Gemeinde* (1934), p. 218—the Church already possesses Jesus' exegesis of the law and in his "But I say unto you!" hears him speak as Messiah. In his words they already have the wisdom and knowledge which according to the belief of the apocalyptic writers the Messiah will someday bestow. *Mt*. 5:17 (*T*. 18-19, *Lk*. 12:32, *Mt*. 10:16, "Behold, I have given you authority to tread upon serpents and scorpions; . . . and nothing shall hurt you" (*Lk*. 10:19). p. 47.

dawn of the consummation of the world is manifested in it. God is speaking his final word.[1]

The first important presupposition is that Jesus brings the final revelation which completes the Law.

The second is that the Matthean Jesus's radicalization of the Law expresses a code of messianic discipleship. It is not intelligible apart from the "realized eschatology" of messianic salvation already achieved in principle.

The Pauline view of Jesus and the Law is based on very different and much more personal presuppositions. Paul saw history as charged with and under the control of sin and death. But if the trespass of Adam is the key to the misery of history, obedience to Christ is the key to the happy resolution of history. The Law had only been a tool of sin and death. With Christ's victory over these powers, a new era has come, stamped with freedom — not only from sin and death, but also from the Law.

Here, the authority of Christ seems to be presented in a way contrary to the Matthean vision of things. But there are important points of contact between the two views. In both instances the cue for the Christian present is the messianic mission of Jesus. And underneath the conceptual opposition between Matthew and Paul lies a common radicalization of God's demand from men. The conceptual schemata differ, but the moral idealism and life style proposed by both meet at almost every point. In part, no doubt, this is due to Paul's assimilation, into his own scheme of things, of "the commands of the Lord."[2]

1. J. Jeremias, *New Testament Theology Part One The Proclamation of Jesus* tr. J, Bowden, pp. 84-85.

2. D.L. Dungan, *The Sayings of Jesus in the Churches of Paul*, "Paul was 'sheltering himself' behind the authority of the Lord because his readers would generally have recognized who was speaking in Paul's words. . . . The warning that many of the parallels (where Paul does not say he is depending upon a word of the Lord) are to be accounted for as common Jewish tradition must still be rigorously heeded. But at least this much may be agreed upon: The alleged contrast between Pauline Christianity and that branch of the early Church which preserved the Palestinian Jesus-tradition that finally ended up in the Synoptic gospels is a

When Jesus cast out devils, the scribes said, "He is possessed by Beelzebub, and by the Prince of Demons he casts out the demons." (*Mk* 2:22). Thus, even enemies are pictured as acknowledging Jesus's authority over the realm of the evil spirits. Campenhausen, therefore, rightly observes:

> The impact of Jesus's authority is shown most directly precisely in the non-human, 'demonic' realm. Jesus possesses 'authority' over the demons.[1]

Jesus and the evangelists conceived of devils as rulers with power over those earthly things, including sickness (*Mt.* 10:25; 12:14; 17; *Mk.* 3:22, Lk. 11:15; 18:7) and death (*Heb.* 2:14), which militated against the rule of God.[2] If one were sick, this was taken as an indication of Satan's power. The devils were presented as commanders of military forces (*Lk.* 10:19) or even as rulers over a kingdom, as indicated by the reference to "Satan as master of the house" (*Mt.* 10:25).[3]

The aim of Jesus's miracles, such as exorcism, healing, and raising from the dead (*Lk.* 21:12 ff.; 10:16, *Mk.* 1:21-28; 9:25) was to fight the devils whose evils made men slaves, and, through God's authority, to gather a people freed from sickness and fear for the coming of God's Kingdom.[4] However, the curing of the sick and the casting out of the devils were also the basis of a dramatic christology (*Mk.* 6:5, *Lk.* 5:17).[5]

When Jesus argued :

> But if it is by the finger of God that I cast out demons, then the kingdom of God has come upon you (*Lk.* 11:20).

figment of the imagination. In fact, they were one and the same branch—for precisely in Paul's careful preservation of, and yet selective and discriminating obedience to, the Lord's commands, do we see prefigured the characteristic traits of the Hellenistic Christian gospel editors." p. 150.

1. Campenhausen, *op. cit.*, p. 5; cf., Kee, *op. cit.*, p. 136.
2. *Loc. cit.*
3. Jeremias, *New Testament Theology*, *op. cit.*, pp. 88-89.
4. Kee, *op. cit.*, p. 136.
5. Campenhausen, *op. cit.*, p. 6.

He presented himself to the Christian consciousness as one whose authority[1] as the Messiah transcended nature and history. The devils he cast out were rank Satanic tools and their dwindled power signified the transfer of the world from that reign to the reign of God.

2. *The old Temple and the New*

The Gospels present several versions of the saying about the destruction of the Temple (cf., *Mt.* 26:61, *Mk.* 14:50; 15:29, *Jn.* 2:19). In the Johannine form Jesus says : "Destroy this temple, and in three days I wlll raise it up" (*Jn.* 2:19). Here the phrase "raise it up" relates to the body of Jesus who was risen. Thus he himself becomes the new temple of the eschaton. Jesus, according to Bertil Gartner,[2] seems to have believed that his authority replaced the authority of the temple which was now obsolete. In the Christian consciousness Jesus's death and resurrection were both seen as a sacrifice and the acceptance of the sacrifice by God. He, therefore, became head of the new assembly of believers which replaced the temple.

At this point we may consider the exchange between Simon and Jesus at Caesarea Philippi as reflected in the consciousness of the Matthean Church. In response to a question posed by Jesus himself, Simon recognized him as, "the Christ, the Son of the living God" (*Mt.* 16:16). Jesus's response included the following words: "And I tell you, you are Peter, and on this rock, I will build my church" (*Mt.* 16:19). Here, the name "Peter" and "this rock" are, etymologically (*Kp*' or Petra), identical. Also, according to *John* 1:42, "So you are Simon the son of John?

1. Williams, *op. cit*., p. 83; cf., Gogel, *op. cit*., Vol. 1: "Jesus did heal the sick, or, according to the interpretation which was given of sickness in the setting in which he lived, that he did cast out demons. There is no need to distinguish between the healing of the sick and the casting out of demons, for according to the ideas of the time sickness was caused by the actions of demons . . . Jesus, it is impossible, to distinguish quite clearly between the activity of the healer and the activity of the prophet or the Messiah." pp. 220-221.

2. B. Gartner, *The Temple and the Community in Qumran and The New Testament*, p. 120.

You shall be called Cephas (which means Peter)." Kêphas transliterates Aramaic *Kepā* whereas Petros (Greek for "Peter") translates it. The word means "massive rock or bed-rock."[1]

Kepā or Képhas is more than merely a personal name. Neither כיפא in Aramaic nor Kephas in Greek was used as a name prior to the Christian period. Purely personal names were not translated from one language into another. But כיפא was not only transliterated (Kephas), it was also translated (Petros, from *petra* but with a change from the feminine ending 'a' to the masculine ending 'os').[2] Kepa or Kephas or Petros is completely a new name. It appears nowhere outside the *New Testament* in Greek literature as a name.[3] When applied to Simon, then, what is the precise meaning of "massive rock" or "bed-rock?"

All the Gospels indicate that Jesus conferred a special status on Peter by calling him the "rock." In the *Old Testament* (*Gn*. 17:5; 32:29, *Is*. 62:3; 65:15) and in rabbinic usage, names were bestowed by God for special purposes, such as to testify to a promise or impose a specific task.[4] The symbol of the "rock" has several possible meanings. First, it possesses a symbolism as the "cosmic rock" or "rock of the world," that is, it is the earth's exact centre or navel. It evokes the divine act of creation, and the theme of the top of the mountain as the point of entry to the heavens. Under the rock is "the nether-world." And, on earth, the rock designates the appropriate site of the central cultic sanctuary or temple.[5] Second, the relation of the "cosmic-rock" symbolism to the *petra-logion* designates

1. Cf., J. Ringger, "Petrus der Fels. Das Felsenwort. Zur Sinndeutung von *Mt*. 16, 18, vor allem in Lichte der Symbolsprache", 271-346, eds. M. Roesle, O. Cullmann, *Begegnung der Christen*, O. Karrer Festschrift, Stuttgart, Frankfurt, 19: "1. Peter refers to Peter personally; 2. Behind the Greek words lie the Aramaic כיפא equivalents, in which the word-play is even more pronounced; 3. One of the translations for the Aramaic Kêpā is "rock." But may not Aramaic Kêpā mean also, or primarily, "stone" in the Matthew text? No. The context supports One does not build on a "stone", but rather on a "rock" foundation." p. 273.
2. Cf., Ringger, *op. cit*., p. 276.
3. *Loc. cit*.
4. Kittle, ed., *Theological Dictionary of the New Testament*, Vol. 1, p. 19.
5. Jeremias, *Golgotha*, pp. 68 ff.

Simon as the "rock-ground" upon which the Messianic community is established.[1] Third, the image of the rock foundation is exactly paralleled in rabbinic literature, where Abraham and the twelve patriarchs are equivalently referred to as the "rock of the world" (*Mt.* 11:7-9, 25-30).[2] The text referring to Abraham is especially interesting: "He is the rock that braves the subterranean floods and bears the House of God."

In the designation of Abraham as the "rock" we discover a Jewish preparation for the view that Jesus, and subsequently the Apostles, became the rock-foundation. So, here, Peter is declared to be the "foundation rock" of the new temple, the Messianic people. When we consider other attributes of the cosmic or "holy" rock, the scriptural portion in *Matthew* 16:18 becomes intelligible as a unit: the rock, the *ekklesia,* which will be built on the rock, the importance of the nether-world, and the reference to the keys to the Kingdom of Heaven are all related.

Although all the Evangelists use the name Peter, only the *Gospel of Matthew* contains the account of the meaning of this name as it was related by Jesus. It should be noted, however, that before Jesus gave Peter this name, the latter had confessed: "You are the Christ, the Son of the Living God" (*Mt.* 16:16); thus the faith of Peter[3] accounts for his having been given

1. Ringger, *op. cit*., p. 282; cf., Ringger's "Das Felsenwort" (section III-IV): This is primarily a detailed analysis of the rock-symbolism in Jewish sources which Jeremias had worked out. In Section IV Ringger adds some extra material: Qumran: 1. The juxtaposition of "gates of Hades" and the "Power of the underworld" as in Mt. 2. God provides for the *devotees* a rock of comfort, safety, etc., which cannot be shaken by the power of the underworld. 3. We have here the same rock-foundation upon which the eschatological community is based as in Matthew. 4. The Qumran literature (especially the Thanksgiving Psalms) makes it clear that Jesus could easily have spoken of "his EKKLESIA" which he would build on the *cosmic rock*. However, in the Qumran community, the rock which could build community is not interpreted in terms of an individual (like Peter) pp. 282-287.

2. J. Jeremias, *Angelos*, pp. 107 ff., and especially A. Oepke, *op. cit.* pp. 150 f. Also note the Rabbinical explanation of *Isaiah* (chapter 53) in Strack Billerbeck, *Kommentar Zum N. T. aus Talmud und Midrasch*, Vol. 1, p. 733; Jeremias "Golgotha", p. 73.

3. Jeremias, *New Testament Theology, op. cit*., p. 238.

this name. The authority to participate in Christ's mission to Israel was given not only to Peter but to all the disciples.

These commissions indicate that their preaching aimed at the proclamation of the coming Kingdom. The authority to cast out demons resided in the fact that the apostles were united with Jesus in his fight against the powers of evil (*Mk*. 3:13-15). Jesus also promised that the Twelve would be with him in the coming Kingdom and would judge with him. He said:

> As my Father appointed a Kingdom for me, so do I appoint for you; that you may eat and drink at my table in my Kingdom and sit on thrones judging the twelve tribes of Israel (*Lk*. 22:29-30).

This indicates that Peter and the other disciples were co-workers with Jesus in the establishment of his Kingdom. Through their faith, they shared in his messianic function and would participate in the Last Judgment and salvation. Not only did they share the power of judging, but also exercised disciplinary power within the Church for the sake of unity.

The true "rock" was Christ (1 *Cor*. 10:14) as the head of the Church. The meaning of Peter as the "rock" is that he would participate in the Messianic function of Jesus as his messenger. Therefore, only Jesus was the source of authority; the others shared in this authority as co-workers.

Peter and the other apostles have, then, a derived authority, and no authority other than what is derived from the authority of Christ. It is because Christ was empowered by God to bring the Church into being that the churchmen—Peter, John, James, Paul—could themselves claim and exercise authority. Hence the rock theme in *Matthew* is merely a representative text, richly paralleled (in terms of the theme of Church authority deriving from Christ's own authority) elsewhere in the *New Testament*. Jesus founded the Church, says the *New Testament*. Indeed, in early Christian consciousness, every aspect of its life was derived from him. We will study only the most significant parallel: the Pauline view of authority.

3. *Pauline Apostleship*

How Paul could defend his claim to apostleship is an important problem. Apostleship had hitherto been claimed only by those who had received it from the historical Jesus, and there was no provision for apostolic succession.[1] Paul had no association whatsoever with the historical Jesus like Peter, who had been the first of the Twelve, and who had been told by Jesus that he would build his Church on him (with his faith). Nor did he have a blood relationship with Jesus, as had James, who, being the first brother of Jesus, had doubtless become an important leader of the Church at Jerusalem on that account.

Under these circumstances, what then was Paul's self-understanding of the basis of his apostleship? Paul claimed that his apostleship had been given to him directly by Jesus after he had risen through his experience (*Gal.* 1:15-16; cf., 1 *Cor.* 9:1-2). Because Jesus had called him directly, Paul's apostleship was independent of his mere human authority.

He believed, therefore, that he could belong to the circle of apostles and have the same authority as the other apostles. He refers to his authority as, "... the authority which the Lord has given me for building up and not for tearing down" (2 *Cor.* 13:10; 11:8). He also said, "... for he who worked through Peter for the mission to the circumcised worked through me also for the Gentiles" (*Gal.* 2:8).

However, from having initially been the leader of those who opposed the Christian movement, Paul had become a missionary

1. Walter Schmithals, *op. cit.*: "Certainly the apostolate of Paul cannot be brought into agreement with the self-interpretation of the Twelve." pp. 58-59. And, on the basis of this awareness K. H. Rengstof's article, in *Theological Dictionary of the New Testament*, I.G. Kittle, ed., tr. by Geoffrey W. Bromiley discusses, "... the special nature of Paul's position among the other apostles of Jesus, 'wherein by the other apostles' are meant the twelve disciples of Jesus. But unfortunately we do not learn on which side all the rest of the apostles stand." pp. 441-442.

preacher of Christ's message. Without his encounter with the risen Christ, this could not have been possible:

> Then I went into the regions of Syria and Cilicia. And I was still not known by sight to the Churches of Christ in Judea. They only heard it said 'He who once persecuted us is now preaching the faith he once tried to destroy' and they glorified God because of me (*Gal.* 1:21-24).

The Apostles and the Jerusalem council recognized Paul as an apostle to the Gentiles and accepted his experience as a commission from Jesus.[1] Therefore, they sent him to the Gentile churches as a missionary even though some of his theological views differed from those of the Jewish Christians on some important points, such as the status of the Law of Moses.[2]

Paul's position as "the thirteenth witness"[3] forced him to argue the basis of his authority in a way which would set him on par with Cephas and the Twelve. He opened his argument in the first chapter of *Galatians* and brought it to a conclusion in the second chapter. Paul's Gospel was not "from man", nor "according to man." Yet, he laid before the Jerusalem authorities "the gospel which I preach among the Gentiles, lest somehow I should be running or had run in vain" (*Gal.* 2:2). A satisfactory resolution of this seeming contradiction was offered by J. B. Lightfoot:[4]

> The words . . . must be taken to express his fear lest the Judaic Christians, by insisting on the Mosaic ritual, might thwart his past and present endeavors to establish a Church on a liberal basis. By conferring with them . . . he might not

1. Campenhausen, *op. cit.*: "The fundamental event, which brought his apostolate, his gospel, and his success, was the encounter with Christ on the Damascus road; it was because of this even the great apostles at Jerusalem could not do otherwise than recognize his authority." p. 35.
2. Bultmann, *op. cit.*, pp. 54-57.
3. C. Burchard, *Der dreizehnte Zeuge*, pp. 174-183.
4. J. B. Lightfoot, *The Epistle of St. Paul to the Galatians*, p. 103.

only quiet such lurking anxiety (*mepos*) as he felt, but also, if there were any lack of unanimity, win them over to his views.

The way in which Paul here deals with the issue of authority is illuminating. His own authority, like that of the Jerusalem authorities, was derived directly and entirely from the risen Lord. But the exercise of authority, once again, was conditioned by humility, practicality, and concern for harmony with others. Paul deliberately evoked the image of the Isaian Servant as his own apostolic model, and offered himself as the model for the life of the Churches he begot in the name of Christ.[1]

1. D. M. Stanley, *The Apostolic Church in the New Testament*, pp. 371-372.

Chapter V

RESPONSE TO THE FOUNDER: ECCLESIAL COMMUNITY

In this chapter ecclesial communion in faith and practice will be considered in relation to Jesus as the "author of salvation" (*Heb.* 10:1-18) and the founder of the Church (*Mt.* 16:17-19).

Jesus's central proclamation bore on the Kingdom of God. The Church was related to the Kingdom, in the early Christian consciousness, as its harbinger and organ. It appeared as the eschatological community, mediating God's act of final salvation. Since Jesus's "holy remnant", destined to be saved, was an open rather than a closed group, the life of the Church was marked by disciples summoned to help propagate Christ's mission, to be his successors in proclaiming the Kingdom. The Church was not, then, the Kingdom itself but the community preparing for the establishment of the Kingdom in the last days.

Our understanding of the ecclesial life of early Christianity is through the *New Testament* writings, each of which represents a certain "field of meaning." These fields of meanings are diverse and variously related to one another. If we are to understand the life of early Christianity, we must take note of this diversity of texts and of the many-sided diversity revealed by the texts, e.g., various groups of different background, different historical and social situations, and diverse responses to Christ.

The most far-reaching diversity in early Christianity was that between "Jew and Greek," or, to be more exact, between Christian-Jew and Christian-Greek. But, as we learn from the *Acts*, the tensions arising from this division were preceded by similar tensions in the all-Jewish Christian Church—tensions arising from the division between *Hebraioi* and *Hellenistai* (*Acts* 6); that is, Aramaic-speaking Christian Jews and Greek-Christian Jews.

No doubt, the whole of primitive Christianity considered itself —its style of life, its faith and hope, its prayer and its mission, its values, aspirations and ambitions—to be nothing other than a response to Christ. The concrete form and thrust of the response, however, differed from one language-zone to another, from group to group, and from generation to generation. Our present purpose is to consider the basic impulses toward unity and diversity, to survey the most fundamental diversity, its character and roots, and to try to discern the meaning of the variety of proposals aimed at effecting a deep and lasting Christian unity.

The great test of early Christian ecclesial life lay rooted, as we have indicated, in the cleavage between the Jews and the Greeks. The Christian response to Christ rightly—indeed, necessarily—took ecclesial form, and the breach between the Jews and the Greeks threatened precisely the *ekklesia.* This situation defines and limits the following survey of Christian ecclesial life as revealed by the various *New Testament* writers.

1. *The Basic Impulse Toward Unity*

Every voice in early Christianity was raised in favour of Christian unity and against divisions in the Church. Paul insisted on the accord between the pillars of the Jerusalem community on the one hand and himself (*Gal.* 2:1-10) on the other. The Markan redaction makes the point (as we shall see) that in and by the Eucharistic, Christ, Jew, and Greek were one (*Mk.* 8:13-21). For Matthew the Church was founded on the single "rock of Peter" (*Mt.* 16:18-19). *Luke/Acts* recounted and celebrated the resolution of Church conflicts (*Acts* 6:1-6; 11:1-18; 15:1-29). Just as the Johannine Jesus was about to embark on the journey to his death, he prayed solemnly for the unity of the Church (*Jn.* 17:1-26). The main theme of the deutero-Pauline master-piece, the *Epistle to the Ephesians*, is precisely unity in the name of, " . . . one body and one spirit . . . one hope ...one Lord, one faith, one baptism, one God and Father of us all" (*Eph.* 4:4-6). To Ignatius of Antioch the faithful were to be " . . . attuned to the bishop as the strings to a harp," so that "Jesus Christ is sung"—Christians taking their "key" from God and singing "with one voice" (*Eph.*4).

Why this profound impulse to unity? Was there a single thrust behind the particularity of circumstances and motivations? Behind the variety of persons and diversity of times, was there a radical oneness in the impulse toward unity? This question is not, perhaps, completely answerable; yet the mass of early Church reflections on unity does seem to exhibit a certain continuity.

Our purpose here is not to demonstrate this continuity. It is, rather, to try to capture the most substantial and permanent issue accepted by all the above writers.

All these writers understood their faith, their worship, and their corporate life to be a response to God, or, more precisely, a response to God's saving act in Christ. The Church was called into being by one God and was united by one common faith in Christ Jesus as Lord and Messiah (cf., *Gal.* 3:26 f.; 1 *Cor.* 1:2). The Church established a continuity between Israel and the new people of God (*Rom.* 9:1 ff.). Thus, as Israel, the chosen people of God, had had religious unity based on their covenant with one God, so the members of the Church, as the new people of God, had unity through the New Covenant with Christ and their belief in "him alone" (*Phil.* 2:10). It should be noted that the New Covenant, being with the people of God as a whole, was oriented to community rather than to individualistic life. The unity of the Church, then, was basically grounded in response to a unified divine act. It was not, in any case, a merely social arrangement.

From this viewpoint, we may allude briefly to the Pauline struggle over whether the Law was necessary for salvation. The conflicting attitudes may be summed up for our purposes as "Paul vs. the Judaizers." And here the issue was defined by Paul's question, "What did God do in Christ?"

So far as we know, the Judaizers' stand was settled, not by answering this question, but simply by reference to the revelational and traditional status of the Mosaic Covenant. Paul's views, on the contrary, turned on the soteriological all-sufficiency of the paschal mysteries of Christ: If Christ was all-sufficient, the *torah* was not necessary. So Paul argued the converse: If the *torah* was necessary for salvation, Christ's paschal mysteries were lacking! But this contradicted the faith formulas of the Jerusalem Church itself, and, worse, it downgraded the cross.

Here, then, we have a dramatic instance of the imperativeness of unity in the sphere of faith. Such internal realities, moreover, inevitably found external expression, which, in the Christian context, primarily consisted in baptism and the Eucharist. Baptism and the Eucharist provided a degree of unity in ritual and substance which counteracted the centrifugal forces of geographic expansion and cultural diversity. When Paul wrote to the Church in Rome in the fifties of the first century, there was, of course, no official formulary creed as yet. The Romans were simply admonished to be obedient from the heart to "the pattern of teaching" (the baptismal confession) (*Rom.* 6:17). Paul was concerned that diversity among individuals and groups should not lead to chaos, but, rather, contribute to unity. This is indicated in the statement that all things should be done for edification (1 *Cor.* 14:26), for "God is not a God of confusion but of peace" (1 *Cor.* 14:33). These lines may indicate an intent on Paul's part to establish fixed liturgical forms (e.g., benedictions, doxologies, and hymns).[1] The "sacraments" have their sense and context in the "People of God"—a single, corporate personality.[2] Ancient Oriental peoples were predominantly concerned with corporate life, in contrast to the modern Westerners' emphasis on individualism. For example, God said, "I am the Lord . . . . I will take you for my people, and I will be your God;" (*Exod.* 6:6 f.). The *Old Testament* attitudes were reflected in the early Church, to which the concept of being the New Israel meant to be a nation with religious unity. The Church was seen as an organism. In the *New Testament* understanding, it was the Church which was a social reality; there was no individualism within it. All of the metaphors relating to the Church are corporate in character, e.g., the Israel of God, the elect, the Body of Christ, the communion of Saints, the fellowship of the Holy Spirit, and the messianic banquet.

Secondary elements in the impulse toward unity include Church

1. J. G. Davies, *The Early Christian Church*, pp. 63-64.
2. A. Schlatter, *The Church in the New Testament Period*, tr. P.P. Levertoff, p. 10.

regimen. The Apostles appear to have had a sort of authority over the management of the churches, the teaching of the Gospel, and the answering of questions from the people. For example, the Apostles and missionaries visited different communities, and were understood to be the leaders of all the churches. Therefore, when Peter visited the Gentile churches, they welcomed him. Also, when Paul visited Jerusalem, he was accepted as a Gentile missionary, even though elements of the Jerusalem community disagreed with his view of the Law. Paul did not build the Roman Church but sent it a letter through his apostolic authority. Through the teachings of the Apostles and missionaries, and through their letters which were sent out from one congregation to another, spiritual unity was developed.

2. *The Major Diversity in Earliest Christianity*

Paul's letter to the Galatians indicates a bitter division among Christians. The controversy was between Paul's Law-free gospel and the Judaizers' insistence on the *tōrah* as necessary for salvation. The controversy involved an attack on Paul, and Paul's defence and conterattack. Here we are not concerned with "who was right" in this debate, but exclusively with the piovotal issue which was the problem of the "Jew and Greek." The Jew thanked God that "Thou hast not made me a Gentile."[1] In one sense he shared the world of Gentile culture, in another he deliberately cut himself off from it. Indeed, the prescriptions of the *torah* divided him from the Gentile world and gave him an identity — now admired, now resented—by the Gentiles. Did Christianity make any difference to the division and antipathy epitomized in the pharse, "Jew and Greek?" Paul maintained that it did: "There is neither Jew nor Greek.... for you are all one in Christ Jesus" (*Gal.*3.28). But concretely, did this not merely mean that the Jew had ceased to be a Jew with the result that, in pragmatic effect, all had become Gentiles (though by pure *theologoumenon* all might be titled "Israel")? So it must have seemed to many a Jewish Christian, who preferred that, in the Christian fellowship, Gentiles, in fact as well as in name, should become Jews.

1. *TDNT,* Vol. I, p. 777.

The sheer power of division between the "Jew and Greek" was felt in various ways within Judaism, e.g., in the form of a division between those who cultivated Greek cultural idealism and those who repudiated it. The single difference of mother tongue (Semitic or Greek) involved numerous other differences even in Jewish religious culture and constituted a division among Jews. When Jews and Gentiles alike became Christians, the old divisions of the Jew and Greek was imported into the inner arena of Christian ecclesial life. This was at the root not only of the bitter conflict reflected in *Galatians*, but of the main tensions recorded in the *Acts*. We will begin our account of the responses of the various *New Testament* writers to the problems rooted in "diversity" by simply fastening on the major diversity summed up in the phrase "Jew and Greek."

3. *New Testament Responses : The Book of Acts on the Earliest Christian Response to the Major Diversity*

Acts 6: 1-6 reveals the existence of tension between Christian "Hebrews", and "Hellenists" i.e., Aramaic-speaking and Greek-speaking Jews. Tensions between the two groups developed as the membership of the Church increased. The Hebrews' neglect of the Hellenists' widows in the daily distribution of alms led to criticism and protest. To avoid disharmony, the particular problem was resolved by the selection of seven Hellenists to administer this service.

The problem of disunity, however, had a more fundamental basis than the problem arising out of any other specific issue. While the Hebrews were conservative, the Hellenists were liberal.[1] Their concepts of Christ, consequently, differed in emphasis. The Hebrews appear to have emphasized the relationship of Christ with the Jewish Temple and the Law. They viewed Jesus as the flowering of Israel and never so much as imagined an existence outside and apart from Judaism. To the Hellenists, in contrast, "Jesus of Nazareth" replaced the Temple and the *torah*, as

1. Cf., L. Goppelt, *Apostolic and Post-Apostolic Times*, tr. R.A.Guelich p. 55; cf., F. C. Grant, *An Introduction to Testament Thought*, p. 271.

Stephen's sermon indicates. In brief, the Hebrews viewed Christ as the crown of Judaism whereas the Hellenists seemingly took him to be its successor.

Acts 8:1 recounts:

> On that day a great persecution arose against the church in Jerusalem: and they were all scattered throughout the reign of Judea and Samaria, except the apostles.

This passage records that, after the death of Stephen, pesrecution by the Jews forced many Hellenists, who had been members of Stephen's circle, to leave Jerusalem. Although these Hellenists left to preach the Gospel in various parts of Judea and Samaria, the Apostles remained in Jerusalem. This appears to indicate a different emphasis on the part of the Apostles from that of the Hellenists, one which was sufficiently acceptable to the Jews that the apostles were permitted to remain in Jerusalem.[1] The Apostles evidently sided with the Jewish Christians in balancing the Temple and the Law with faith in Christ, whereas Stephen had rejected the importance of the Temple and the Law, and had emphasized faith in Christ only. This interpretation is supported by Stephen's own sermon, and in the charge levelled against him by those who condemned him to death, that, "This man never ceases to speak words against this holy place and the law" (*Acts* 6:13). Jewish persecution, however, appears to have been selective rather than general, being directed specifically against Stephen's circle and other progressive elements. The *Hebraioi* seem to have achieved peaceful coexistence with officialdom by observing the Law and attending the Temple.

It appears very significant, that the Hellenists took a positive attitude toward the Gentile mission, as indicated in the *Acts* 11: 19-20, where it is recorded that:

> Those who were scattered...travelled...speaking the word to none except Jews. But there were some of them, men of

1. Cf., S. Yamatani, *Kristokyo no Gigen*, (*Origin of Christianity*), Vol. 1, pp. 216-219.

> Cyprus and Cyrene, who coming to Antioch spoke to the Greeks also, preaching the Lord Jesus.

With the preaching of Jesus to the Greeks and the founding of the church at Antioch, the Gentiles were admitted to membership in the Christian community for the first time without the requirement that they be circumcised as Jews.[1] Thus it was accepted that one could believe in Christ without subjection to the Jewish Law. It should also be noted that the Church at Antioch, which was "legitimized" under Barnabas, with the help of Saul, was the first to include Jews and Gentiles together (vv. 22-26). Schlatter has observed that Jews and Greeks had equal rights within the church at Antioch:

> Since the time of Seleucid Kings, the Jews at Antioch had enjoyed 'isopolicity', i.e., equal political right with the Greeks, a privilege of which they were very jealous (Josephus, Bell. *Jud.* VII, 43-5). In the same way now the Christian church gave Jews and Greeks equal rights in their fellows?[2]

Because of the departure of the community at Antioch from the Law-and-Temple-orientation of Judaeo-Christianity, it was here that the disciples were first called "Christians," and the worship of Christ replaced Temple-worship, thus reflecting the movement toward universalism.

It should be noted that the Cornelius affair, recorded in *Luke* (10:1-11:18), indicates that the Gentile mission had not been unquestioningly accepted by the earliest Palestinian church. Such passages as *Mt.* 28:18f.; *Mk.* 16:16; *Lk.* 24;45; *Acts* 1:8, which indicate that the Church had received a universal mission from Christ, appear not to be historical, as indicated by the views widely held in the early Church. Instead, the early community seems to have assumed that the Gentiles might be saved by divine intervention in the last hour of the world. Peter, however, claimed that he had baptized and eaten with the uncircumcised Gentile Cornelius because of a divine revelation to him through a vision at

1. Schlatter, *op. cit.*, p. 108.
2. *Loc. cit.*

Joppa. With the acceptance of Peter's communitarian change of heart by the Church, a new departure was launched in the mission of the Church to the Gentiles.

The first journey of Paul and Barnabas in their world mission was preceded by the gathering of a group of prophets and teachers at Antioch, who said that, "The Holy Spirit said, 'Set apart for me Barnabas and Saul for the work to which I have called them' " (*Acts* 13:2). The "prophets and teachers" then laid their hands upon Paul and Barnabas and sent them on their way, but, significantly enough, Paul and Barnabas saw themselves as having been divinely appointed by the Holy Spirit, with the "prophets and teachers" having acted only as the Holy Spirit's agents. Paul, the real leader, acting as God's initiate, established the new mission of Messianic salvation for the world. The Church thus accepted its world mission as constituting a continuation of God's previous activity in history, and as being a response to divine inspiration transmitted by the Holy Spirit.[1]

It is not without significance, however, that the Church's acceptance of its mission to the Gentiles was to lead to problems of disagreement between the Gentiles and the Jews on such issues as the importance of the Law and the Temple. These problems are discussed more fully in the following paragraphs.

In *Acts* 15:1-2, the problem of diversity within the Church, which had developed as a consequence of the Gentile mission, appears more serious. There appear to have been two basic reasons for the existence of this problem. One is indicated in *Acts* 15:1:

> Some men came down from Judea, and were teaching the brethren, 'unless you are circumcised according to the custom of Moses, you cannot be saved.'

Whether these men had come with the right of supervision or not, it seems probable that their attitude toward the Law reflected that which prevailed in Jerusalem. The second reason was the matter of ritual purity. Dupont comments:

1. Cf., J. Weiss, *Earliest Christianity*, Vol. I, p. 174.

Of all the laws of purity James wished (Gentile Christians) to retain only those whose religious significance seemed universal: the eating of meat offered to idols involved a certain participation in sacrilegious cult (cf., 1 *Cor.* 8-10). Blood *in concreto* is life and this belongs to God alone. Hence the Law's prohibition concerning it (cf., *Gen.* 9:4; *Lev.* 17:10-14) was of such character as to explain the repugnance of the Jew toward dispensing the Gentiles from it. The meat of strangled animals is an analogous case. Irregular marriage unions figure in the present context in virtue not of morals but of legal purity.[1]

The basic disagreement, however, was between Paul's position of "freedom from the Law by faith in Christ," and the opposite position which called for a balance between Christ and the Mosaic Law of God as a condition for salvation which the Gentile Christians should have to obey. The Church was faced with a choice between formal unification and acceptance of different conditions for Jewish and Gentile members. Paul did not deny that the Law expressed what God willed in the moral life of man. He refused to accept the Law as being a condition required for salvation through Christ. He did not, therefore, accept circumcision as being a necessary condition for a Gentile to become a Christian. Following considerable discussion and debate, Paul and Barnabas and some others went to Jerusalem to discuss this question with the Apostles and elders there. The basic division within the Church at this time was really whether Christ or the Law *and* Christ was the ground of salvation.

The Hebrews understood the Gospel to be a source for them of a unique privilege, and therefore continued to attend the Temple and to keep the Law. James, for example, was called a "righteous man" in the Jewish sense, because of his adherence to the Law.[2] The conservative Hebrews were opposed to Paul's idea of a Law-free life transcending the bounds of race and making salvation available to all. They believed that it was

1. J. Dupont, *Les Actes des Apotres*, p. 140.
2. Yamatani, *op. cit.*, p. 196.

through fulfilling the Law that one would share in messianic salvation through the grace of God. They contended that to share in this messianic salvation, one must become one of the "chosen people" of God, Israel, which meant that one must be circumcised. They argued, therefore, for circumcision as a condition of entry into the Church. Paul, in contrast, believed that only Christ was central and primary and that such matters as succession from the Church at Jerusalem and the keeping of the Law by the Gentiles were secondary. The differences between Paul's understanding of Christ and that of the conservative Hebrews (the party of the Pharisees) who tried to suppress Paul's teaching (15:4) led to the threat of a serious disruption within the early Church.

The diversity found within the earliest Christianity signified by the phrase "Jew and Greek" was at bottom a diversity in the understanding of Christ and His role. It probably never occurred to the most conservative elements of the earliest Palestinian Church that the coming of the Messiah could signify anything other than the final validation of the Mosaic economy of religion. If, as we saw above, faith in Christ was the ultimate ground of Christian unity, differences in the theological explication of that faith were a source of tensions.

Those who, according to the *Acts*, responded to the tensions were the leaders of the Jerusalem community — the Twelve and, later, James "the brother of the Lord". What did their responses consist of? First, the Twelve, when faced with complaint over inequities in "the daily distribution," responded with the introduction of a structural re-organization of the community, giving the *Hellenistai* their own community officers. Secondly, the community followed the interpretation of Peter in approving, as already divinely validated, the entry of the Gentiles within the Christian fellowship without reference to circumcision or *torah* observances. If we correct in understanding the *Acts* 15 as an account telescoping two distinct issues — that of circumcision (15:4-12) and that of observance of the ritual Law (15:13 ff.) — the Jerusalem community decided, under Peter, that, as a general principle and not merely by way of exception, the circumcision of the Gentile converts was unnecessary, and they again decided, under James, that the Gentile Christians need observe only the most fundamental and universal of the prescriptions of the ritual of the *torah.* These responses to the practical problems raised by the underlying issue of "Jew and Greek" were diverse in character (structural re-organization, conversion policy, prescriptions on life-style) but one in inspiration. They were all aimed at securing and preserving *ecclesiastical* unity. The basic impulse toward unity overrode the divisions of "Jew and Greek."

4. *The Response of Paul*

According to Paul, the members of the Galatian churches were "turning to a different gospel" (*Gal.* 1:16; cf., *Gal.* 1:2; 1 *Cor.* 16:1), and straying from the Gospel of Christ. The Jewish Christians were legalistically oriented, and followed the "Law."[1] Paul, therefore, told them that they would have to choose between "law" and "faith" (*Gal.* 3:2). Evidently, a split developed between Paul, who presented the Gospel of salvation through faith in Christ, without the Law, and the "Judaizers" who insisted that adherence to the Law was essential to salvation. Because of Paul's desire for unity among the churches, he viewed this division as a serious crisis and emphasized that there was only one Gospel. Anyone preaching another gospel should be cursed (*Gal.* 1:7-9).

Those who challenged Paul's claim to apostleship seemed to consider his mission to be dependent on its recognition by the leaders at Jerusalem. Paul, then, should have to obey the dictates of Jerusalem regarding all matters of importance.[2] They may also have argued that, since Paul had not lived with Jesus like the other Apostles, how could he know the true Gospel? How could he reject the traditions which the Apostles had received directly from Jesus? His antilegalism was seen as

1. Grant, *op. cit.* : "The normal Jewish response, and likewise the Christian Jewish, is the still later one of the *Epistle of James* (2:18-26). 'Show me your faith apart from your works, and I by my works will show you my faith . . . A man is justified by works and not by faith alone . . . For as the body apart from the spirit is dead, so faith apart from works is dead'. " p. 310.

2. Schlatter, *op, cit,*, p. 170.

a rejection of tradition in favor of his own self-styled gospel. Another question was also posed: If the people rejected righteousness according to the Law, how could Christianity endure by faith alone?[1] They insisted, therefore, that the Jerusalem leaders be followed and both Gospel and Law be lived. The challenge to Paul presented by these legalists had an import throughout the Galatian churches. Many rejected Paul's teaching and adopted *torah* observances, just like the Jerusalem Church.

Insofar as "Gospel without Law" versus "Gospel plus Law" was the basis of the division within the Galatian churches, Paul's opponents did not deny the Gospel as such.[2] *Kerygma* was of importance to them, because the original apostles believed in Jesus as Lord, in his atoning death, and in his future coming.

Paul, therefore, had to decide between his desire for unity within and among the churches and his position on "Gospel only." He stood for "Gospel only" and said that there was none other. In support of this stand, he argued that his apostleship was independent of tradition and that both his apostleship and the word had been received from Christ (*Gal.* 1:1; 1:12), not through tradition.

Rejecting the adequacy of the Law for salvation, he said, "No man is justified before God by the Law" (*Gal.* 3:11) and "Law was our custodian until Christ came ... we are no longer under a custodian" (*Gal.* 3:24-25). By arguing against the necessity of the law, Paul also argued against the universal supremacy of the Jerusalem Church. He criticized Cephas because the latter had eaten with Gentiles, before men came from James, but then drew back and ceased to eat with the Gentiles (cf., *Gal.* 2:11 ff.). This appears to indicate that Paul wanted complete acceptance of the truth of the Gospel (*Gal.* 11:14), unmodified by the Law.[3]

1. Grant, *op. cit.*, pp. 310-311.
2. Schlatter, *op. cit.*, p. 170.
3. Cf., H. Lietzmann, *A History of the Early Church*, Vol. I, tr. B.L. Woolf, "Paul . . . began to avoid table-fellowship with the 'unclean.' The logical result was, plainly that the Lord's Supper could not be observed in common, and two sections of the church became distinct and separate communities." p. 108.

Because the Gospel was independent of the Law on some points, such as eating with the Gentiles, Paul in this episode appears to be demonstrating in his own sphere that he was no less an authority than the great Apostle Peter. Peter's dining with Cornelius (*Acts* 10: 11:3) indicates that he did not differ with Paul on the propriety of eating with the Gentiles, but that Peter respected the authority of James, whereas Paul did not. Luke wrote that "Paul and Barnabas (were) appointed to go up to Jerusalem" (*Acts* 15:2), but Paul said that he went to Jerusalem "by revelation", i.e., because Christ, and not the leaders at Jerusalem, had told him to do so (*Gal.* 2:1-2). Although Paul emphasized his independence of Jerusalem, he did not entirely rule out a relationship with the Jerusalem Church.

Why, then, did Paul openly reject the "Gospel-plus-Law" position of the Jerusalem leaders, rather than accept its being taught for the sake of an external appearance of unity ? Paul appears to have believed that without the spiritual "unity of the Gospel," which meant salvation through faith only, Christianity could not have stood on its own. If the Gospel were balanced with the Law, and Christ's redemptive power through the cross and resurrection were not seen as the only route to salvation, then Christianity would remain just a sect within Judaism. Also, through the Law, the Jews claimed their superiority as the elect by birth. This belief would have made impossible any real equality and unity through faith in Christ. Finally, if one could be saved through obedience to the Law, human pride would predominate over the grace of Christ.

Paul, therefore, appears to have believed that, in the Galatian situation, spiritual unity by faith in Christ without the Law was essential (cf., *Gal.* 3 : 14; 6 : 29). He strove for this spiritual unity through emphasis on his apostolic authority and on Christ's teachings. Ethical qualities were presented as being the gift of the Holy Spirit (cf., *Gal.* 5 : 1-6 : 10).

Paul's emphasis on the "Gospel alone" in the Galatian situation freed Christianity from being a sect of Judaism and established Christian unity based on "Christ alone".

There is neither Jew nor Greek,
There is neither slave nor free,
There is neither male nor female;
for you are all one in Christ Jesus (*Gal.* 3:28).

Although this attitude was essential to spiritual unity, Paul was not entirely successful in his relationship with the Jerusalem Church. Therefore, even though he did not entirely reject tradition, the seeds of disunity among the earliest churches were sown.

In Corinth unity was endangered by the dependence of the people upon their favourite leaders. Theological differences had developed. In this situation, Paul emphasized that Christ was the source of unity, for the Church was the "body of Chirst"

In speaking to the divided Corinthians, he asked, "Is Christ divided?" Groups had arisen within the Church which said, "I belong to Paul" (those emphasizing the Gospel of pure faith?) "I belong to Apollos" (Christianity as wisdom?), "I belong to Cephas" (Jewish Christianity?) or, simply, "I belong to Christ." This diversity related to both cultural and theological factors: the reference of religious allegiances to particular teachers. Paul explicitly disengaged himself from "the Pauline party," asking, "Was Paul crucified for you? or were you baptized in the name of Paul?" (1 *Cor.* 1:13). Paul's point: The centre of unity is Christ and no other; his authority as crucified and risen was unique and non-transferable; no one but Christ could be the head of the Church.

Paul's explanation of the Church as "The Body of Christ" represents Christ as the center of the Church and Church unity as comparable to that of a living organism (1 *Cor.* 10:16-17).

His source for the conception of the Church as "body" need not detain us.[1] But it is important to know what his use of the theme tells us of his response to the crises of unity. He drew on the "body-of-Christ" theme in a variety of contexts, all of them parenthetic. We will consider three cases. First, he argues: "Because there is one bread, we who are many are one body, for we all partake of the one bread" (1 *Cor.* 10-17). Here, as the

1. W.L. Knox, *St. Paul and the Church of the Gentiles*, "The church as a body, of which the individuals were members, was derived from the stoic common-place of state as a body in which each member had his part to play . . . ." p. 161.

unity of the Church is wholly derived from unity with Christ, unity may have a "sociological" aspect, but it is essentially a theological category. It does not belong under the rubric "response to Christ"; rather, it creates the new rubric "Extension of Christ," and extension is effected by participation in the Eucharist. Secondly, what Paul says of the Eucharist has its parallel in what he says of baptism: "For by one Spirit we were all baptized into one body—Jews or Greeks, slaves or free—and all were made to drink of one Spirit" (1 *Cor* 12:13). Once again, unity is conceived theologically, for it is brought about sacramentally. The achievement of unity, therefore, is an instance of "become what you are". Concretely, the imperative is an imperative to bridge gulfs, to transcend differences, to live in peace and to work together without jealousy or self-seeking; and this imperative is rooted in sacramental fact. Out of the fact of baptism and the eucharist must arise a shared life:

> There are many parts, yet one body. The eye cannot say to the hand, "I have no need of you", nor again the head to the feet, "I have no need of you."
>
> (I *Cor*. 12:20-21)

Christian vocations, such as apostleship, administration, and preaching of the Word, are seen here as gifts of the Holy Spirit. There were "varieties of gifts," Paul wrote, "but the same spirit" (1 *Cor*.12:4). Since the diverse vocations were all seen as gifts of the Spirit, different classes of community leaders should respect one another and work together for the community. Much of what Paul says of leadership roles within the Church correlates very well with his body-of-Christ theme. Thus:

> ...God has appointed in the church first apostles second prophets, third teachers, then workers of miracles, then healers, helpers, administrators, speakers in various kinds of tongues (1 *Cor*. 12:28-29).

The vocations of all these persons were seen as gifts of the Spirit (1 *Cor*. 12:4) and their functions were guided by the Spirit. Paul believed that all these vocations were precisely for the sake of order in the Church.

We have been discussing Paul's response to the problem of ecclesial divisions, and we have been discussing it in the larger context of ecclesial unity as a response to Christ. The theme of "the body of Christ," stands somewhat outside the limits of the rubric "response to Christ" but it does so, as it were, by excess. The theme is not only relevant to our larger concerns but also illustrates the usefulness of distinguishing between one response and another within the community to its founder. The response of Paul is that of a theologian. As such, it is a response whose significance abides as a resource for the post-Pauline Church (as the *Epistle to the Ephesians* richly corroborates).

We have already referred to the common impulse of the *New Testament* writers in regard to Church unity. Now we will take up in somewhat greater detail the responses of writers other than Paul to the difficulties arising from the division between Jew and Greek. The writers are the Synoptic evangelists and the unknown author of the *Epistle to the Ephesians.*

5. *The Synoptics' Responses*

Without pretending to break new ground, we may recall that for Mark it was *in the church* and specifically by common participation in the one loaf that is Christ (cf., 1. *Cor.* 10:17) that the antipathy of Jew and Greek was resolved and healed. In ch. 6-8 Mark offers a sequence of narratives bound together by the catchword "bread" or "loaf". The sequence, which prominently includes the two multiplications of bread, ends with the story of the disciples' crossing the Lake with Jesus:

> Now they had forgotten to bring bread; and they had only one loaf with them in the boat. And he cautioned them, saying, "Take heed, beware of the leaven of the Pharisees and the leaven of Herod." And they discussed it with one another, saying, "We have no bread." And being aware of it, Jesus said to them, "Why do you discuss the fact that you have no bread? Do you not yet perceive or understand? Are your hearts hardened? Having eyes, do you not see, and having ears, do you not hear? And do you not remember? When I broke the five loaves for the five thousand, how many

> baskets full of broken pieces did you take up?" They said to him, "Twelve," "And the seven for the four thousand, how many baskets full of broken pieces did you take up?" And they said to him, "Seven." And he said to them, "Do you not yet understand?" (*Mk* 8:14-21).

The text is enigmatic in certain details. Why is Jesus represented as cautioning the disciples against the leaven of the pharisees and the leaven of Herod ? There would seem to be some conscious play of ideas linking the "leaven" of Jesus's question with the "bread" the disciples had forgotten to bring. And why the detail that there was (after all) one loaf in the boat? Finally, what is the sense of the last questions put by Jesus.

The mystery is resolved with the recognition that the key to the text is a set of related symbols.

That the disciples "have no bread" is refuted, in Jesus's view, by the memory of bread aplenty. But this sets us already on the plane of symbols, practically excluding a non-symbolic reading of the passage. A further observation confirms this: The final questions of Jesus imply that the riddle of bread galore *vs.* "no bread" is somehow resolved and illuminated not only by remembering the multiplications of bread but also by answering the question of how many baskets full of broken pieces were gathered after each occasion. These numbers are, as the text states, "twelve" and "seven". Now, we know that "twelve" has special reference, in *Mark* as in the rest of the *New Testament* to Israel *Mk* 3:13-19; *Mt.* 19:28 *par.*; *Acts* 26:7 etc.); it should be noted that "seven" has special reference to the Gentiles (cf., the seven nations God destroyed in the land of Canaan, *Acts* 13:19, and the seven nations of the Gentiles which the Essenes thought God would destroy through Israel in the last great War, *IOM* 11:8-9) These two symbolic numbers correlate with the observation that the second multiplication of bread took place in Gentile lands ("the region of the Decapolis" *Mk*. 8:31). The multiplications, then, relate respectively to Jew and Greek. Jesus himself is their provider. Indeed, it is he to whom the "one loaf" refers. "No bread"? On the contrary, Jesus is bread sufficient—bread of life for the whole world! Concretely, it is the Eucharistic Christ who represents this for the Church, and it is in the Church that the division of Jew and Greek is broken down. The Eucharistic motifs in 6:41 and 8:6 (blessing, breaking, giving: cf., 14:22) support this reading. The "leaven" of Herod and of the Pharisees is, accordingly, to be interpreted in all probability along lines of political and racial separatism or nationalism, reinforcing the old division of Jew and Greek.

We look in vain for a comparable theme in the *Gospel of Matthew*. Rather than the pattern of reconciliation, in the Church, of Jew and Greek, we find the substitution of Greek and Jew:

> I tell you, many will come from east and west and sit at table with Abraham, Isaac, Jacob in the kingdom of heaven, while the sons of the kingdom will be thrown into the outer darkness; there men will weep and gnash their teeth.
>
> (*Mt.* 8:11-12)

The sequence of missions is also remarkable: first, Jesus (15:24) and his disciples (10:5) are divinely sent to Israel along. Then once risen from the dead, Jesus sends his disciples to the world of the Greek:

> All authority in heaven and on earth has been given to me. Go therefore and make disciples of all nations, baptizing them in the name of the Father and of the Son and of the Holy Spirit, teaching them to observe all that I have commanded you... (*Mt.* 28:18-20a).

No provision is made here for a second try with the Israel which had rejected and crucified Jesus. Though some scholars see an implicit reference to Israel in the expression "non-believers" Matthew at any rate does not make the reference clear. Nevertheless, the Church which issues from the work of Jesus is in fact created around the nucleus of the Twelve whose eschatological function was to judge "the twelve tribes of Israel" (*Mt.* 19:28), and who themselves were Jews. The Church is the rightful prolongation of the life of Israel. Its charter is a code of discipleship in which the *torah* comes to full flower. Its life is modelled on that of the Lord, so fulfilling the word of promise and prophecy which was Israel's heritage. What Matthew offers, then, is the vision of a universal Church. Israel is not excluded from it by design. But the vision reflects the harsh fact that Israel did not come into this Church.

The Lukan scheme of things similarly features the passage of salvation from the Jewish to the Greek world. It is, however, note-worthy that in the *Acts of the Apostles* the tensions between Jewish and Greek Christians are explicitly narrated and their resolution emphasized. Here the response to what we have called "the major diversity" in early Christianity was unambiguously grounded in a common response to Christ: even more fundamentally, it was grounded in God's saving action in Christ. Thus, it was not the Law that had saved the Jewish Christians and, as time showed, it was not so much as a prerequisite condition of this saving action. Peter speaks to the Jerusalem community about the baptism of Cornelius and his entourage:

> ...the Holy Spirit fell on them just as on us at the beginning. And I remembered the word of the Lord, how he said, 'John baptized with water, but you shall be baptized with the Holy Spirit'. If then God gave the same gift to them as to us when we believed in the Lord Jesus Christ, who was I that I could withstand God (*Acts* 11:15-17).

The entry of the Greek into the community of messianic salvation is represented by Luke as legitimized in advance by the divinely granted vision of Peter at Joppa, from which he concluded that "God shows no partiality." Thus, the opening to the world of the Greeks throws a powerful light on the economy by which the Jew was saved as well. That is, God's action and man's response are clarified in terms of "faith alone" (*Acts* 15:11).Perhaps this was conceived, by the first Jewish Christians who acknowledge it, as grounding a church of two "peoples" (Jew and Greek). It may be, in short, that Luke has preserved a fragment of Jerusalemite tradition in the words he attributes to James in *Acts* 15:14:

> Symeon has related how God first visited the Gentiles, to take out of them *a people for his name.*

What is clear, in any case, is the Synoptics' common conviction that the problems relating to unity in the Church are not grounded in the will of God but are obstacles to God's will and are to be dealt with as such; that the division of Jew and Greek in the Church is just such an obstacle; that the victory of unity over division is comprehended in the action of God saving and sustaining the Church; that the Church's own effort to heal divisions and find solutions is no mere social instinct but precisely a response to the saving action of God.

6. *The Response to The Epistle to the Ephesians*

The situation to which the *Epistle to the Ephesians* is addressed seems to be an atmosphere of Gentile-Christian indifference of Jewish Christianity. This is the reverse of the problem which Paul faced, and yet he himself glimpsed it in the *Epistle to the Romans*, where he warned Gentile believers not "to boast", and told them "do not become proud, but stand in awe" (11:20).

Ephesians seeks to recover the moment of wonder that even the Greek had been saved. At one time the problem had been to win a place for the Greek in the Church. Now it was to keep a place for the Jew. The tack taken by the writer is to recall the course of the Greek from his origins in the darkness of idolatry to his entry into the light of Israel's heritage:

> And you he made alive, when you were dead through the trespasses and sins in which you once walked, following the course of this world, following the prince of the power of the air, the spirit that is now at work in the sons of disobedience... Therefore remember that at one time you Gentiles in the flesh called the uncircumcision by what is called the circumcision, which is made in the flesh by hands, remember that you were at that time separated from Christ, alienated from the commonwealth of Israel, and strangers to the covenants of promise having no hope and without God in the world (2:1-2, 11-12).

God's solution to the problem of division between the Jews and Greeks had been a Secret kept through the ages until the fullness of time. But now the Secret is cried out from the housetops: Christ had died for all men "and you who once were far off have been brought near in the blood of Christ" (2:13). Therefore, Christ "is our peace, who has made us both one and has broken down the dividing wall of hostility" (2:14). The economy of "the Secret that is Christ" is one of unity in salvation. Jew and Greek alike live in and by the body of Christ and as co-sharers of the promised Spirit (3:6).

The significant point is that, though the roles are changed, Jew and Greek are once again summoned to unity in Christ as response to Christ. Thus the theme of unity is seen in a theological perspective. Our contention that, in the self-understanding of early Christianity, the very being of the community relates to its founder as a response to a call, is verified by all relevant sources from the earliest to the latest. (*Ephesians* probably dates from the 80's of the first century, and thus belongs to the later letters of the epistolary corpus attributed to Paul.) In the most generic sense of "structure", the structure of Christianity is, by its own testimony and in its own self-understanding, the result of a response to its founder.

CHAPTER VI

THE AUTHORITY OF DISCIPLINARY DECISIONS IN EARLY CHRISTIANITY

The treatment of the subject-matter in this chapter has been so designed as to provide materials for a comparative study of early Christianity and early Buddhism, since it is in respect of the authority of disciplinary decisions that similarities and dissimilarities between the two religions become readily apparent. This accounts for the choice of the topic: "the community's discipline"; here we find materials for ready comparison. But we are also concerned here with comparative materials susceptible of treatment in terms of our basic inquiry: the relation of the community to its founder as conceived by the community itself (or, as expressed in the community's own self-understanding). Hence the precise question determining how we are to deal with this material: "What is the authority of early Christian discipline?" Insofar as, in the early Christian self-understanding, the authority for disciplinary arrangements is Christ himself, the whole question of discipline is situated in the context of the "response to the founder."

Now, we will deal with "discipline" in two ways: (a) as a total set of arrangements which define a life style and (b) as a set of particular decisions made to meet *ad hoc* problems. As we are concerned with "the authority" which stands behind disciplinary arrangements, particular disciplinary decisions should prove to be especially helpful: Decision-makers imposing some disciplinary decree are usually summoned to offer a justification for it. Thus we learn what "warrants" are held in honour by the community.

To discuss discipline in the first sense, we shall examine *Mt.* 5; *Mt.* 18; *Acts.* 5; 1 *Cor.* 5-6. In the second sense, special and important disciplinary cases appear in *Acts* 15: 12-29; 1 *Cor.* 7:10-16.

1. *Life Style*

Matthew 5 presents a code of discipleship. Is this the equivalent of an ecclesial discipline characterizing the life style of the Matthean Church? First of all, it would seem that there are here no specific "rules for discipline", such as excommunication. We do find, however, a variety of references to concrete particulars (monogamous marriages, prohibition of oaths, etc.) as well as the general principle that "not an iota, not a dot,will pass from the law" and the proclamation that Jesus himself has come "not to abolish" but "to fulfill" (*plerosai*) the law and the prophets (5:17-18). There is a genuine "discipline" being spelled out in *Mt.* 5, evidently because the Church is the real audience of the Sermon, and the Church is considered to be, not a conglomeration of individuals, but a community of saints. Thus the "discipline" of the Matthean Church embraces every topic occurring in the Sermon, and the whole of this discipline is presented as charged with the authority of Christ.

Let us consider some aspects of this life-style. It is a life oriented toward interior and secret piety as conditioning entry into the Kingdom. For achieving self-discipline, Matthew evidently believed that the *torah* was compatible with the Christian faith. Jesus said that he had come "not to abolish . . . but to fulfill" the law and the prophets (*Mt.* 5:17), and: "Unless your righteousness exceeds that of the scribes and Pharisees, you will never enter the Kingdom of Heaven" (*Mt.* 5:20). This appears to present the *torah* as basic to the direction taken by the Church and Jesus as the true interpreter of the *torah*. But more than an interpreter, he is also the proclaimer of the *torah* brought to its completion.

Christ as the "fulfiller" of the Law defines a new righteousness as the condition of entry into the kingdom; for "fulfiller" here means "one who fills it to the full." It is Christ who brings the *torah* to its divinely appointed fullness or measure of perfection.[1] The Matthean Christ, then, asked that Christians should not only obey the prescriptions forbidding lying, murder,

1. J. Jeremias, *New Testament Theology*, The Proclamation of Jesus, "The concluding revelation," pp. 82-85.

and adultery, but also transcend them by not even thinking about such acts. He said, for instance:

> You have heard . . . 'You shall not kill'; . . . But I say to you that every one who is angry with his brother shall be liable to judgment. You have heard . . . 'You shall not commit adultery. But I say to you that every one who looks at a woman lustfully has already committed adultery with her in his heart. (*Mt.* 5:21-28)

Christ positively promoted the development of individual moral perfection, to be sought through a saintly life style modelled after God's perfection. He strongly emphasized such virtues as "purity of heart," holiness, humility, honesty, sincerity, love of one's neighbour, and love even of one's enemies. He called upon his followers to "Let your light so shine before men that they may see your good works and give glory to your Father who is in heaven" (*Mt.*5:16).

These passages may be interpreted as indicating, first, that religious discipline was based on believing discipleship by which the disciple accepted the completed *torah*, and, second, that sanctification through inner discipline was more dependent on moral purity rather than on ritual practices (e.g., *Mt.* 5:23-26). They indicate, moreover, that discipline was inwardly directed and that it did not consist of conformity to legalistic rules imposed and enforced by the community. Righteousness was seen as derived, not from the Law, but from the response of faith in Christ. This faith was directed toward the seeking of God's kingdom. It required repentence, recreation, divine orientation, and God's forgiveness.[1]

The life style required by Christian discipline, as presented by Matthew, was divinely oriented and characterized by a piety that concealed its asceticism (*Mt.* 6:1-6, 16-18). It was a rigorous life style, exacting renunciation, in which individual acts were set in the social context of the believing community. Discipline was Church discipline, as both the *Gospels* and the *New Testament* letters testify. Its rigour was intended to bring about an

1. J.G. Davies, *The Early Christian Church*, p. 22.

orderly and pure community with high standards, one made up of persons responding to an eschatological call.

The discipline implied in the Gospel according to Matthew does not seem to have remained sufficient for the needs of the growing community. As its membership increased, specific disciplinary regulations came into being, motivated by a certain communitarian self-understanding. It was necessary for the sanctity of the community that the incorrigible sinner be excluded. Matthew presents Jesus as having asserted that the divine authority of "binding and loosing," belonged to the Apostles.[1] Historical critique (the question of to whom Jesus gave this authority) is not the issue here. For our purposes we may note simply that the origin of this disciplinary authority was attributed to Jesus by the early disciples for the sake of a sanctified and united community.

Perhaps we should discuss, at this point, two repeatedly observable phenomena relevant to early Christian discipline, which require explanation: "unhistorical attribution" and "chain of command." By "unhistorical attribution" we refer to the readiness of the Christian community to attribute to Jesus disciplinary dispositions which the historical critique assigns to early Palestinian Jewish Christian communities. Chapter 18 is a case in point:

> In the first place it is improbable that Jesus should have given detailed instructions for church discipline to be observed in the post-Easter community, and v. 17c.
>
> "Let him be to you as a Gentile and a tax collector" seems strange on the lips of one who sought out precisely the company of tax collectors and sinners; secondly, from the standpoint of literary criticism, the comparison with LK.17:3 f. shows that the logion preserved there in its original form— which merely gave point to the duty of forgiveness in personal relationships— has been recast in Mt. 10:15-17 to become, in secondary fashion, an instruction on the disciplinary treatment of sinful members of the community.[2]

1. Ch. 18 is directed to community leaders, not to the community as such. Cf., J. Jeremias, *op. cit.*, p. 238.

2. C. H. Hunziger, *Judisches Erbe in der urchristlichen Kirchenzucht* (unpublished, Habilitations schrift), Part III, pp. 3-5.

It is evident that the discipline of the community has been considered as something charged with the authority of Christ. What does this tell us of the self-understanding of those unknown Christians who made this kind of connection? It tells us that Jesus was taken to be the all-sufficient and exclusive source of Christian life. For he was not only the God-given model of the Church and the spokesman divinely authorized to define God's will for Christians, but also uniquely those things. Everything which, for whatever reason or from whatever source, seemed to point to the right way to the Church was therefore spontaneously considered to derive somehow from him, "for there is no other name under heaven given among men by which we must be saved" (*Acts* 4:12). "Unhistorical attribution" is accordingly a precious index to the self-understanding of the earliest Church as enshrined in its disciplinary code.

The "chain of command" indicates a second important facet of this self-understanding. More proximate sources of authority were either reduced to the authority of Jesus, as we have just seen, or they were grounded in that authority on the principle that,

He who hears you hears me
and he who rejects you rejects me,
and he who rejects me
rejects him who sent me (*Lk.* 10:16).

Thus three points emerge with clarity: (1) The authority of those who functioned as leaders in the Church was an authority derived from Christ; (2) the authority of Christ was, however, not absolute or ultimate, but was itself derived from God the Father; (3) these derivations were such that, in the case of Christ as in the case of those whom he commissioned, no less an authority than that of God himself was operative. This correlates well with the total "economy" of salvation presupposed in early Christian life. Prayer, for example, was directed to God the Father. In Christian thought the call to salvation originated with the Father; the scheme of history was defined by his "sending" Moses and the prophets and, climactically, the Son; and numerous titles (such as "saviour") fundamentally belonging to the Father were bestowed on Christ precisely insofar as he was conceived to be the Father's chosen instrument. In this way, the "chain of command" situates the discipline of early Christian communities in an explicitly "theological" or "God-the-Father-centered" context.

Now we may consider the style of life and thought implied by the discipline of "binding and loosing".[1]

The authority of "binding and loosing," as expressed in the Semitic languages, was authority to prohibit and to allow, to reject and to accept, to condemn and to acquit. The rabbis claimed the power to bind and to loose, especially in the sense of taking decisions about how the Law was binding and how it loosened and freed. In the *New Testament* "binding and loosing" is Christ-centered. It takes its meaning from the *New Testament* conception of the mission of Christ. The authority which the Gospel according to Matthew represents as given to the Apostles includes, it would seem, all the senses of "binding and loosing": the power to declare what is prohibited and what is allowed, to admit into the community and to exclude from it, and (in close accord with the latter function) to mediate the forgiveness of sins (Cf., *Acts* on baptism) in the row of the Church's life. It is difficult, at any rate, to find the point at which "binding and loosing" in *Matthew* is limited. Thus, in some sense the reign of God entered the world through Christ's grace and power. As expressed in *John* 20:22-23, the Apostles are armed with the Holy Spirit : "Receive the Holy Spirit. If you forgive the sins of any, they are forgiven; if you retain the sins of any, they are retained." The authority of the disciples, then, was expressed in terms of the gift of Christ, namely, the Holy Spirit. The words of Christ, as recorded in *Matthew* 18:20 ("Where two or three are gathered in my name, there am I in the midst of them"), indicate that the authority of judgment, of forgiveness, and of excommunication was exercised in the name of Christ and was based upon Jesus's authority to forgive sins (*Mk*. 2:5-10). This maximalist reading of the text, we propose, is probable.

Acts 5:1-11 relates the story of Ananias and his wife, Sapphira, both members of the Jerusalem community, who pre-

1. J. Jeremias, *op. cit.*, p. 238.

tended to give the total proceeds from a property sale to the community, while actually holding back a part of the money. They were condemned by Peter, and they lost their lives as punishment. What does this episode tell us of early Christian discipline and of the self-understanding implied by it?

The Ananias and Sapphira affair offers us privileged access to the idealism of early Christian discipline. In the restored community of Israel, no one was to be poor (*Deut*. 15:4), for his brother would open his hand out to him (cf., *Deut*. 15:8) in a practical application of the precept: Love the neighbour as thyself.[1] This ideal is reflected particularly in the story of the rich young man, the Matthean form of which betrays a specific *Sitz im Leben*, namely, the test of those petitioning entry into a Palestinian Christian Community.[2] "Community of goods" (in some less than absolute form, cf., *Acts*. 5:4) is thus made to derive from Jesus himself as guide to the "way" variously described as the way to "life" (*Mt*. 19:16 f.) and as the "perfect" way (*Mt*. 19:21).[3] We meet once again the early Christian trait of tracing communitarian idealism and practice back to the authoritative word of Christ.

Let us next discuss the life style in the Pauline Church and its relationship with the authority of Christ. Generally, Paul seems to have emphasized that divine discipline consisted of two aspects, namely, baptismal and external discipline. The aim of both aspects was to develop the Church as the body of Christ, i.e., as a community of the purified, with an eschatological outlook. This discipline included an element of asceticism, but did not call for renunciation of life in the world. Thus the discipline appears to have reflected the spirit of Jesus (cf., 2 *Cor*. 6:14). Loyalty to the authority of Christ as head of the community was of paramount importance.

Baptismal discipline was inner discipline. It consisted of living in a new spirit as part of Christ's body, to bear "the fruit of the spirit" (*Gal*. 5:22-23), and to practice moral behavior

1. J. Schmitt, "L'organisation de l'eglise primitive et Qumran" *La secte de Aumran et les origines du christianisme* 217-231; p. 222.
2. Cf., Schmitt, *art. cit*., 228-230. Cp. *IOS*. 1.
3. *Op. cit*. p. 228.

(cf., 1 *Thess*. 4:1-12). This means that the Holy Spirit dwelt within the Church through the discipline of the members, who repented and were sanctified by faith. Their loyalty to Christ through the Holy Spirit required them to live according to a high moral standard, and to maintain their purity of life. Baptismal discipline, therefore, was Christological and divinely-oriented rather than being a purely human discipline.

Although this inner, baptismal discipline was of fundamental importance in the Pauline Church, outer, or communal, discipline became necessary as increasing membership brought with it increasing problems of disunity and unethical conduct.

Evidently, Paul imposed an outer discipline, consisting of prohibitory rules, and enforced it through the penalty of excommunication, as did the synagogue (1 *Cor*. 16 : 22; *Gal*. 1 : 8).[1] He used the primary laws from Jewish tradition as the basic framework of his discipline. He developed modifications, however, in the light of Christ's teachings. Numerous pragmatic considerations, moreover, are evident in his instructions.

We might consider the Pauline style of communitarian discipline in a couple of illustrations provided by 1 *Corinthians*.

In 1 *Cor*. 5 : 1-15, we find Paul urging that gross sinners such as the man "living with his father's wife" be excommunicated for the sake of the purity of the fellowship. If a member was judged to have sinned, the Church could decide, through the divine power of the Holy Spirit, whether to excommunicate him or whether to accept his confession and repentence before the assembly.[2] Paul's words, "Shall I come to you with a rod . . . (1 *Cor*. 4 : 21), are indicative of Apostolic authority which was based fundamentally on the Spirit and was employed as the sacred Law of God by charismatic individuals such as Paul.

The excommunication of sinners (1 *Cor*. 16 : 22; *Gal*. 1:8) followed the practice of the synogogue, which was based on the commandment in *Deuteronomy* 17 : 7 : "So shall you purge the evil from the midst of you." Of one living with his father's

1. A. Schlatter, *The Church in the New Testament Period*, tr. Paul P. Levertoff, pp. 179-180.

2. Bultmann, *Theology of the New Testament*, Vol. II, p. 233.

wife (1 *Cor*. 5 : 1 ff.) Paul said that the community should "deliver him to Satan" that, at the last day, his spirit might be saved.

Paul specifically told the Corinthian Christians to refrain from disputes before secular tribunals (1 *Cor*. 6 : 1-8) because he knew that traditionally "Greeks love to go to law."[1] This injunction appears to be related to the practice among the communities of the Jewish Diaspora of deciding disputes among their members before their own forum. Paul believed that the response of the Church as a community of saints to Christ should lead its members into a higher order of ethical practices than that of the secular community. Consequently, he felt that it would bring shame upon the Christian community if its members were judged by outsiders. Moreover, the Christian community, being instructed by the words of Christ through the Spirit, should be qualified to judge not only itself, but also non-Christians, and even angels (1 *Cor*. 7:25, 40; 14:37). By Christian standards, the judgments reached by non-Christians might be unjust.

Paul himself does not here make explicit the grounds on which he instructs his community. He seems to expect that the community to which he writes will itself perceive the incompatibility with Christian life and ideals of the stand opposed to his own. The situation, that is, speaks of itself against the incestuous man and against public litigation. At the same time it is clear that Paul speaks with authority. In 1 *Cor*. 2:1-16 this is "pneumatic" authority, and in 1 *Cor*. 7:40 he says: "And I think I have the Spirit of God." Such divine gifts should not, however, be artificially separated from Paul's authority as an "apostle" (9:1-7), as one divinely sent to bring men to the obedience of faith. In the end, this is Paul's final word about himself as it is the first word in his letters (*Rom*. 1:1; 1 *Cor*. 1:1;2 *Cor*. 1:1; *Gal*. 1:1; *etc*).

2. *Test Cases of Discipline*

It is clear that the authority of the Apostolic Decree recorded in the *Acts* 15 (cf., *Acts* 21:25) is divine. True, it represented

1. A. Schlatter, *op. cit*., p. 180.

the consensus of the community, but this must be balanced by the extraordinary word of James: "It seemed good to the Holy Spirit and to us" (*Acts* 15:28). The authority of the decree may correctly be regarded as "communitarian" and "Apostolic" and "pneumatic." Indeed, these are concretely one.

As presented in the *Acts* 15:29, the Apostolic Decree required Christians "to abstain from what has been sacrificed to idols, and from blood and from what is strangled, and from unchastity." These rules were derived primarily from the *Old Testament* Holiness Code, recorded in *Leviticus* 17:18-13; 18:1; 26 and in *Genesis* 9:4-6.

The prohibition against eating food which had been offered to pagan idols did not, then, originate with Jesus. The disciples who followed him during his earthly life were Jews, who had not been faced with this decision. This problem arose later after the Gentiles joined the Christian community. J. Dupont comments:

> . . . of all the laws of purity James wished (Gentile Christians) to retain only those whose religious significance seemed universal: the eating of meat offered to idols involved a certain participation in sacrilegious cult (Cf., 1 Cor. 8-10). Concretely, blood is life and this belongs to God alone. Hence the Law's prohibition concerning it (Cf., Gen. 9:4: Lev. 17:10-14) was of such a character as to explain the repugnance of the Jew toward dispersing Gentiles from it. The meat of strangled animals is an analogous case. Irregular marriage unions figure in the present context in virtue not of morals but of legal purity.[1]

It is significant that the Apostolic Decree presented by James maintained the tradition of "binding and loosing" in terms of the Holy Spirit. James, in presenting these decrees, attributed them to the judgement of "the Holy Spirit and [of] us." It is clear that the decision was authorized, in the Christian view, by divine discernment and authority. In short, the words, "It seemed good to the Holy Spirit and to us" appear to say that the Spirit transcends individuals and rules, and that the decisions of the Council expressed this. Ultimately, it was Christ who rules as

1. See Chapter III, p. 90, *fn*. 3, this work.

Lord and head and who was the chief author of the decisions, for ultimately it was he who sent—or rather "poured out"—the Spirit on the community (*Acts* 2:33).

In 1 *Corinthians* 7:10, Paul gave the Corinthian Church disciplinary instructions concerned with marriage, saying, "I give charge, not I but the Lord." This is followed by a prohibitory decree forbidding divorce and remarriage. Now, this is presented, not as Paul's own idea, but no doubt on the basis of Christ's commandment: "What . . . God has joined together, let not man put asunder" (*Mk*. 10:9), and his statement that "everyone who divorces his wife and marries another commits adultery" (*Lk*. 16:18; *Mt*. 19:9). Paul's instruction indicates that the words of Christ were remembered as authoritative. In form the words "not I but the Lord" recall the *Septuagint* and the *torah*. Jesus's prohibition of divorce (*Mk*. 10:11 ff.; *Mt*. 5:32; 19:9; *Luke* 19:18) completed and perfected the *torah*, but in a way which practically repealed it, for, according to the *torah*, a husband could divorce his wife on his own volition (*Deut*. 24:1).[1] Thus the authority of Christ as the basis of discipline is here explicit in Paul.[2] He evidently established the basis of the prohibition to prevent anyone from contesting it in a community where sexual immorality and a devalued attitude toward marriage had led to problems concerned with divorce.

In discussing mixed marriages, on the other hand, Paul wrote "To the rest I say, not the Lord . . . ." (1 *Cor*, 7:12). Here it appears that Paul imposed rules through his own authority and transmitted those proclaimed by Jesus. This distinction and the fact that the Paul himself made this distinction are important. The question arises as to whether the authority by which Paul made such rules was "apostolic" and "theological" or merely human and "sociological." The answer must be the former. For, what did Paul do to make this rule except that he extended the spirit of Jesus's teachings to a situation not specifically covered by the words of Jesus himself ? The rule was imposed by Paul in the context of divine authority through carefully distinguishing the words of Jesus from the word by which the Holy Spirit

1. Jeremias, *op. cit*., p. 10.
2. Cf., D. L. Duncan, *The Sayings of Jesus in the Churches of Paul*, pp. 81-93.

guided the Church: "I have no command of the Lord, but I give my opinion as one who by the Lord's mercy is trustworthy" (1 *Cor.* 7:25).

An example of Paul's pragmatic attitude is seen in his position on mixed marriages, and divorce. Ideally, in the light of Jesus's teaching, there should be no divorce. But Paul said that in a mixed marriage, if the non-Christian member wanted a divorce, the couple could separate. If they did not, the ensuing strife and ill-will could adversely affect family life and the faith of the Christian partner and might spread to become a disruptive influence in the congregation. Paul wanted to apply the basic principles of Jesus's teaching to the exigencies of the actual situation in order to foster peace and unity within the Church.

In conclusion, it will hardly be amiss to summarize and to offer complementary reflections on the authority of early Christian discipline.

"Unhistorical attribution" to Jesus himself of particulars in the early Christian life style shows that what counted for the first Christians was not so much the Church's *memory of Jesus* enshrined in the *New Testament* as its present possession of the *Spirit*.

The "chain of command" motif situates early Christian discipline in an explicitly theological context. At the same time it is clear from Paul that there was some point in distinguishing a Word of the Lord himself and a word of Church leaders.

It should now be clear that from the point of view of its essential purpose, early Christian discipline was unequivocally religious. Its first purpose was to preserve the unity and purity of the Church community as it came to be challenged and experience strain, first in the transition from the pre-paschal discipleship of Jesus to the Easter Church, and then in the transition from *torah* culture to the Gentile culture of the Mediterranean basin. It should further be borne in mind that the discipline of the early Church, a part of "the obedience of faith", thus retained its prophetic character even as it came to terms with new particular problems.

Lastly, we should note that the *New Testament* Church's conception of the moral life of man is ultimately irreducible to matters of Church discipline. Thus, Matthew's Gospel teaches that the eschatological destiny of mankind finally hinges on the service of one's neighbour in such wise that the saved and the damned will be equally astonished on the day of judgment that all their lives they had dealt with an anonymous Lord. "Lord, when did we see thee hungry or thirsty or a stranger or naked or sick or in prison....?" The final answer is: "As you did it to one of the least of these my brethren, you did it to me" (*Matt*. 25:31-46).

PART III

COMPARATIVE STUDY

CHAPTER VII

CONCLUSION

In the foregoing pages we have been studying Buddhism and Christianity from the very early beginnings to about a hundred years in each case, in terms of three specific and distinct aspects of both religions, *viz.*, the authority of the founder, the community, and discipline. In each case we have been aided by the respective scriptures which record them within the bounds of uncertainties which, due to the imperfections of historical and literary critical study, still persist, a situation which is even more true of the Buddhist texts than the Christian. Such a special investigation seems to be warranted because of both striking similarities and equally glaring dissimilarities. It need not be demonstrated that Buddhism and Christianity are two of the greatest of world religions and the very first to claim global and universal allegiance and that a comparison of the two at this basic level is somehow in order.

So far we have been examining the points common to both as well as those in which they differ. What we have noted leads us to point out an important religious phenomenon, namely that there are two great missionary world-religions, taking their origin from two of the greatest spiritual figures in world history, with many parallel ideas of ethics, communitarian structure and life-style, ideas that manifest striking similarities in secondary characteristics although in the primary ones, they would appear to be vastly different. That such a significant phenomenon lies here is the thesis which is being worked out in these pages. Not a few similar traits appearing in two widely different religions which arose in two different areas of the world, in time removed from each other by about five hundred years, are enough to make a research worker stop and look closer. But as one looks closer, one also sees that the headwaters of each stream are very different from the other, revealing very different spiritual worlds. The results of the investigation have been appropriately distributed, according to a scheme, in the foregoing pages. We may now do no more than summarize and focus the important issues already dealt with.

1. *The Authority of the Two Founders*

In comparing early Buddhism and early Christianity we must first concentrate on the question of authority, which naturally calls for a comparison of the authority of the two founders.

As understood by the first Christians the basis of Jesus's authority was the fact of the Resurrection. Being above the Law and equivalent to that of God himself Jesus's authority was heteronomously oriented. His disciples accepted his authority through faith. The authority of the Buddha, in contrast, was based on doctrine (*dharma*) and on his own position as a law-giver. His authority was autonomously oriented, with no claim to be divine. It was accepted by his disciples through wisdom.

Let us now compare the divine-heteronomous, faith-oriented authority of Christ with the human-autonomous, wisdom-oriented authority of Buddha. Jesus's authority was based on the belief entertained by the disciples that as Christ he was the Son of God who had risen from the dead and who was Lord of all things. The authority of the founder as the risen one had to be accepted by faith rather than by reason. The disciples' experience of the risen Christ is transcendent of reason in nature. The Christian scriptural documents say that it was initiated by Christ and accepted by his followers. Christ's divine authority as expressed through such acts as his healing the sick and raising the dead had to be accepted by faith.

Jesus's earthly life was held to be consistent with his divine nature, as indicated by his teaching, his performance of miracles, his casting out of demons. Therefore, the *kerygma* — his life, death, and resurrection — had to be accepted primarily through faith rather than through analytical knowledge; they did not belong, essentially to the realm of reason. Because such events as the miracles and the resurrection could be accepted only through faith, not through reason; the establishment of Christianity depended upon divinely revealed authority. The developing *kerygma* of the resurrection of Jesus provided the basis for his authority to the earliest disciples. In was necessary for

Christ's disciples to receive him through the "confessional formula." His messianic authority was not like that of Buddha who taught *dharma*. It differed in that he was above the laws and teaching, having equal authority with God himself. Briefly speaking, the authority of Jesus had, in the understanding of his disciples, the following constituent parts:

The belief that Jesus rose from the dead was obviously the most fundamental, as already observed, and it was based not on any rational analysis but on faith. There was the belief that Jesus was the saviour of Israel which was based on Jewish theocratic politics, involving the kingship of the Messiah. This was a very basic notion. There was the acceptance of the authority of Jesus as a teacher — as a Rabbi. The Church combined the authority of Christ, with the *Old Testament* model for it, *viz*., the Servant of Yahweh; it also combined it with the laws of Moses — not to annul but to fulfill. Further, the Church looked upon Jesus as the one sent by God to found the Kingdom; his authority was accordingly exercised in both teaching and action and hence was superior to that of the teachers and prophets and carried with it the "royal power," the power to cast out demons.

Buddha's authority, by contrast, was fundamentally dependent on the *dharma-vinaya*,[1] which consisted of universal principles which he had discovered through his experience of enlightenment (wisdom); divinity was not a factor at all. One led by "knowing eyes" attained *nirvāṇa* through wisdom, with help from no one else. By following this pattern and through their own efforts, Buddha's disciples attained the power to live according to *dharma*. Buddha's personal authority was secondary to that of *dharma*, although his disciples were dependent upon his teaching (*dharma-vinaya*) that could lead them to their ultimate goal. Their faith differed from that of Christ's disciples in that it was based on understanding (initially faith and later wisdom). The *sūtra* thus requires "entering through faith and attaining through wisdom."[2]

1. *Saṁyutta-Nikāya*, (*Kindred Sayings*) *op. cit.*, Part I ; "This Norm (dharma) then, wherein I (Buddha) am supremely enlightened—what if I were to live under it, paying it honour and respect!" p. 175.

2. *Ta-chih-tu-lun* [Mahāprajñāpāramitā-śāstra], *Taisho*, vol. 25, p. 63.

The existence of *dharma* was independent of Buddha. He was respected because he was fully enlightened; that is, his followers respected him because they respected *dharma*, and he had attained *dharma* and exemplified it. A *sūtra* says, "For us, Lord, these things have the Exalted One as their guide, their resort."[1] This passage implies the feeling widespread among his disciples that if there were no Buddha, there could also be no *dharma*.[2] They were dependent upon the Master in order to understand *dharma* and had faith in his person.[3] This faith in him, however, differed from faith in Christ in that Buddha was not himself an end but only a means to *dharma*, whereas Christ was understood by the first Christians to be the end itself.

During Buddha's lifetime, his disciples were dependent on his personality for the development of the community. After his death, the *dharma-vinaya* was emphasized as the ultimate authority for the community. His teachings were accepted not through divine faith but through rational analysis. They could be experienced through wisdom.

Buddha said that truth was not hidden from the diligent seeker. Each disciple could learn and know the *dharma* through his own efforts. The earliest disciples did not, therefore, lay primary emphasis on faith in Buddha himself, but stressed instead the understanding of his teachings (law and discipline) and the practice of these teachings for the purpose of attaining *nirvāṇa* through their own efforts.

Why did Buddha's disciples obey the discipline ? Their position was not like that of the Christians, who were dependent

1. *Saṁyutta-Nikāya*, (*Kindred Sayings*) *op. cit*., Part II, p. 19.

2. *Majjhima-Nikāya*, (*Middle Length Sayings*) *op. cit.*, Vol. 1, 317: "For us, Lord, things (dharma) are rooted in the Lord for their conduit, the Lord for their arbiter." p. 379.

3. *Suttanipāta*, (*A Collection of Discourses*) *op. cit.*: "Thou hast passed to the end of and beyond pain, thou art a saint, perfectly enlightened, I consider thee one that has destroyed his passions, thou art glorious, thoughtful, of great understanding, O thou who puts an end to pain, thou has carried me across." p. 93. Cf., Keith : "he (Buddha) is the finder of the way, who taught the saving texts, and founded the order within whose bosom alone is sainthood to be won." p. 133. Kitagawa, *op. cit.*, "Not only was he the discoverer of the centural doctrine, the one who has lived it and reached the goal." p. 175.

on the divine authority of Jesus and had absolute faith in him. The Buddhists' obedience was not a heteronomous response to the duty imposed by God, but, instead, was practised primarily for the liberation of each individual. Autonomy was emphasized—Buddha and communal faith were secondary. The heteronomous "other-power"-oriented authority of Christianity, and the autonomous, "self-power"-oriented authority of Buddhism, led to soteriological differences. A comparison of the following episodes provides contrasting pictures of the soteriological authority of Buddha and Christ.

According to the "mustard seed story," Gautamī, a woman, brought her dead boy to Buddha and begged him for help. Buddha did not use a miracle to raise the boy from the dead, but said :

> You did well, Gautamī, in coming hither for medicine. Go enter the city, make the rounds of the entire city, beginning at the beginning and in whatever house no one has ever died, from that house fetch tiny grains of mustard seed.[1]

Gautamī had faith in him and visited every house in the city, but she could find no house in which no one had ever died. So she realized that death had not come only to her family but everybody was subject to it. Thus relieved of her sorrow she laid her son away in the burial ground. She sought to become a disciple of the Enlightened One and was accepted by him.

When Jesus heard that a ruler's daughter had died he said, "Do not fear, only believe, and she shall be well." He came to the ruler's home and said, "Do not weep, for she is not dead but sleeping." They laughed at him, knowing that she was dead. But, taking her by the hand he called, saying "Child, arise", and her spirit returned and her parents were amazed.[2]

The "mustard seed story" tells us that Buddha as the great teacher did not use miracles to give life back to the dead child or to solve the problem of the woman's heavy heart. Instead, he made her solve the problem of death through her reason and

1. E. A. Burtt, *The Teaching of the Compassionate Buddha*, p. 115.
2. *Luke* 8:49.

her psychological experience of impermanency of human life and freed her from anxiety over death and converted her to be his disciple. That means that he was regarded as a teacher whose wisdom was far superior to that of others, but he was not looked upon as God. Therefore, he did not use miracles. It was a rational trust, neither absolute faith in him nor trust in divine authority that he asked of his disciples.

The story of Jesus differs from that of the Buddha. Jesus was the Son of God and also had absolute divine authority. Thus he invited belief in himself, and raised the dead child through a miracle. He demonstrated his power to win even over death. Christ's authority was divine, as creator and redeemer, because of his miracles, and the resurrection, and his authoritative teaching. The *New Testament* presents Jesus 'Messianic authority as being his own, in his God-appointed capacity accepted through faith by his disciples. Buddha's authority was not considered divine by his disciples, although it was considered above that of gods or other men. Hence his authority is abstract in character—that of the Truth (*dharma*) itself. He rejected the concept of the creation of the world or of the immortal soul. He was a redeemer through his soteriological doctrine, but this does not imply that people were expected to be saved through him. Instead, they saved themselves by following his soteriological doctrine (*dharma*) and his examples through wisdom.

Buddha's teachings (law and discipline) were also akin to basically universal moral principles, "stopping evil, doing good,"[1] although they did not form the core of the teachings. They provided a moral foundation for the requisite discipline cultivated for the goal of liberation in *nirvāṇa*. Buddha and his disciples did not seek *nirvāṇa* through the help of any extraneous power. Rather, through wisdom, meditation, and the practice of moral discipline did they seek their own liberation.

Christianity depended on the authority of Christ, which was the foundation of its faith. Without faith in the crucifixion and resurrection of Christ, there could be no salvation—so the

1. *Dhammapada:* "An evil deed is better left undone, . . . a good deed is better done, . . ." 314, p. 48.

early Christians held. Faith in Christ was primary, moral perfection dependent on it.

In Buddhism, on the contrary, faith in Buddha himself was not primary; the emphasis was on understanding his teaching and on the practices of meditation and moral discipline. Moral perfection was of primary importance for the liberation which Buddha himself exemplified. Thus the sources of Buddhist wisdom and Christian belief are very different. In early Buddhism prayer was never addressed to Buddha, nor for that matter to any god who controls human destiny. Buddhists do not ask gods for grace, but, instead, seek inner self-enlightenment through meditation and moral discipline. Christianity, on the other hand, has an essential orientation towards God so that man as a sinner needs God's forgiveness through his faith for salvation. Buddhism, to the extent that it does not consider any idea or original condition of human existence, takes no account of the conception of sin. It proceeds from the framework of the actuality of human life alone and seeks a path of liberation entirely within its boundaries. It implies no notion of restoration; *nirvāṇa* is not restoration but something beyond it. Liberation is dependent on introspection, in which one destroys and frees oneself from ignorance (*avidyā*), (*avijjā*) and desire (*tṛṣṇā*), (*taṇhā*). One's mind and consciousness permit one to attain the final solution. The Buddhist, therefore, is not dependent on a god or gods.

The dualism of good and evil is basic to Christianity but not to Buddhism. This difference has far-reaching effects on the idea of the founders' authority in early Christianity and in early Buddhism. The demons spoken of in Christianity may be contrasted with Māra of Buddhism. The demon of Christianity can be described as an evil power in the universe, opposed to God, and controlling the world. It is destroyed by Christ. The early Christians recognized Christ's authority even over the demons. Māra, in contrast, is seen as a psychological temptation which arises within the individual as an expression of his inner psyche, interfering with his practice of moral discipline.

Buddha's authority is related to enlightenment; the understanding of *dharma* is of primary importance. Christ's authority, in contrast, is related to faith. Christ, therefore, was hailed as the God-man, whereas Buddha was the *dharma*-man. As the above discussions have indicated, there were indeed certain similarities between early Buddhism and Christianity. The disciples in both communities regarded the founders as great persons in relation to soteriology. The teachings of both founders, and the communities they gathered, became the power of their respective movements. It would therefore be very difficult to discuss discipline in these communities without considering the authority of their respective founders.

The authority of both founders was soteriologically oriented. The basic difference is that Christ's authority was his own, and his followers believed in him, whereas Buddha used *dharma* and taught that one could save oneself through enlightenment by following his (Buddha's) own example.

While Buddha's soteriological objective was *nirvāṇa*, "the ultimate peace", Christ's was "the Kingdom of Heaven" or "the everlasting life." The orientation of Christian discipline is largely historical in context, whereas Buddhist discipline is universally oriented.

These two religions are similar in that their founders had authority as soteriological, historical personalities. In both, the disciples were dependent upon the personality of the founder. Both developed as universal religions. Buddha and Christ were independent teachers, although they were spiritual Kings. Their leadership was unique in history. Christ differed from other prophets in the Judaic tradition in that, whereas his predecessors had presented themselves as servants of God who transmitted God's own words, Christ claimed to be the Son of God and the Messiah, and to have divine nature like that of God Himself through his resurrection. Unlike the prophets, he proclaimed laws on his own authority as the creator of law. No prophet or priest had claimed, like Christ, to be equal to God.

Buddha had a powerful personality though it was not regarded as divine in the early tradition. In the Hindu tradition, teachers, priests, and gods had not been sharply distinguished. Some humans had been in part priests but had also been, themselves, the objects of prayer and divine worship. Other gods had not been historical personalities; rather, they were powers of cosmic existence. The sages of Brahmanism had taught the secrets of

Reality as hidden truth, but, unlike Buddha, they had not taught with personal authority, and none had become the founder or leader of a religion.

Judaism differed from Brahmanism in that none of its historical personalities had been considered divine. Both traditions were alike, however, in that their historical personalities had spoken as teachers. No personality in either case had had the unique authority like that of Buddha, or had claimed to be equal to one God above all gods, like Christ. Both Buddha and Christ transformed traditional, ceremonial religion into personal religion.

Having discussed the soteriological differences between the two founders' authorities, let us now discuss the soteriological similarities. Both Buddha and Christ were the founders of their communities and had powerful personalities of authority. Both present soteriological patterns as saviours, as teachers of righteousness, and as spiritual kings of their communities (or kingdoms). Both were teachers and had numerous disciples, and both believed that their mission was to establish righteousness. Each community was formed after teacher-and-disciple pattern and was soteriologically oriented. Both Buddha and Christ asked their disciples to "Come and see," although Christ called them to himself, whereas Buddha called them to his *dharma*.[1]

The authority of Buddha, as teacher of *dharma*, was primarily grounded in his *dharma*. However, since his teaching authority was higher than that of the gods, it was claimed that as a liberated man, he was praised even by the highest god. His authority, therefore, was human, as teacher of men and of gods. He had developed it as a human teacher through long spiritual cultivation. The development of his authority culminated in his enlightenment experience and in his becoming the teacher of the Law. From a soteriological standpoint, salvation was not reached through Buddha himself but through *dharma*. Thus *dharma* was

1. E. O. James, *Comparative Religion*, New York, 1938, reprinted 1961: "Founder Buddha . . . did say 'Come unto me.' Gauttama was content to give his disciples dharma and leave them to work out their own salvation not as redeemed sons of God but as creatures bound to earth by the law of Karma till they could secure release by their own unaided efforts, and thus enter the passionless peace of Nirvana." p. 313.

supreme, and Buddha was subordinate to it. *Dharma* existed as a universal principle independent of the existence of the founder. It should be noted, however, that Buddhist *dharma* became manifest and was taught only as a result of Buddha's enlightenment. From a practical view-point, therefore *dharma* was established by Buddha. Prior to Buddha's enlightenment *dharma* did indeed exist according to Buddhist belief, but mankind knew nothing of it. Buddha disciples claimed that their *dharma* had originated with Buddha, and they were, therefore dependent on him. Without Buddha, *dharma* had no meaning for them. Even though they might develop an understanding of *dharma* through analytical and intuitive knowledge, their reasoning was grounded in trust in Buddha's personality and patterned after his personal example. The disciples received the teacher as a father, and desired liberation through following his law. Liberated *arahats* who had received the Law from Buddha himself and attained enlightenment wanted to become equals of their teacher. Buddha however, was uniquely omniscient and perfect in virtue and wisdom as a result of spiritual cultivation in former lives which his disciples had not practised. An *arahat* might attain equality with Buddha in a spiritual sense but not historically.

It should also be noted that, after Buddha's death *dharma-vinaya* was proclaimed to be the final authority, whether *dharma* was right or wrong depended on whether or not it was really Buddha's own word. Without the backing of Buddha's authority, *dharma* was not accepted as being true *dharma*.

The divine authority of the risen Christ had to be accepted by faith in the light of the divine life of Jesus, reflected in his teaching miracles, and the casting out of devils. Jesus, like Buddha and others, was called a teacher, but he exercised divine power. His authority as a teacher was derived from his having been sent by God. He taught new laws. His prophetic authority was not merely that of a human teacher. He taught a divine personal authority, his words and deeds were his own. He was the fulfillment of Law and prophecy. As the sign of his being a God-teacher, he performed miracles, curing the sick, raising the dead, and driving out the demons.

Jesus wanted to fulfill the Law, not to destroy it. Laws were dominant in the *Old-Testament* tradition, and they were exceeded only by God's own authority. No one could change the Law. Jesus, however, did change the Law. He forgave sins against the Law. He gave new commandments. His interpretation of the Law was different. The laws of the *Old Testament* emphasized outward obedience to specific rules; Jesus's emphasis was that inner motivation was more important. His interpretation of the laws is focused on the spirit of the laws in the light of God and man; the teachers of his time, on the contrary concentrated on minor details.

He was the teacher of righteousness and the fulfiller and interpreter of the law as well as the creator of a new law with divine authority. He accepted the value of the law, but at the same time transcended it. As he was the risen Christ and the Messiah messianic salvation was achieved through him. He was the saviour-teacher of his people.

The divine authority of Christ was faith-oriented, in contrast to that of Buddha, which was essentially philosophical and wisdom-oriented. Buddha, however, did have authority. When he asked his disciples to come, they obeyed because of his omniscience and his ethical purity. He was, therefore, the matrix of the community. He referred to the members of the community as his people or his sons.[1] His disciples left their homes to follow him because they respected his historical person, his teachings, and his living example as teacher of men and gods. Because he exemplified the *dharma* through his personal authority his disciples followed him and his teachings in order to keep the *dharma*.

When it is said that Buddha's disciples followed him, what is meant, more precisely, is that they followed his soteriological personality. The Buddhist ideal of *nirvāṇa* is sought through the Four Noble Truths and analysis of self. These approaches are not so much related to wisdom and analytical reason as they are to the following of Buddha's personal example. It was because of the disciples' faith in him and their dependence upon him

1. *Majjhima-Nikāya*, Vol. III, 29: "Monks, if anyone speaking rightly could say of a man: 'He is the Lord's own son, born of his mouth, born of dhamma, formed by dhamma, an heir to dhamma, not an heir to material things'—speaking rightly he could say of Sariputta: 'He is the Lord's own son, born of his mouth, born of dhamma, formed by dhamma, an heir to dhamma, not an heir to material things'." p. 81.

that they developed soteriological convictions and decided to follow him and practise his teachings.

Buddha and Christ were both teachers of their disciples, and both appear to have viewed their missions as being the fulfillment of what lay behind them in their respective religious traditions. Although Christ gave "new" commandments and Buddha presented "new" universal principles, the messages were similar in some respects. Both placed ultimate demands upon their followers in the form of selfabnegation, non-violence, sexual purity, minimization of human needs, preference for the higher to the lower, fearlessness, etc. Buddha preached the *dharma* as its transmitter and as judge, presenting such principles as the Four Noble Truths, purity of mind, and moral perfection. He emphasized wisdom, meditation, and moral purity, so that the *arahat* might be free from suffering. He preached righteousness for the spiritual kingdom and gave his followers the vision of *nirvāṇa*. Christ desired not to abolish the law but to deepen it and extend its application. He presented a radically new kind of righteousness as the means by which man would become perfect and free from sin, and would enter the Kingdom of God. It should be noted that Matthew and Paul express different ethical emphases; the former laid more stress on human, moral perfection, the latter on the fruits of the spirit, but both present Christ's moral commandments as being absolute.

Both were soteriological personalities. Their "words and acts" provided the models of how to live up to the law which they transmitted to their disciples. Buddha was a teacher who preached the *dharma*, it lived in him and through him, although this relationship was considered only accidental and of no essential value, except for facilitating meditations. Those who followed his example would achieve liberation (*nirvāṇa*). Likewise, Christ's disciples followed the Law of Christ, which they accepted as a code for messianic disciples. The code of morality, however, as far as early Christianity was concerned, was in no way separable from Christ. The code lived in him and through him. But he himself was its spirit and essence, and the relationship of the code to him was essential and not accidental. It not only facilitated meditation but called for belief. Both Buddha and Christ were believed by their disciples to be omniscient teachers. Buddha's virtues and wisdom were held to be perfect, and he was seen as a being possessed of supranatural character, with fore-knowledge of events, such as his death. Christ, also, appears as being perfect and having fore-knowledge of his death (*Mark* 8:31; *John* 1:45-51;2:24-25). Both had great disciples, such as Sariputta and Peter while Sariputta confessed the Buddha as greatest of men, Peter confessed Jesus as the Christ. Both were regarded as the greatest teachers and religious examples, but while Christ was worshipped as the "God man", Buddha was looked upon as the "*dharma*-man". Both said, "Come unto me." Gotama taught his followers that their salvation depended on them, and that through their own efforts they could attain *nirvāṇa*; Jesus, as the divine man, asked his followers to believe in him, and stated that he would free them from sin and prepare them for salvation in his Kingdom. Jesus used miracles for the sake of salvation. Buddha forbade the performance of miracles by his disciples. In brief, both Buddha and Christ had soteriological authority as saviour-teachers who preached righteousness in order to establish a spiritual kingdom. The vision of both was primarily not this-worldly. Each appears to have projected almost an identical image of himself as ruler of his kingdom. This similarity in self-conception is reflected in the similarity of the kingdoms which each sought to establish. Neither Buddha nor Christ was born with a royal status. Though Buddha was born in a noble family and was associated with people of the upper classes, he was not actually a king. Christ, who was born in a lower-class family, drew his disciples generally from the lower classes. Both developed a kingly consciousness on their own, and this self-understanding was reflected in the attitudes of their disciples toward them.

There is also a marked similarity in the life-stories of Buddha and Christ. If the question of the historical accuracy of these stories is disregarded, the accounts of the birth of Buddha and Christ are similar, and each is said to have been exceptionally precocious during his early years. Each renounced worldly wealth and power for soteriological reasons. Each was tempted—Buddha by Māra, Christ by Satan. Buddha experienced the *dharma*, Christ God's will.

Buddha, as the King of Dharma, saw it to be his duty to teach his people the principles of good conduct. He strove to guide the world through righteousness rather than force, and to save and protect his people through his own moral example. Also, in referring to his disciples as his people or as his sons, Buddha established a relationship comparable to that of a father and his sons. He called Sariputta his general for the presentation of his *dharma*. Buddha's status as the King of Dharma was *in effect* that of a saviour.

As the Messiah, Christ not only taught his people but also judged them and forgave their sins. Through his cleansing of the temple and his casting out of demons, he established God's rule and his Kingdom. Christ, like Buddha, did not become a secular ruler or leader. His disciples were disappointed in this because, in the view of the Jewish "theocracy politics," the "Saviour of Israel" was to be a secular ruler who would defeat the enemies of the Jews and establish a secular Jewish kingdom.

To sum up, both Buddha and Christ had spiritual authority derived from their soteriological power as rulers of their respective kingdoms. Buddha's personal authority as the founder of his community was similar to Christ's authority as Teacher and King. An important difference, however, is that the authority of Buddha was strictly anthropocentric; he did not, like Christ, claim divine authority. He adhered to the Hindu pattern in that he recognized *dharma* as being higher than himself, but he did not accept the theology and ontology of Hinduism.

2. *Unity of the Community*

In the early Christian and Buddhist communities, unity was primarily a response to authority and the teaching of the founders, even though these communities differed in their theological and human understanding of their respective founders, and in their relative emphasis on the person of the founder rather than on his teaching. In both communities, the founder was accepted as the head of the community, as teacher, and as the only true lawgiver and judge. Unity was based on the unchallenged authority of Christ in the Christian community and on the *dharma-vinaya* personified by Buddha in the Buddhist community.

Each of these communities comprised spiritual family of those who had responded to the call of the founder. The followers of the risen Christ, or the *dharma-vinaya* as personified by Buddha, had a common loyalty which served as a unifying factor in the community. In doctrinal, ethical, and disciplinary matters, the commandments of Christ, and of Buddha as the personification of *dharma-vinaya,* were accepted as binding by all the members of the community. This resulted in a common practice of the founder's teaching, and a common adherence to the founder's goals, these being the guiding factors towards a common purpose, pursued with a congenial spirit in common purity.

Both Christianity and Buddhism emphasized discipline, in response to the founder, as a source of unity. Ethics, communal laws, and punishment were accepted as the founder's directions for holding the community together. In cases when disunity presented problems, the final judgment was always based on obedience to Buddha's teaching of the *dharma-vinaya* in the Buddhist community, and on obedience to the commandments of Christ in the Christian community. At least, decisions were always expressed in terms of adherence to the founders commandments, although the historicity of the words attributed to the founders may in some cases be questionable. This common loyalty to the respective founders' teachings was essential to the unity of the communities; otherwise, diversity could arise and persist unchallenged.

In both communities, unity was promoted by the emphasis on the "new race" in which all were equal. In Christianity, all were equal through faith; in Buddhism, through virtue. This new equality transcended the old inequalities based on caste or nationality.

Inner and outer discipline, as a reflection of the founder's teachings, was essential to the development of each community as a community of the elect, with inner discipline being of greater importance in both. The members of each community, in their drive toward sainthood, modelled their life style after that of the founder.

Although Buddhism had no notion of divinely instituted legislation, and although Christianity developed no lengthy list of specific rules comparable to those of Buddhism, both communities imposed punishments upon violators for the sake of preserving the community. The ultimate punishment was ex-communication.

Another similarity between the two communities is that both included leaders who transmitted the authority of the founders and led and taught the people. The Christian Apostles, however, differed from the Buddhist monk-teachers in that the Apostles were charismatic, divinely oriented leaders, whereas the monk teachers were humanly oriented. The role of the Apostles in perpetuating and spreading the words of Christ, and that of Ananda and Upali in transmitting the *dharma-vinaya* are comparable in their contributions to the unity of their respective communities. The role of James and the Apostolic Council in restoring unity when dissension arose between the Jewish and Gentile Christians has its counterpart in Sariputta's reuniting the separatist followers of Devadatta with the Buddhist community.

As well as being identical with respect to their unifying influences, the two communities were also similar in the nature of the diversity which arose within them. In both communities, differences were primarily between liberal and conservative responses to the founder, with social and cultural factors having been of secondary importance. In the Christian community, differences developed between the liberal Greeks who followed Paul, and the conservative, law-observing Jews. There was no comparable situation in early Buddhism.

There was, in both Buddhism and Christianity, considerable anxiety to preserve the existence of the community. This was accomplished only through resisting any tendency toward division or disobedience. Also, there was a sense of the vulnerability and precariousness of the community, which made tolerance of schisms within the community almost impossible. This means that there was always a sense of persecution. The response to persecution reflected the ideal of the founder in each community. The Christians felt it was their supreme privilege to court martyrdom, while the Buddhists reacted more rationalistically.

In Christianity the authority of Christ was expressed ontologically—in *logos*, doctrine, etc. In Buddhism, there was no such ontology. In Christianity, the founder's role in relation to the law is essential (*agape*), whereas in Buddhism, the founder's role is instrumental (*maitrī*). The question may be asked: Did discipline develop in each case through gradual response to situation, which was not anticipated from the beginning, rather than through appreciation of a pre-existent body of knowledge ?

In Christianity, the ultimate norm was held to be above any law. But all discipline was in some sense engendered by the community measuring itself by its transcendent norm, Christ. Law and discipline, although important, were not integral to the truth itself, but the community, as the bearer of the truth, enforced law and discipline in order to survive as a community. In early Buddhism, discipline was more integral to the teaching; it was in fact part of the teaching and was credited to the founder himself.

In Christianity, the ground of unity was Christ himself, who was head of the Church, with the members forming an integral part of his body. The community was theologically and ontologically oriented, regarding its faith, sacraments, liturgical forms, and communal life as a response to God's redeeming acts through Christ. The doctrine of the Holy Spirit gave the members of the community a sense of unity in that they saw themselves as being led by one Spirit, who bound them into one body as the people of God in the New Covenant.

In Buddhism, the ground of unity was the *dharma-vinaya*, personified by the Buddha, who was regarded as an omniscient teacher of *dharma*. The Buddhist community was a pluralistic, humanly oriented group of individuals who had gathered to learn and practise *dharma* as exemplified by the Buddha. Loyalty to *dharma* was of paramount importance, and apart from it there was no independent notion of loyalty to Buddha as such. *Dharma* was personified by Buddha, and Buddha himself was what he was because of it, not the other way round.

A fundamental difference between Buddhism and Christianity is that while Christianity was ontologically and divinely oriented, Buddhism taught *dharma* as being represented by the "Middle Path" and adhered to the principle of "dependent origination." It sought unity through avoiding extremes, by rejecting a clear-cut distinction between "right" and "wrong" ideas and through the denial of the self in order to coexist with other persons and groups within the community.

The Christian community, comprising the "people of God," represented deductive unity. The Buddhist community, which emphasized individual self-discipline, was in contrast characterized by inductive unity. This was the basis for the soteriological differences between the two communities. The Church was communally oriented toward the Kingdom of God, whereas in *saṁgha* it was the individual who sought *nirvāṇa*.

The concept of the Church in the *New Testament* community of Christians would be hardly comprehensible without the idea of the Kingdom of God. As the Gospel according to *Luke* puts it, using the words of Jesus: "As my Father appointed a kingdom for me, so do I appoint for you that you may eat and drink at my table in my Kingdom, and sit on thrones judging the twelve tribes of Israel." (*Lk*. 22:29-30). Further, Christ was empowered by God to bring the Church into being. Jesus founded the Church, says the *New Testament* explicitly; every aspect of its life in early Christian consciousness was derived from Him.

The ideal of the Kingdom, as the *telos*, determined the character of the Church. In Buddhism, the ideal goal of all striving was *nirvāṇa*, and that determined in turn the character of the *saṁgha*. *nirvāṇa* was in no way related to the Buddha as the founder of the *saṁgha*; the founder has no role as founder in respect of *nirvāṇa*. In Christianity, as the *New Testament* understands it, Christ the founder of the Church had also a special relation to the Kingdom because his work was primarily to found the Kingdom. The whole Church itself was a response to the founder. The *saṁgha*, on the other hand, was only a functional community and the response there was merely to the human authority of the founder, to his wisdom.

The Church was clearly depicted as a response to a divine act. The Church established a historic continuity with Israel, a historic community, as this-worldly replica of a transcendent community, and this was far from being a merely human arrangement.

The Church valued the concept of "the people of God" made real by the Sacraments, which in turn received in it their sense and context. The Church was clearly conceived as an organism. All the metaphors of the Church, such as the Israel of God, the body of Christ, the elect, the Communion of Saints, the fellowship of Christ, etc., were corporate in character.

In Christianity, where Christ is primary and the Law secondary, loyalty to Christ is emphasized (more than is loyalty to Buddha in Buddhism). This is expressed not only in Christ's command to "follow me," but also in the symbolism which portrays Christ as a husband and head of the community and the Church as a bride. In Buddhism, Buddha is regarded as a father who teaches his sons the ethical discipline which they must practise if they are to know *dharma* and experience the enlightenment necessary in order to attain *nirvāṇa.*

The intimate relationship between Christ and the Church was one of the essential ideas in the *New Testament.* This intimate relation imposed a wholly new character upon the corporate community. It always saw its foundation elsewhere, in the person of Jesus Christ. Here we notice a radical difference in Buddhism. This may be also because Buddhism emanated from a religion (Brāhmaṇism) without a conception of a visible (and transcendent) centre of corporate identity as a people, as was present in Judaism in the form of the Temple and Yahweh. In Brāhmaṇism the centre of identity was a metaphysical one, which co-existed with a heterogeneous pluralistic ritual structure, both of which Buddha totally rejected. The great issues that divided Buddhism from Brāhmaṇism were ritual and metaphysical.

But when we turn to early Christianity we note that the very fact that there was a controversy between Paul and the Judaizers on the question of Law or Faith centered around the Jerusalem Christians, and their practice had no parallel anywhere within early Buddhism. Whether the Buddhist *saṁgha* retained Hindu ritual laws was not an issue; rather it was an indifferent and fundamentally irrelevant matter. For one thing, there was no issue of absorbing the community back to Brāhmaṇism until about the early medieval period of the *Purāṇas.* There was no late-comer like Paul. (Later, in the *Purāṇas* it was the Buddha who was absorbed into Hinduism as an *avatāra.*)

"Peace" in the Christian community was due to God's saving action through Christ's death and the response of the members to it. It was, therefore, divinely bestowed. In Buddhism, however, the members sought to establish a common purpose with a congenial spirit in common purity, through their following the *dharma-vinaya* and the example of the Buddha. Unity, therefore, was achieved through the members' own initiative.

The first Christian leaders were depicted as charismatic. They were said to have been led by the Holy Spirit by whom they were given all authority. The idea of the community as the extension of Christ is uniquely Christian, without any parallel in early Buddhism. Although the accounts of decision-making in the Jerusalem Church indicate the existence of an element of democracy, the leadership of the Holy Spirit made this element unnecessary. The Buddhist community, in contrast, adopted *gaṇa* — "political union on a republican model." It promoted unity through democratic decisions made in the light of teachings based on the question of discipline. The monk teachers had leadership functions, but their leadership was not regarded as being charismatic, nor as essential.

The major rules regarding conduct, e.g., not to kill, not to commit adultery, or lie, were identical in the Buddhist and Christian communities. The many strict rules of Buddhism, e.g., the 250 rules of *pātimokkha*, along with its judges and courts of law, and its general meeting of monks (*upavasatha*) provided Buddhism with additional basis of unity which were lacking in early Christianity.

3. *Discipline in the Community*

Discipline constituted a response to the founder's authority in both the Buddhist and Christian communities. The nature of discipline in the respective communities, however, was intrinsically different. First of all, the difference between the human autonomous orientations and divine must be made clear. It should be noted that heteronomous orientations hold good in the case of discipline as in the case of the authority of the founder and the community. In Christianity, discipline was related to a chain of command, from God to Christ, through the Holy Spirit. Discipline, therefore, was achieved through the help of the Holy Spirit rather than strictly through human effort, the latter being secondary in importance. In Buddhism, the commands were essentially rational precepts, almost self-explanatory, and the origin of it was Buddha's own historic (or rather "cosmic") discovery, and there is no power to back it up other than the power of the individual in concert with the community as such.

Early Buddhist discipline, unlike that of Christianity, was based on "self-power". In practising this discipline, the members of the community followed Buddha's example and his disciplinary directives in order to achieve enlightenment and attain *nirvāṇa*. Discipline was balanced with wisdom and meditation. Early Christian discipline, in contrast, was based on "power." According to its tradition, since the prophets had been chosen and sent by God, they represented the theological, God-centered nature of this discipline. Christian discipline required faith in Christ. The life-style which it required was modelled after the perfection of God ("Be ye perfect even as my heavenly Father is perfect" *Mt.* 5:48), and was to be practised through the Holy Spirit, the gift of God for this purpose.

At *patimokkha*, the Buddhist monks confessed their sins, repented before the assembly, and were forgiven by the assembly. In the early Christian community, in contrast, one made confessions of sins in the community and was forgiven ultimately by the Holy Spirit. Therefore, Christianity practised the external discipline of baptism to purify the members of the community as members of the body of Christ.

Both Buddhism and Christianity used expulsion from the community as a last resort of punishment for sins such as murder, adultery, and lying. In both communities, expulsion constituted a spiritual death sentence. In Buddhism, punishment was imposed by the assembly of members. In Christianity, punishment was imposed by the charismatic Apostles or by the community through the guidance of the Holy Spirit, as the expression of the will of the Spirit.

Discipline in both communities had ascetic elements. In the Buddhist community, the monks were required to renounce worldly life. The laymen, of whom this was not required, were of secondary importance in the community, and therefore Buddhism was little concerned with family life, marriage, and divorce. Christianity on the other hand, did not require renunciation of worldly life, which is why matters pertaining to family life, therefore, figured prominently in its discipline.

The difference in the disciplines of the early Buddhist and Christian communities have become more evident as we consider them in the light of the difference between the respective religious communities, a task which we have already undertaken. The Christian community included all members of the Church. It was an open community, and all who joined followed the same disciplinary practices and aimed at the same kingdom. There were, to be sure, inner groups, such as the Twelve Apostles, but their importance was secondary, the existence and functions of these inner groups being oriented toward the good of the community as a whole. The Buddhist community, while theoretically open to all, was primarily a monastic community. This monastic community was a closed one, consisting of elected members. The aim of the monks was *nirvāṇa.* The place of the laity in early Buddhism was definitely secondary, their primary function being to provide material assistance to the monks and nuns. Since the achievements of the monks and nuns would be difficult for the laity to emulate in their secular environment, their immediate aim was to attain to a heaven, rather than *nirvāṇa.* This basic difference in the nature and composition of the two communities was responsible for a basic difference in their disciplinary practices. In Christianity, the same discipline applied to all members, whereas in Buddhism, discipline was primarily concerned with the monks and nuns, rather than with the laity. Although discipline in the early Buddhist and Christian communities differed in certain fundamental aspects, there were significant similarities in secondary aspects. These similarities will be considered in the following paragraphs.

Disciplinary authority in both communities was derived from the founder, without whom there would have been no reason for disciplinary practice. No disciple in either community replaced the founder in having authority as the final source of discipline. In both communities, the purpose of discipline was to achieve unity and purity, to establish a community of saints as "new men", who would be purified through doing good and avoiding evil. In both ritualistic practices were therefore rejected and spiritual and moral discipline was emphasized. Buddhism did make use of laws taken from Brāhmaṇism and Jainism, these laws being adapted in the light of Buddha's example. Likewise, Christianity adapted the laws of Moses, which were reinterpreted in the spirit of Christ.

In both communities, discipline was more inwardly directed than it had been in previous societies. In their earliest years, neither community had many strict or well-defined rules; they depended instead upon the righteousness of the members. This situation changed in both, however, as membership increased. The Buddhist community became troubled by the entry of incorrigible sinners and other unqualified persons into its ranks, and consequently developed the rules of *vinaya.* The Christian community gradually changed from a *torah*-oriented one, with its members being mostly Jewish, into a Gentile one. As its membership came to consist largely of people who had no background of following the rules of the *torah*, the Christian community found it necessary to establish its own rules, Under the influence of Paul, both moral and organizational disciplines were increasingly emphasized and specific rules were formulated and enforced.

In both, the objective of an extraordinarily pure community with high moral standards was sought to be achieved through an ascetic life style, with material interests renounced. The Christian community, however, in doing so did not accept a two-level system as did the Buddhists.

Economic discipline also followed the two-level system in Buddhism, while it retained the one-level approach in Christianity. The Buddhist monastic system was similar to the Christian in that both emphasized common possession of all property. But at the lay level in Buddhism there was room for capitalistic accumulation and individual ownership of wealth. The practices in these communities differed from purely materialistic communism in that the purpose of the communitarian practices was spiritual and moral, and not physical well-being of the members. In both the *saṅgha* and in the Church, material goods were shared for the sake of brotherhood, so that peace could be established without quarrels arising over possessions; and so that the members could devote themselves to the spiritual life without worrying about material things.

In the Christian community, emphasis was laid on the use of material things to serve others. In the Buddhist community, on the other hand, laymen were encouraged to acquire material possessions through their work. In this community, also, material goods were not valued out of self-interest but for use in the service of others, so that the person so using them might acquire merit.

In both communities, the purposes of discipline were primarily non-worldly in their orientation. It should be noted, however, that in neither community were material needs and persons outside the community ignored. The withdrawal from the world as practised by the Buddhist monks may appear self-centered, but the monks acted as teachers, i.e., as morally qualified leaders who could lead others out of social suffering. Laymen in the Buddhist community used their money in social service as a token of their "compassion for life." The role of deacons in the New Testament Christianity in "serving tables" is comparable in the sense that by providing for the material needs of the people, they freed them from slavery to material goods.

Finally, a few sentences may be devoted to summing up the outcome of the present research. We have considered an aspect of history of two of the world's leading missionary religions in their original formative periods. Needless to say, Buddhism and Christianity were both founded and developed as universal religions. Each sought to replace the great, earlier traditions, which go back to antiquity, through the authority of a great figure who became the founder, leader and ultimate source of all that is essential in each. The followers of each founder elected to join together as a community in order to practise and propagate the founder's message. They have spread through history, covering the major part of the globe in each case—two world-religions, offering different routes to the solution of our ultimate ills. A close look at their early histories, at the time of their seminal formations and immediately after that has been found to be both instructive and revealing.

Their dissimilarities are as striking as their similarities. The ground upon which the dissimilarities are to be placed contributes to the ultimate difference in their spiritual outlook: In Buddhism it is gnostic, in Christianity it is eschatological. This great difference cannot be overcome. This, then, seems to account ultimately for the differences in the conceptions of the authority of the founders, communitarian structures, discipline, and life-styles. It is indeed fascinating, however, that from two widely different outlooks, strikingly similar moral teachings, human organizations, disciplines, life-styles, and personalities could emerge, as indeed has seemed to be the case with Buddhism and Christianity.

Further, there is another fruit that this study has yielded. It has seldom been realized that such things as authority and community have had a very important place in early Buddhism; they have been held to be primary aspects of Christianity, and Buddhism was commonly thought to be a fairly rationalistic and individualistic religion. This study has shown that such a notion as that, i.e., that early Buddhism was merely individualistic and analytically rational and ethical without a proper "religious" authority and community, is too one-sided to be correct. Buddhism—in having a foundation of authority, as well as a pattern of disciplined life of common responsibility in a community and a community structure which harked back to that foundation—qualifies to be called a "religion", rather than an ethical or philosophical system. In that it was rather like early Christianity itself, one can see how they became two of the greatest and most influential of the world religions.

SELECTED BIBLIOGRAPHY

PART I

ON BUDDHISM

A. PRIMARY SOURCES

Pali Texts :

Aṅguttara-Nikāya. 6 vols. Edited by R.M. Morris, E. Hardy, and C.A.F. Rhys Davids. Pali Text Society. London : Oxford University Press, 1883, 1955, 1958, 1960.

The Book of the Gradual Sayings. 5 vols. Translated by F.L. Woodward and E.M. Hare. Pali Text Society. London : Luzac and Co., 1951, 1952, 1955.

Dīgha-Nikāya. 3 vols. Edited by T.W. Rhys Davids and J.E. Carpenter. Pali Text Society. London : Oxford University Press, 1890, 1947, 1960.

Dialogues of the Buddha. 3 vols. Translated by T.W. Rhys Davids and C.A.F. Rhys Davids. *The Sacred Books of the Buddhists.* Vols. II to IV. London : Luzac and Co., 1956, 1957, 1959.

Majjhima-Nikāya. 4 vols. Edited by V. Trenckner. Pali Text Society. London : Oxford University Press, 1948, 1960.

The Middle Length Sayings. 3 vols. Translated by I.B. Horner, Pali Text Society. London : Luzac and Co., 1954, 1957, 1959.

Saṁyutta-Nikāya. 6 vols. Edited by M. Leon Feer. Pali Text Society. London : Luzac and Co., 1960.

The Book of the Kindred Sayings. 5 vols. Translated by Mrs. Rhys Davids and F.L. Woodward. Pali Text Society. London : Luzac and Co., 1950, 1952, 1954, 1956.

Vinaya Text. 3 vols. Tr. by T. W. Rhys Davids and H. Oldenberg. *Sacred Books of the East.* XIII, XVII, XX. Oxford, 1881, reprinted 1965.

The Book of the Discipline. 5 vols. Tr. by I.B. Horner. *Sacred Books of the Buddhists.* X, XI, XIII, XVI, XX, 1938 etc.

The Dhammapada. Tr. by I. Babbitt. New York, 1936, 1965.

Chinese Texts :

Cheng-shih-ih-san-sen-ching. (長十一善生経) *Taisho Daizokyo*. Vol. 1. (referred as *Taishō*).

Chu-shē-lun. (俱舎論) *Taishō*, 29.

Fu-ban-nieh-huan-ching. (佛般泥洹経). *Taishō*, 1.

Kokuyaku Issaikyō. (國譯一功経) Japanese Translations of the Buddhist Canons). *Vinaya* Parts 1-4. Tokyo, 1929, etc.

Mo-ho-ŝeng-chih-lū.(摩訶僧祇律 Mahāsaṅghika-Vinaya) *Taishō*, 22.

Nanten Daizokyō. (南傳大藏経) Vols. 3, 4.

Pi-ni-mu-ching. (毘尼母経) *Taishō*, 24.

Shan-Chien-Pi-Po-Sha. (善見毘婆沙). A Chinese Version by Saṅghabhadra of Samantapāsādikā). Tr. by P.V. Bapat and A. Hirakawa. Poona, 1970.

Shih-fên-lü. (十分律) *Taishō*, 22.

Shi-sung-lü. (十誦律) *Taishō*, 23.

Ssu-fên-lü. (四分律) *Taishō*, 40.

Ta-chib-tu-lun. (大智度論) *Taishō*, 25.

Ta-shih-ching. (大事経) *Taishō*, 17.

Ta-p'i-p'o-shah-lun. (大毘婆沙論) *Taishō*, 27.

Tsa-a-han-ching. (雜阿含経) *Taishō*, 2.

Chung-a-han-ching. (中阿含経) *Taishō*, 1.

Tseng-i-a-han-ching. (增一阿含経) *Taishō*, 2.

Wu-fen-lū. (五分律) *Taishō*, 22.

B. Lexica And Encyclopaedias

The Concise Encyclopaedia of Living Faith. R.C. Zaehner, ed.

Bulkyo Sajun. (A Dictionary of Buddhism). Unhu. Seoul, 1968.

A Dictionary of the Chinese Buddhist Terms. (中英佛学辭典) Ed. W.E. Soothill and L. Hodous. Taipei, Taiwan, 1934.

Encyclopaedia of Religion and Ethics. Ed. J. Hastings, IV (1912).

Japanese-English Buddhist Dictionary. Tokyo, 1965.

Mochizuki Bukkyo Daijiten (*Mochizuki Buddhist Great Dictionary*) 8 vols. Tokyo, 1936, reprint 1963.

Pali-English Dictionary. Ed. T.W. Rhys Davids and W. Stede. London, 1921, reprint 1959.

A Practical Sanskrit Dictionary. Macdonell. Oxford, 1929, reprint 1969.

A Sanskrit-English Dictionary. M. Monier-Williams. Oxford, 1899, reprint 1960.

Shin Bukkyo Jiten (*New Buddhist Dictionary*) S. Ishida et al. Tokyo, 1962.

C. SECONDARY SOURCES

Anesaki, M. (姉崎正治). *Kompon Bukkyo* (根本佛教 A Primitive Buddhism). Tokyo, 1910.

Bahm, A.T. *Philosophy of the Buddha*. New York, 1958.

Bapat, P.V. 2500 *Years of Buddhism*. Delhi, 1959.

Banerjee, S. C. *Dharma Sūtras—A Study in Their Origin and Development*. Calcutta, 1962.

Barua, B.M. "Faith in Buddhism", B.C. Law, ed., *Buddhistic Studies*. Calcutta, India, 1931.

Beck, H. *Buddhismus*: *Buddha und seine Lehre*. 1, Berlin, Leipzig, 1916.

Bhandarkar, R.D. *Lectures on the Ancient History of India*. Calcutta, India, 1919.

Conze, E. *Buddhism*: *Its Essence and Development*. New York, 1951, reprint 1959.

———. *Buddhist Thought in India*. Ann Arbor, 1962, reprint 1967.

Dutt, S. *The Buddha and Five After-Centuries*. Ahmedabad; 1955.

———. *Buddhist Monks and Monasteries of India*. Ahmedabad, 1955.

———. *Early Buddhist Monachism*. Bombay, India, 1960.

———. "Vinaya Piṭakam." *Journal of the Department of Letters*. Vol. X, Calcutta, India, 1923.

Eliot, C. *Hinduism and Buddhism*. Vol. 1. London, 1921, reprint 1962.

Frauwallner, E. *The Earliest Vinaya and Beginnings of Buddhist Literature*. Rome, 1956.

Gard, R.A. "Buddhism." *A Reader's Guide to the Great Religions*. Ed. Charles Adams. pp. 83-160.

Hayajima, K. (早島鏡正). *Shoki Bukkyo to Sahkai Seikatzu* (初期佛教と社会生活 Early Buddhism and Social Life). Tokyo. 1934.

Hirakawa, A. (平川彰). Genshi Bukkyo No Kenkyu (佛教教団の 研究)A Study of Primitive Buddhism). Tokyo, 1964.

——— . *Ritsuzo no Kenkyu* (A Study of the Vinaya-Piṭaka). Tokyo, 1970.

———. *Shoki Tacho Bukkyo no Kenkyu* (初期大乗佛教の研究 A Study of Early Mahāyāna Buddhism). Tokyo, 1968.

———. "Kairitsu mitaru Bukkyo no shinrikawn" (A Buddhist view of truth in the light of discipline). S. Miyamodo, ed. *Bukkyo no Kombon Shinri* (佛教の根本眞理 The *Fundamental Truth of Buddhism*). Tokyo, 1957.

Hume, R.E. *The Thirteen Principal Upaniṣads*. Oxford, 1921, reprint 1965.

Humphreys, C. *A Popular Dictionary of Buddhism*. London, 1926.

Hunabashi, K. (宮本正尊) "Genshi Bukkyo no Okeru Shukkedo to Zaikado." (原始佛教における出家道え在家道 Ways of Monks and Ways of Laymen in Early Buddhism. *Indogaku Bukkyo gaku Kenkyu*. (印度学佛教学研究) A Study of Indian and Buddhistic Sciences). Vol. 3, No. 1, Tokyo, 1954.

Jaini, P.S. "Śramaṇas", *Chapters in Indian Civilization* Vol. 1. *Classical and Medieval India*, Joseph W. Elder, Ed. A.K. Narain. P. 78.

Jayatilleke, K. N. *Early Buddhist Theory of Knowledge*. London, 1963.

Jayaswal, K.P. *Hindu Polity*. India, 1934, ed.

Keith, A.B. *Buddhist Philosophy in India and Ceylon*. India, 1962.

Kern, J.H. *Manual of Indian Buddhism*. Strassburg, 1896, reprint Varanasi, India, 1968.

Kimura, T. (木村泰賢). *Genshi Bukkyo Shisoron*. (原始佛教思想論 The Theory of the Thought of Primitive Buddhism). Tokyo, 1936.

Kitagawa, J.M. *Religions of the East*. Philadelphia, 1960.

Kyono, G. (境野黄洋). Tr. *Ritsu Bu*. I. 律部一 'Shibunritsu Kaidai'' 四分律解題) *Kokuyaku Issaikyo* 國譯一功経 Tokyo, 1929.

Law, B.C. *Buddhistic Studies*. Calcutta, 1931.

———. "Early Buddhist Brothers and Sisters." *Journal of the Asiatic Society of Bengal*. Vol. XI, 1945.

Law, N.N. *Gautama Buddha 25th Centenary Volume*. 1956.

Masunagai, L. (増永霊鳳) *Kompon Bukkyo no Kenkyu* (根本佛教の研究 A Study of Primitive Buddhism). Chita, Japan, 1948.

Matzumoto, B. (松本文三郎). *Bukkyoshi no Kenkyu* (佛教史の研究 A Study of History). Kyoto, Japan, 1928.

Matzutani, H. (増谷文雄). *Bukkyo Kairon* (佛教概論 Introduction to Buddhism). Tokyo, 1968.

———. *Toyo Shiso no Keisei* (東洋思想の形成 Formation of Eastern Thought). Tokyo, 1964.

Miyamoto, S. (ed. 宮本正尊) *Bukkyo no Kompon Shinri* (佛教の根本眞理 A Fundamental Truth of Buddhism). Tokyo, 1957.

———.*Chudo Shiso oyobi Sono Hattatsu* (中道思想及びその発達 The Thought of Middle Path and Its Development). Tokyo, 1944.

Mizuno, K. *Primitive Buddhism*. Tr. K. Yamamoto, Ube, Japan, 1969.

Monier-Williams. M. *Buddhism*. 1889, reprint Varanasi, India, 1964.

Muller, M. "Buddha and Buddhism". Ed. Muller, M. *Studies in Buddhism*. Calcutta, India, 1953.

Murti, T.R.V. *The Central Philosophy of Buddhism*. London, 1955, 1968.

Nakamura, H. (中村元). *Bukkyo Kyodan no Kenkyu* (佛教教団の研究) A Study of Buddhist Community. Kyoto, Japan, 1968.

———. *Gotama Buddha* (ゴタマブッタ). Tokyo, 1969.

———. *Genshi Bukkyo* (原始佛教 Early Buddhism). Tokyo, 1970.

———. *Genshi Bukkyo no Sei-Ritsu*. (原始佛教の成立 The Formation of Early Buddhism). Tokyo, 1969.

———. *Genshi Bukkyo no Shiso*, II (原始佛教の思想 Thought of Early Buddhism). Tokyo, 1971.

———. *Genshi Bukkyo Sono Shiso to Seikatsu.* 原始佛教その思想と生活 The Thought and Life in Early Buddhism). Tokyo, 1970.

———. *Indo Kotaishi.* (印度古代史第一巻 Ancient History of India). Vol. I. Tokyo, 1963.

———. "Keisei tojo no kyotan" (形成途上の教団 The Formation of the Community). Ed. S. Yoshimura. (芳村修基), *Bukkyo Kyodan no Kenkyu*(佛教教団の研究 A Study of Buddhist Community). Kyoto, Japan, 1968.

Oldenberg, H. *Buddha : His Life, His Doctrine, His Order.* Tr. W. Hoey. London, 1882.

Parrinder, G. *Comparative Religion.* London, 1962.

Radhakrishnan, S. *The Principal Upaniṣads.* London, 1953.

Raychaudhuri, H. C. *Political History of Ancient India.* Calcutta, 1953.

Rhys Davids, T. W. *Buddhist India.* New York, 1903.

———. *Theragatha.* (Psalms of the Early Buddhist Brethren). London, 1909 reprint 1964.

———. *The Sacred Books of the East.* Vol. XI, Oxford, 1881, reprint New York, 1969.

———. *Early Buddhism.* London, 1908.

———. *A Buddhist Manual of Psychological Ethics.* London, 1923.

Saṅgharakṣita, B. *Three Jewels*, London 1967.

Sato, M. *Bukkyo Kyodan no Seiritsu to Tenkai.* (佛教教団の成立と Formation and Development of Buddhist Community). Tokyo, 1967.

———. "Genshi Bukkyo no Kyodan Rinen." (原始佛教の教團理念, The Community Idea in Early Buddhism). Ed. Yoshimura S.(芳村修基), *Bukkyo Kyodan no Kenkyu.* (佛教教団の研究 A Study of Buddhist Community). Kyoto, Japan, 1968.

———. *Genshi Bukkyo Kyodan no Kenkyu.* (原始佛教教団の研究 A Study of the Early Buddhist Order Tokyo, 1963.

Sharma, R. S. *Aspects of Political Ideas and Institutions In Ancient India.* Motilal Banarsidass, 1955.

Shastri, A. M. *An Outline of Early Buddhism*. Varanasi, India, 1965.

Stcherbatsky, Th. *The Central Conception of Buddhism*. London, 1923.

Takahashi, Y. (高橋堯昭), ("Kai To Sono Kiban 戒とその基盤, Discipline and its Foundation: Problems in Discipline). Ed. Nihon Bukkyo Gakukai (日本佛教学会) *Bukkyo Ni Okeru Kai no Mondai* (佛教における戒の問題 Problems in Buddhist Discipline). Kyoto, Japan, 1967.

Thomas, E. J. *The History of Buddhist Thought*. London, 1933, reprint 1967.

———. *The Life of Buddha as Legend and History*. London, 1927, reprint 1969.

Tsukamoto, K. (塚本啓祥), *Shoki Bukkyo Kyodanshi no Kenkyu*. (初期佛教教団史の 研究 A History of the Early Buddhist Order). Tokyo, 1966.

Ui, H. *Bukkyo*. (佛教 Buddhism). Tokyo, 1967.

———. *Bukkyo Kyoten Shi* (佛教教団史 A History of Buddhist Community). Tokyo, 1957.

———. *Indo Tetsugaku Kenkyu* (印度哲学研究 A Study in Indian Philosophy). V. 4, Tokyo, reprint, 1965.

Walleser, M. *Die Philosophische Grundlage des altern Buddhismus*. 1904.

Warder, A. K. *Indian Buddhism*. Delhi, 1970.

Watanabe, G. (渡邊棋雄) *Bukkyo no Kyosetzu*. (佛教の 教説 Teachings of Buddha). Tokyo, 1935.

Watsuji, (和辻哲郎). *Genshi Bukkyo no Jissen Tetsu gaku*. (原始佛教の 実践哲学 Practical Philosophies in Primitive Buddhism). Tokyo, 1927.

Yoshimura, S. (芳村修基). Ed. *Bukkyo Kodan no Kenkyu*. (佛教教団の 研究 A Study of Buddhist Community). Kyoto, Japan, 1968.

Part II

ON CHRISTIANITY

A. Primary Sources

The Holy Bible (Revised Standard Version).

B. Lexica and Encyclopedias

Dictionary of Apostolic Church. 2 Vols. Ed. J. Hastings. Edinburgh, 1915-1918.

Dictionary of the Bible. 5 Vols. Ed. J. Hastings. Edinburgh, 1898-1904.

Dictionary of Christ and the Gospels. 2 Vols. Ed. J. Hastings. Edinburgh, 1906-1908.

The Interpreter's Dictionary of the Bible. 4 Vols. New York, 1967.

Theological Dictionary of the New Testament. 5 Vols. Ed. G. Kittel. Eerdman's, 1964-1968.

The Vocabulary of the Greek Testament Illustrated from the Papyri and Other Non-Literary Sources. Ed. H. J. Moulton and G. Milligan. London, 1914-1929.

C. Secondary Sources

Allmen, J. J. *Vocabulary of the Bible.* London, 1958.

Andrews, E. *The Meaning of Christ for Paul.* New York, 1949.

Barrett, C. K. *Jesus and the Gospel Tradition.* London, 1967.

Benoit, P. *The Passion and Resurrection of Jesus Christ.* Tr. B. Weatherhead, New York, 1969.

Bornkamm, G. *Jesus of Nazareth.* Tr. J. M. Robinson, London, 1969.

Bouttier, M. *Christianity According to Paul.* London, 1966.

Bultmann, R. *Theology of the New Testament.* Tr. K. Gróbel, New York, 1955.

Burchard, C. *Der dreizehnte Zeuge.* Gottingen, Vanden Noech U, Ruprecht, 1970.

Campenhausen, H. *Ecclesiastical Authority and Spiritual Power in the Church of the First Three Centuries*. Tr. J. A. Baker. Stanford, 1969.

Coates, T. *Authority in the Church*. St. Louis, 1964.

Cullmann, O. *Early Christian Worship*. London, 1953.

———. *The Early Church*. London, 1956.

Cunliffe, J. *The Authority of the Biblical Revelation*. London, 1945.

Davies, J. G. *The Early Christian Church*. London, 1965.

Duncan, D. L. *The Sayings of Jesus in the Churches of Paul*. Philadelphia, 1971.

Dupont, J. *Les Actes des Apotres*. Paris, 1958.

Evans, C. F. "The Kerygma", J. T. S. 7, 1956. *Resurrection and the New Testament Studies in Biblical Theology*. Second Series, 12. Naperville, 1970.

Freyne, S. *The Twelve : Disciples and Apostles*. London, 1968.

Fuller, R. H. *The Formation of the Resurrection Narratives*. 1963 reprinted 1971.

———. *The Foundations of New Testament Christology*. New York, 1965.

———. *The Mission and Achievement of Jesus*. 1954.

———. *The New Testament in Current Study*. New York, 1962.

Giblet, J. et al. *The Birth of the Church*. New York, 1968.

Gogel, M. *Jesus and the Origins of Christianity*. 2 Vols. New York, 1960.

Goodspeed, E. J. *A History of Early Christian Literature*. Chicago, 1966.

Goppelt, L. *Apostolic and Post-Apostolic Times*. Tr. R. A. Guelich. London, 1970.

Grant, F. C. *An Introduction to New Testament*. New York.

Greenslade, S. L. *Shepherding the Flock*. Naperville, 1967.

Hanson, A. T. *Jesus Christ in the Old Testament*. London : S.P.C.K., 1965.

Higgins, A.J.B. *The Lord's Supper in the New Testament*. London : SCM Press, 1952. Reprint 1960.

Holbrook, "The Problem of Authority in Christian Ethics", *Catholic Biblical Quarterly* 29, 1967. V.I., XXIX, Washington.

Hunziger, C.H. *Judisches Erbe in der urchristlichen Kirchenzucht.* (Unpublished Habilitationsschrift), Gottingen, 1955.

Hurd, J.C. *The Origin of I Corinthians.* New York, 1965.

Jeremias, J. *The Eucharistic Words of Jesus.* London, 1966.

———. *New Testament Theology. Part One The Proclamation of Jesus.* Tr. J. Bowden, London, 1971.

———. Golgotha. Leipzig, 1926.

Kahler, M. *The So-Called Historical Jesus and the Historic Biblical Christ.* Tr. C.E. Braaten. Philadelphia, 1966.

Kasemann, E. *Essays on New Testament Themes.* Tr. W. J. Montague. London, 1964.

Kee, H.C. Jesus in History : *An Approach to the Study of the Gospels,* New York, 1970.

Knox, J. *St. Paul and the Church of the Gentiles.* Cambridge, 1939.

Kramer, W. *Christ, Lord, Son of God.* Tr. B. Hardy, Naperville, 1966.

Lightfoot, J. B. *The Epistle of St. Paul to the Galatians.* 1865. Reprint Grand Rapids, 1962.

Lietzmann, H. *A History of the Early Church.* Tr. B. L. Woolf. New York, 1963. Vol. I.

Martin, R. P. *Carmen Christi.* Cambridge 1967.

McArthur, H.K. *Understanding the Sermon on the Mount.* New York, 1960.

Mckenzie, J.L. *Authority in the Church.* New York, 1966.

Mignard, J.E. *Jewish and Christian Cultic Discipline to the Middle of the Second Century.* (Unpublished Ph.D. Thesis). Boston University, 1966.

Minear, P.S. *Commands of Christ.* New York, 1972.

Moule, C.F.D. The Phenomenon of the New Testament. Studies in Biblical Theology. Second Series 1. London, 1967.

Pollard, T.E. *Johannine Christology and the Early Church.* London, 1970.

Ringger, J. "Petrus des Fels Das Felsenwort Zur Sinndeutung von Mt. 16, 18, vor allem in Lichte der Symbolsprache.' *Begegnung der Christen.* Stuttgart, 19.

Robinson, J.M. *A New Quest of the Historical Jesus.* London, 1166.

Schlatter, A. *The Church in the New Testament Period.* Tr. Paul P. Levertoff. London, 1961.

Schmitt, J. "L'organization de l'eglise primitive et Qumran," *La secte de Aumran et les origines du Christianisme.* Bruges, 1969.

Schmithals, W. *The Office of Apostle in the Early Church.* Tr. J. Steely. New York, 1969.

———. *Paul and James.* Tr. D. M. Barton. London, 1965.

Schnackenburg, R. *The Church in the New Testament.* Tr. W.J.O'Hara. Montreal, 1965.

Schweizer, E. *Church Order in the New Testament.* London, 1961.

Stanley, D.M. *The Apostolic Church in the New Testament.* Westminster, Maryland, 1967.

Williams, R.R. *Authority in the Apostolic Age.* London, 1950.

Yamatani, S. *Kristokyo no Kigen.* (Origin of Christianity), Vol. 1.

Zahrnt, H. *The Historical Jesus.* Tr. J.S. Bouwden. London, 1963.

Zimmerli, W. and J. Jeremias. *The Servant of God.* London, 1957.

PART III

ON COMPARATIVE STUDIES

Berry, T.S. *Christianity and Buddhism.* London, 1891.

Ebersole, M.C. *Christian Faith and Man's Religion.* New York, 1961.

Edmunds and Anesaki. *Buddhist and Christian Gospels.* Vol. II. Philadelphia, 1935.

Eliade, M. *Patterns in Comparative Religion.* New York, 1963.

Eliade, M. and Kitagawa, J.M. ed. *The History of Religions.* Chicago, 1959.

Garbe, R. *India and Christendom.* La Salle, 1959.

Graham, D.A. *Conversations: Christian and Buddhist.* New York, 1968.

Ishizu, T. et al. *Religious Studies in Japan.* Tokyo, 1959.

James, E.O. *Comparative Religion.* London, 1938, 1961.

Johnston, W. *Christian Zen.* New York, 1971.

King, W.L. *Buddhism and Christianity.* Philadelphia, 1962.

Krester, B.D. *Man in Buddhism and Christianity.* Calcutta, 1954.

Matzutani, F. *A Comparative Study of Buddhism.* Tokyo, 1957.

Nakamura, H. *Hikaku Shiso Ron* (A Study of Comparative Thoughts). Tokyo, 1960, 1968.

———. *Ways of Thinking of Eastern Peoples.* Honolulu, 1964.

Neill, S. *Christian Faith and Other Faiths.* Oxford, 1961.

Niles, D.T. *Buddhism and the Claims of Christ.* Richmond, 1967.

Northrop, F.S.C. *The Meeting of East and West.* New York, 1946, 1966.

Noss, John B. *Living Religions.* Philadelphia, 1957, 1962.

Parrinder, G. *Comparative Religion.* London, 1962.

Radhakrishnan, S. *Eastern Religions and Western Thought.* Oxford, 1959.

Scott, A. *Buddhism and Christianity.* Edinburgh, 1890.

Tillich, P. *Christianity and the Encounter of the World Religions.* New York, 1963.

Toynbee, A. *Christianity Among the Religions of the World.* New York, 1957.

Wach, J. *The Comparative Study of Religions.* New York, 1958, 1963.

Zaehner, R.C. *The Comparison of Religions.* Boston, 1958.

INDEX